Lee

from Anna 2a  e

with very mu

for reading - a

1993

Talking To Myself

Talking to Myself
Anna Raeburn

ELM TREE BOOKS · LONDON

First published in Great Britain 1984
by Elm Tree Books/Hamish Hamilton Ltd
Garden House, 57-59 Long Acre London WC2E 9JZ

British Library Cataloguing in Publication Data

Raeburn, Anna
  Talking to myself.
  1. Raeburn, Anna   2. Journalists—Great
  Britain—Biography
  I. Title
  070'.92'4   PN5123.R3

  ISBN 0-241-11084-X

Phototypeset by Falcon Graphic Art Ltd
Wallington, Surrey
Printed in Great Britain by
Billings, Worcester

Foreword

To begin with . . .

'Make up your mind,' said my father. 'Either you master time or time masters you.' He made me see that I always had time.

I come from a long line of late developers. My mother became her own woman more after 50 than before. My sister got it together by 40 or so and they both pushed me in the nicest possible way so that I began to cut some kind of mustard a bit earlier. But still I was 27 before I began to be as whole as I'm ever going to be. At 27 I still didn't know what I wanted but I began to know what I didn't want. I stopped looking for endorsement, I stopped looking for permission. I began to offer what I was, what I had. I began to refuse to be told that my values were of less worth than another's because they weren't academically sanctified or were drawn from less-than-Holy Writ. I stopped filling my life with people in the negative way of the lonely who'd rather be with anybody than be alone. I became more aware of my loneliness and I began to live with it instead of against it. And I think that theory about no man being an island is inaccurate. The natural human condition is to be lonely and we're all islands: it's just that some of us build better bridges or boats than others, some find a causeway, some learn to swim and others to fly. It's not true that there is no island, it's just a question of whether you find your way off it or whether others come to share yours with you. I learned that paradox was a very important human law, that when I acknowledged my greatest fears they were not so fearful. And I learned too that for most of us the exchange of views, conversation, a few words, are often profoundly therapeutic against the bruises of life, no matter how minor or major.

This seachange, of working with what I'd got rather than recriminating over what I lacked, has begun to happen in the last ten years of my life. And the intensity of the change telescoped so that the last two years have been more productive than the preceding two and so on. The field of journalism in which I became involved, the value of which I believe in implicitly, offered me a chance to make contact with many different people in many different ways. Both sides benefited. So when I came to write this book, it was first of all in love and appreciation of my husband Nick, my son, my mother, my sister and to the memory of my father.

And then it was as a kind of thank you to all the people who helped me along what I call the journey. Some of them did it by default and names have been changed to protect the innocent, if there are any!

But mostly I wrote it for the public who buy the magazines and newspapers I've worked for, who listen to the radio and televion shows I've contributed to, many of whom I'll never meet or hear from again. For people like the floor manager at Southern Television (as it was then) who didn't like the sound of me but couldn't get a replacement and so had to do a show with me. After the show, he came after me as I prepared to leave. 'You weren't what I was expecting at all,' he said, beaming. 'You're just like my wife!' It's for the television technician who came up to me after a broadcast to thank me for helping him and his wife over the Capital Radio 'phone-in in which I had participated two years before. It's for the boys who lined up for an autograph and a kiss at the only disco I've ever attended. It's for the girl who saw me walking heavily pregnant, recognised me and squeezed my hand as she went past, without a word. It's for Vince who, two years after he threatened to kill himself, leaped out of his car to hug me and for Carl who still sends me a postcard of Rio de Janeiro every time he goes there with the airline. It's for Elaine and Sheila from whom I hear every couple of years as if we were old friends, though I've never met either of them. It's for the girl who wrote to me at *Cosmopolitan* saying, 'I shall feel less safe as a woman when you stop speaking up for me.' It's for the man who rang me at *Forum* after we'd exchanged two long letters on the subject, to tell me how young I sounded and that I'd saved his marriage. How many times have I walked past his shop longing to go in and say, 'Mr X? I'm Anna Raeburn – how are you?' It's for the two women who drove me back from a speaking engagement outside London because they didn't like the idea of my being alone on the train late at night. And for so many more – thank you all, I hope you enjoy reading it. Writing it was *most* instructive!

Chapter 1

When I was a child I dreamed a lot. Say 'dreaming' and most people think of sleep. Say daydreaming and it implies a passivity, which in this case doesn't apply. What it really was was talking to myself. I called it playing. I can hear myself from quite far back, my voice getting younger and younger, saying firmly, 'I'm going upstairs now, to play.'

Upstairs meant my parents' room, where there was an old ottoman full of remnants of Ma's never-very-expensive dance dresses from years ago and a dressing table with a triple mirror. There I would kneel for hours and make myself over from the waist up (I had to kneel to see myself clearly), change my hair, my face, my speech and my role, aided first by the judicious use of cosmetics wheedled from the local chemist's and later by greasepaints. My first mentor in their application was a now defunct magazine called *Woman and Beauty*, which also taught me that if I couldn't sew then at least I could learn to drape imaginatively. Later I was influenced by *Photoplay* and *Plays and Players*.

Part of this 'play' was to do with consolation. I was shortsighted and I could kneel close enough to the little mirror to see myself in every detail without effort and the hated spectacles. It was also because I didn't fit in with my own ideas of beauty. To aim at, much less settle for, being pretty never crossed my mind. My face was a canvas which could be converted into an infinite number of masks. Once the mask was assumed, it might become beautiful of itself. I was always striving for that but I don't think this had much to do with vanity. The mask wasn't me. I just felt a certain proprietorial or even professional pride that I could make something out of what seemed to me to be nothing.

The mirror was a true friend. If it distorted, as my

children's encyclopaedia indicated, then it was for the better and at least it didn't answer back or demand anything of me. I still take refuge in the mirror when I want reassurance or there's an important telephone call I don't know quite how to handle. I rehearse for life but then, when the moment I've been rehearsing for comes, it's never quite as planned. I don't live in the mirror, I escape into it and the mirror reflects the person I'd like to be.

If I wasn't 'playing' and didn't have my nose in a book, I was talking to my parents. I remember noticing very early that we used words in our house that were not familiar to anybody else I knew. What we called the kitchen, they called the breakfast room. What we called the scullery, they called the kitchen. What they called the lounge, we called the front room, presumably because it was on the front of the house. I never thought about it very much. All I knew was that these mannerisms marked my parents out as quite different from everybody else. In Middlesbrough they were foreigners, from the south of England. They didn't want to forget it and I wasn't allowed to.

My mother was born in the Goldhawk Road in Shepherd's Bush. Amy Burdett (her mother whom I never met) assured my mother that she was cockney but as the definition of cockney is 'born within the sound of Bow Bells', mother took leave to doubt her.

My grandfather, Edward Burdett, a newspaper writer, was descended from gypsies and dramatically handsome. In the absence of contraception Amy grew tired of endless pregnancy and miscarriage, as did many women of her day. When my mother was born, in between a child who died and another 'mis', Amy slapped the baby into her husband's arms saying 'Now, you bring this one up' and he took her at her word.

He was a thoughtful man, a man, my mother always said, fifty years ahead of his time. To which end he worried not one whit about Mother playing with the Scots boys next door who really didn't wear anything under their kilts and who walked about naked at home. If Amy was a good cook, it was Edward who knew more about nutrition. And if Amy kept my mother clean and fed, it was Edward who encouraged her to think and explore and never to sacrifice intelligence on the altar of being 'nice'.

His mother had gypsy blood and Ma remembers her as a tiny lady, whose hair remained black well into her seventies. My mother's own hair wasn't so dark but her skin was and is a lovely shade of apricot. She was pretty and as a young woman people stopped her in the street to tell her so. As she has grown older however, she has become a beauty with white hair, bright blue eyes and enviable eyebrows. When I was a child, there was a princess in one of my stories who had finely arched eyebrows so perfect, they looked as if they were cut out of mouseskin and I remember thinking proudly, 'Just like Mummy.'

Things did not go well between Amy and Edward. It's impossible to judge when you're a child and in the middle of such a situation but my mother inevitably sympathised more with her father than her mother. And she has regretted all her life that, when he left, he asked her to go with him and she didn't have the courage. He died of kidney disease, is buried heaven knows where and this probably more than any religious teaching shaped my mother's dismissive attitude towards graves. 'They aren't where the people you love really are,' she explains.

It is fair to say that, having remained loyal in the circumstances of a separation, as would most adolescent girls to this day, Ma was disappointed in her relationship with her own mother. Amy was, she says, 'a good mother' – but her heart wasn't in it. I reaped direct benefit of that. My mother endorsed me to be myself, gave credence in the most practical and helpful manner to what I wanted to do at different times in my life, encouraged me and made me believe unfailingly that she was there for me – all, in short, that her mother had not done for her.

Mother really wanted to act but that wasn't even to be thought of, so she went to Goldsmiths' College on a combined matriculation and degree course to become a teacher. There she met her fate in the shape of my father. He was big and attractive, an electric personality, four years her senior, mahogany dark from years in India and what was then called Mesopotamia, where he'd spent the duration of the Great War. He was also still bandy from riding and he was already nearly bald. I never knew my father with hair or my mother other than grey.

When he took her home to meet his family, Mother discovered something she hadn't had before – a real mother, my paternal grandmother, known to everyone as Mammy. She ran the junior section of the village school while my grandfather, George Alfred (The Old Man) ran the rest of it.

My father George Leslie, variously known as Young Skipper, Leslie and Pim, was the eldest, and the only son. There were three sisters – the eldest the beautiful Razel, Mysie (known as Mikie) who was better than pretty and Georgina Julie who had a perfect nose and the sort of personality guaranteed to blind you to all other imperfections ('such as,' said Ma waspishly, 'a jowl reminiscent of Churchill's and an unfortunate habit of wearing magenta lipstick with a mustard yellow suit!') All three sisters thought their brother the most wonderful creature walking on earth and it is to my father's great credit that he handled their adoration with his usual mixture of intelligence and deprecation.

The first thing my mother noticed about them as a family was the noise. Walking up the path to the house named Lovejoy for the first time, she became aware of shouts and screams of laughter. She put down her case, squared her shoulders and rang the bell. My father opened the door to her, hung about with the writhing bodies of his three sisters – they were all over five feet eight. Somewhat taken aback Ma inquired what they were doing. 'Oh,' they said airily, 'playing rugby with a loaf of bread.'

My mother was far too wise to compete with her sisters-in-law. As she has grown older, I have often heard her speak of her incredible naiveté, even stupidity, and while at eighty odd you can call yourself whatever you please, those epithets are inappropriate. In words attributed to the country and western star Loretta Lynn, my mother may have been ignorant but she was never dumb. She was 44 when I was born and she often emphasises that both she and the world had changed a good deal by then and that I got all the advantages of the changes in both. But she was never anybody's fool and she has always had a strong sense of herself. She would not have survived without it, still less have been able to give of herself so generously to both her children.

My father was on the same course at Goldsmiths' so they did their training and they got married. Apparently he initiated her into the mysteries of the marriage bed the night before the wedding whereupon Mother decided the whole thing was great fun if a bit unwieldy. They set out the next morning to be married in a cold church. Mother wore biscuit and soft blue wool crepe with silk cockades in her hat and I expect Pop looked wonderful. He usually did.

They were poor and they were happy. They had friends, they were young and they managed. They danced a lot and drank a bit and Pop played rugby while Ma watched and cheered. Seven years later Pop went away on a training course and Ma had one of those scares that something was going to happen to him. As soon as he came back she announced that she wanted a baby and he was delighted to oblige. My sister Lesley's entry into the world took 36 hours and was eventually made with the aid of forceps – no laughing matter in those days. Mother couldn't have cared less. She says now that the first few years of Lesley's life were the happiest she's ever known.

Lesley was square and solid and dark, my idea of lovely, but she was a shy, withdrawn child and when the war broke out she suffered badly from the bombing. As a small child myself years later, I remember listening to some radio programme in which part of the soundtrack caused my sister to blench visibly. When I asked her what was the matter, she replied briefly 'Bombs'. Such distress did all this cause her that it was decided that my mother would take her to the country, where the bombing was less, while Pop stayed in town to work for the Air Training Corps – he was already too old for the regular services. This meant that my parents were separated for the duration of the war. There is an idea that absence makes the heart grow fonder and for some part of the human race, this may be true. The rest of us operate more on the basis of out of sight meaning out of mind. In any case, if you aren't together, you don't grow together. Eight years of occasional weekends and odd nights together, living very different lives, dented my parents' marriage and when they were reunited, it cost them a lot of effort to make a go of it.

Some time later my mother decided she was beginning the 'change' and went to the doctor. He examined her and beamed 'Congratulations!' Mother looked puzzled. She was five months pregnant. Typically she held on to me past April 1 –

'No child of mine is being born on April Fools' Day!' – but on the evening of April 3, she announced to my father that she was going to get on and have this child. She drank castor oil and scrubbed the kitchen floor and I was born three and a half hours later.

My sister, then not quite 13, was left with the job of combing the house from top to bottom for cigarette ends so that my father could have a puff or two. He'd run out but would not go out to buy any for fear that he'd miss the telephone call from the nursing home. His first words upon seeing me were 'Oh, look at her beautiful nose!' and he stuck to that sentiment all his life.

That I talk about my parents quite a lot has been remarked upon and not always with great favour. I am too close to analyse why I do. All I know is that they seem to have given me a much better deal than the parents of many of the people I know. Although they never left me in any doubt when they disapproved, neither did they let me doubt that they loved me, or that they saw me as a person in my own right. I loved them as my parents but I liked them and found them interesting as people apart from that. In some ways their very age was fascinating. I remember going to the Victoria and Albert Museum with my mother where, in the costume section, was a wedding dress dated 1919. Ma was vastly amused. 'Another 20 years,' she grinned, 'and I'll be in a museum!'

But unlike the much younger parents of many of my contemporaries they didn't spend their lives harking back to the 'good old days'. In fact if they had a secret for living which they imparted to me with force it was that looking forward was essential. To use a truism, they were in love with life, my father in a reflective fitting-in-with-the-perspective-of-history kind of way, my mother more earthily in keeping with the words her elder sister had pinned up in her kitchen – 'Life ain't always what you want – but it's all you've got: so stick a geranium in your 'at and be happy.'

My mother and sister would agree that I got the best of my father. His height and the splendour of his physique were ordinary matters in comparison with the force of his personality. He could talk to you quite quietly and after about 20 minutes you were exhausted by his sheer intensity. This feeling of concentrated energy was of course enhanced by his size and his ability to express himself. Pop liked knowledge, it gave him the kind of pleasure more tangible acquisition gives others, and as he was a natural teacher, he communicated that pleasure vividly. I loved to ask him questions because besides replying, he embroidered the theme, brought in variations, added a couple of footnotes for interest and suggested a reading list to encompass all the main points he'd raised.

When I was at grammar school between the ages of 12 and 16, I continued to come home for lunch every day and we often got into long conversations while waiting for the potatoes to boil. But by the time the meal was on the table, Ma would hiss at me, 'I'll shoot you! What do you have to start him on that for now? The food'll be cold.'

My father was a one woman man. The finest compliment he ever paid me on my appearance was when I came downstairs aged 16 wearing my first silk dress and he said I looked nearly as good as my mother. My parents were opposites in some ways. My mother's temper was quick to rise and just as quick to disperse. My father's took much longer to rouse but once up, he went on rumbling for days. They were both quite clear and tough about bringing about an end, whether of a topic of conversation or a friendship. They were not, I came to feel later, very civilised and later still I came to be proud of them for their lack of social compromise.

My early memories of my relationship with my parents are all good. They talked to me, played with me, encouraged me. It is alleged that I walked at one year, spoke in sentences three months later and have only stopped moving and talking since in order to read. I hardly knew my sister. Thirteen years my senior, she refused to go to university despite her considerable ability, and went into the Meteorological Office when I was 4. I adored her and yet resented how special she seemed to be. When she sent her laundry home from Prestwick where she was stationed, Ma made special cakes – apple batter and date chews – to be sent back to her in the clean clothes. But I loved her smell and always asked to sleep in her bed before the clothes were changed when she'd been home on leave. When I was a small child, she was an extra benefactor. We were opposites in height – she was tall, I was average. We were opposites in structure – I was slight, she ranged from frankly heavy to generous. If only our differences had stopped there, but when we grew older, things were more difficult.

One of the few long shadows cast over my childhood was my precarious health. I had diphtheria and pneumonia as well as measles and mumps. I didn't sleep and I wouldn't eat. And when I was three, more thorough investigations into my never-ending catarrh revealed what was then called a lung shadow. The scene is quite clear in my memory, like a frozen frame from a film. The doctor sent us to a chest clinic and when the X-ray plate was produced, I was sitting on the examination table so that I was more or less on a level with the physician and my mother. He indicated the X-ray and I remember that the print of my chest was almost totally obscured by a cloud of white. What looked white on the negative was in fact dark grey but I didn't know that. All I remember is my mother saying in her indomitable way, 'I see, and what do we do about it?' She told me years later that when she saw the picture, her heart froze.

When my sister was small, she had contracted scarlet fever. My father was by that time Director of Physical Training, spending a lot of his time inspecting the teaching of games and gymnastics in schools, in constant contact with many children. The doctor therefore advised that my sister was sent to fever hospital. When she came home, she brought with her, among other mementoes, a lifelong fear of electricity – having been shut in a room alone with a hairdryer which shorted and exploded – and a fine crop of lice. Determined that I was not going to be sent away anywhere, Ma put me through a ritual of breathing exercises every night and every morning outside the back door. My bedroom was awash with coal tar waft from the vaporiser, balanced on top of a paraffin heater which gave out nice moist heat. Once a month we got on a bus and rode out to Hemlington Hospital where a nurse put me on a bed with my feet higher than my head and slapped me rhythmically down one side of my chest while I coughed and spat. When I'd half-filled the enamel bowl beside the bed, I was turned so that the other side could be attacked. This grisly routine completed, I had ten minutes' ultra-violet light which accounts in part, I'm told, for the thickness of my hair.

Once again, I can only now appreciate the effort of all this for my mother. Of course there were times, many I suspect,

16

when the last thing in the world I wanted to do was practise breathing or when the trip to the hospital was just another bus journey which made me feel sick and tired. But Ma stuck to it and my chest cleared. It came as quite a shock to discover when I was 19 and applying for a visa to go to America, that I had visible scars on both lungs.

Chapter 2

Schooldays can be the best days of your life or if you're made of more rebellious stuff, you hate them. I got through mine. To begin with there were long absences from school when I was still ill. Then there was the fact that both parents were or had been teachers or educational administrators, so perhaps I had a more informed picture of the highs and lows of formal education than many. I don't remember much about lessons though I felt that for the most part the books I had at home were more interesting. My mother always swore that the only reason I stuck on one of my early readers for so long was not that I couldn't read it but that I wasn't interested enough to try.

There was a junior school twinned with the infants' I attended, so I came into contact with both my peers and some much older children. Generally I got on well with the kids in my class but some of the older girls took a sinister exception to me. I can't remember how it all began but I obviously varied from some expected response. Perhaps I didn't do as I was asked or, more likely, questioned what was asked of me. They didn't like my not fitting in and the easy focus of this dislike was the way I spoke. I was quite deferential to my elders so one or other of this group found it easy to lure me on to a bus as being 'a short way home'. I walked to and from school and didn't know of a relevant bus – maybe I was too intimidated to disagree, but trustingly I fell for this trick again and again. Several stops along an unfamiliar route, the bus would stop and I would leap off or the conductor would check where I was going and tell me to get off, but nobody ever seemed to know how to direct me back home. So I would start walking and looking for a policeman while my parents became frantic on the other side of town.

Eventually my mother simply forbade me to get on the bus, *any* bus, without her. Inevitably this led to confrontation with my tormentors. Having failed to persuade me, they mocked me for a goody-goody, always does what her mother tells her and then, after several other unflattering remarks, they concluded that my trouble was that I talked posh. I could hardly wait for them to go and then I rushed home to my mother to ask what posh meant. 'It means,' said my mother, he blue eyes taking on a steely glint I've come to know and love, 'that you speak differently from them, thank God.'

My best friend at this time was a girl called Rosemary Buxton. Not only was she nice to know but her father had a car and often we were whisked away to play for a happy gritty day on the beach at Saltburn, Marske or Redcar. There are photographs of us absorbed in sandcastles and conversation and once or twice I think we went to the circus together. She was as round as I was flat and when we met again, thirty years later on a programme for Tyne Tees Television, she told me that one of the reasons she'd liked me so much was that I hadn't seemed even to notice her weight. Of course I hadn't – I was so used to people fussing about how thin I was. Had other people fussed about her weight? She raised her eyes expressively. How unobservant. Her weight wasn't Rosemary's most outstanding characteristic. She had a husky voice and smelt of sage and honey and she didn't notice my accent specially, probably because her father was a Geordie and that was different again.

At the beginning of my first year of junior school, my father pulled rank (the first of only two occasions on which he ever did such a thing) and demanded that I went to school in a cleaner air zone. The primary to which I was originally assigned backed on to a laundry which belched black smoke all day long and he felt my lungs couldn't take the extra strain.

It was a struggle but at the age of nine I was assigned to Whinney Banks Junior School, a bus ride away, K bus down and J bus back. Near the bus stand at the school end was a baker's where I discovered a lifelong addiction to bread. Let everyone else buy all the gobstoppers and liquorice bootlaces and sherbet (which we called 'kaylie') they liked. I bought fresh milk bread rolls at one and one half old pence a time and gorged on them.

19

I didn't know it but one of the reasons that this school was regarded askance was that it was in a slum clearance area. Not all my little peers were the world's nicest or brightest people but at least some of them were what I needed. Looking back on it, Jean Dunn, Susan Sanderson, Lesley Gill and I probably didn't have a great deal in common. What drew us together was a running fantasy, best nurtured in classes where we could talk, like art or handicrafts. (As I typed that last word, I saw before me the truly horrible yellow and purple slippers I was encouraged to weave on a cardboard back and I wonder to this day how we can expect anything of our young unless we instil some aesthetic discernment in them from an early age. My family's reception of these gifts left me in no doubt that weaving them killed time. Wearing them might kill feet!)

Anyway there we sat, quite happy and busy, and talked about clothes. We pretended to be four sisters and told the story of what was happening to us by turns. Continuity was not important, nor was history for I seem to remember we had quite different tastes. What mattered was that each of us described in lavish detail what she was wearing, drew illicit sketches to illustrate the odd detail and changed as many times as possible. We weren't much influenced by television, more by what contact we had with the cinema through film annuals and Saturday morning matinees, whatever we saw in the way of ballets or plays and those magazines our mothers subscribed to. I cannot remember a time when I was not fascinated by magazines. We were after all still very much guided by our mothers in terms of what we wore but it was also the beginning of the 'youthquake' when for the first time in history, the young dictated what was worn. It is fair to say that an interest in clothes was probably all that drew us together.

Although I called these girls my friends, I didn't see them all that much once we were away from school. I was already a confirmed bookworm and my family alternated between pride and concern for my eyesight.

Officially I was supposed to wear glasses for a year to correct the impairment, but when I went for a check up at the end of that year, the specialist recommended that I wear them all the time. I was a bit upset by this but was trying to accept it when, the moment we were outside the hospital gates, my mother removed the pink wire-framed horrors from my nose and put them in my pocket. 'But mummy,' I expostulated, 'the man just said –' 'I heard what he said,' she acknowledged, 'but I let them do that to Lesley and now she can't move without them. Keep them handy and learn to make do.' As far as I know, my mother didn't hear Dorothy Parker's famous line that 'men don't make passes at girls who wear wear glasses' until much later. She just knew what a bind specs were to Lesley. And having gone the whole route of different frames and contact lenses and wasted much fruitless energy hating the darned things, isn't it ironical that the love of my life likes me in glasses?

* * *

The headmistress of Whinney Banks was Miss Rose Gibson, a Scot from the Isle of Mull, who looked at you over her fine aquiline nose with a mixture of severity and affection which won my heart for ever. She sat on the Juvenile Bench for 43 years and only had her own pupils come up before her twice. She was so fair that even when she ruled against you, you felt you could live with it.

According to Miss Gibson I settled in well at school and was generally well liked although I was an outsider. Enlarging on these comments some 25 years later, she remarked that I was really always an adult, a remark which fascinated me as well as proving her generosity. In one affair I know I disappointed her.

There were still children who gave me a hard time, either about my voice or about the fact that my parents were so much older than everybody else's. A boy caught my arm as I ran into line at the beginning of afternoon school. 'I've just seen your dad,' he said, 'and he can't be your dad because he's too old.' I asked him to let go of me. He refused. I tried to pull away and I couldn't. He then remarked that the real reason I wasn't my parents' child was that I was a nigger. I was much darker in complexion when I was younger and in that part of the world, any foreigner could be so described. It was my left arm he held, so I raised my right one and smacked my elbow into his nose. I broke it. We were both marched smartly off to give account of ourselves.

Miss Gibson told us how much she disliked this kind of behaviour. Would we please apologise to each other freely in due course? It is a measure of the love I bore her that, as soon as we were outside the door, I offered him my hand and said, 'I'm sorry I hurt your nose.' He sneered at me, said something about not being sorry really and walked away.

That afternoon was awful. I was embarrassed because I knew a report would have to be made and I didn't want to upset or displease my father. I was furious with the other child for being so mucky minded. I remember thinking quite clearly that I didn't know how being a nigger could be a bad thing if Paul Robeson was one and both my parents thought the world of him. I was damned if I could see what was so terrible about my parents being older than somebody else's. I do not truly remember, brought up in my father's love of the Western, Kipling and Sir Henry Newbolt, feeling one shred of remorse about the broken nose. It was just punishment. I met the boy as a teenager and his nose was set slightly to one side. I hoped to feel remorse. I regret to report I felt only a small fierce satisfaction.

In spite of this I was a good child at school, largely because I saw nothing to be bad about. I didn't like shinty, which is a rehearsal for hockey, but then I didn't like gym or games much. But I did like the school play in which I was cast as a witch and announced that no, I would not be carrying on a toy cat to pretend it was real. I would talk to the cat and make everyone believe it was invisible. My talent and volume received equal praise. Upon the basis of years of 'playing', this and half a dozen films I'd seen, I decided I would be an actress.

Meantime over us loomed the Intelligence Test and the 11 Plus. The first wasn't so frightening because you could go on staying at your school regardless of how you did in it, but the second would decide in the old-fashioned way of streaming whether you future educational needs were best met in a grammar or high school, at a technical college or in a secondary modern, and those needs quite definitely marked you as 'A', 'B' or 'C' stream.

It is once again greatly to my parents' credit that learning was so ingrained in me generally as a good thing that the appearance of 'extra coaching' books to help me out with my mental and mechanical arithmetic and for that matter reassure me about the technical aspects of my English, far from appalling me, were just a fact to be taken in and dealt with. I never felt academically pressured in my life. I was encouraged to believe that it was just as silly for the parents to push the child unendingly, whether through threats, bribes or nagging, as it was for you, the child, to do less well than you were capable of doing.

I do remember the 11 Plus because we had to wait for the results and they came through on Friday the 13th. I had passed. I waited for the bus in a daze and rushed home, running up Briarvale Avenue to where my father was leaning on the gate. 'I passed, I passed,' I shouted. 'Yes,' he said, looking deeply pleased, 'I know.' I stared at him. My beautiful surprise fell in ruins. 'How?' He took me inside to the hall and told me that he and Mummy had had a lot of pressure about my career as a schoolchild because of the illness. I had missed so much that they had even been advised not to let me take the exam but just to settle for putting me into 'another school'. Neither he nor Ma had been able to accept that I shouldn't have a go at it, which was why they'd bought home tuition books. And when the exams were marked, for the second and last time in his life, he rang the examining board and pleaded special privilege, years of service to the town, concern for my welfare and anything else he could think of until they told him – 90 per cent in both maths papers, higher in English and General Knowledge.

And typically he made me promise that this was a private matter and not to discuss it with anyone. We went into the kitchen. My mother turned round from the stove, smiling. 'You know too,' I said, still a bit crushed. She nodded. 'Look.' Every other child I knew was promised a bicycle if they passed the 11 Plus. I got a coral wool skirt and a pound of Black Magic chocolates. Two months later, my father, afraid that I was missing out, bought me a magnificent bike. I think I rode it six times.

Chapter 3

Wherever my sister was posted in the service of the Meteorological Office, it always seemed to be far away. By now she was at Northolt, the other end of England and might just as well have been abroad because, except for high days and holidays when she was on leave, we didn't see her. My parents were always quick to seize her letters (unlike me, she was a good correspondent) and discussed them in great detail. I accepted their concern for her as natural although, because she was older than me, I always thought of her as completely competent. That they thought she was special seemed perfectly reasonable. So did I. I didn't understand their reasons for quite some time to come but to me she was special because she was so much more forbearing than I (in my own mind I decided she was nicer). I recall that once we had a row and I left to fling myself on the bed sobbing in my best 'Sarah Bloody Bernhardt' manner. A little while later she came to comfort me and make peace. By now I was reading *Girl*, a superior comic on the back of which the improving lives of various outstanding women were serialised, one after the other. I remember hugging Lesley and telling her that I thought she was a bit like Mary Slessor, ignoring her demur. I didn't even try to emulate her. I decided she was above me in every way. The comparative rarity of her visits, hedged about with specialness, only added to her sense of 'otherness' in my perception of her.

I went to the same local grammar school she had attended, resplendent in the most unbecoming grey pinafore dress known to mankind. The school is still there, though not quite as it was. It was a pleasant enough collection of buildings within walking distance of home one way and the local shops the other.

Homework was a bit of a blow but once I'd accepted its inevitability, it didn't pose any great problem. I came home, ate something (I seem to recall a passion for cold toast and mayonnaise or sandwich spread) along with a cup of tea or a glass of milk, did some work, ate a more substantial meal with my mother and father when he came in, and did some more. The temptation of the telly didn't exist and although I was a fan of the Children's Hour on the old Home Service, I was seriously in thrall to the printed word. Was, am and always will be. Other women want diamonds, food processors and Robert Redford. I've got diamonds, a Magimix and Nick Lilley – and I still want books.

My mother had gone back to work when I was nine, as a clerk at the Women's Educational Centres, the evening school classes for women held at the old Hugh Bell School a bus ride away. We all joke that the real reason she got the job was because of one of her better *bon mots*. Having taken note of her qualifications, will to work and experience, the interviewer asked, 'And you can type, Mrs Taylor?', to which Mrs. Taylor replied firmly, 'No, but I can use a typewriter!' This candour carried the day and although it meant relentless rushing to get food cooked, clothes washed and the vacuum pushed round occasionally, within a very short time she'd been offered teaching work during the day and was soon the deputy in charge of the whole operation.

This meant that we had more money. My father, dear man, was never any good with money. He wasn't deliberately silly about it, he just didn't like it very much. He was poorly paid anyway and he gave up on the issue. Mother instead took the bull by the horns and by the time I'd gone to grammar school, she had persuaded Pop that it would not be to his detriment if she were allowed to handle the money from now on. Accordingly he would cash his pay cheque and bring home what they taught me to call a 'Chicago roll' (a bundle of money the bootleggers used to carry during Prohibition). He would then amusedly ask for his pocket money which she doled out, keeping and administering the remainder.

About this time my first dog died and we acquired a bull terrier, a breed (in case you're unfamiliar with them) of great humour and with the texture of a torpedo. We also had the excitement of our first car, a 1937 Standard which looked like a Hollywood jalopy. But then my father couldn't drive. He had done during the war, but he had no licence. He took the driving test, and, to his fury, failed. This was followed by some crisis or other among the oil producing nations which led to petrol rationing and he got his confidence back because, although he rarely drove without an authorised person sitting beside him, he didn't have to show 'L' plates. He walked through his second attempt to qualify and from then on, every weekend that the weather was tolerable, Ma packed a picnic and we headed out of town. Ma liked the travelling and I liked the destination, being happiest if told we were heading for a river of some kind. Water of any kind has always had a reassuring feel to me, particularly in the form of a spring, steam or river, where you can if necessary drink it. Is this survival instinct or a longing to get back to the womb? I remember being very impressed by my father's account of a novel called *Earth Abides* in which there is some kind of catastrophe which destroys all the systems we take so much for granted in city life, including heating, lighting and the water supply. The idea of turning on a tap and having nothing come out nagged at me. To this day I prefer to live within walking distance of some form of natural water supply. It makes me feel safer.

My early days at secondary school passed peacefully enough. I enjoyed particularly Miss Travis who taught French and Miss Phillips who taught history. I once got 10 out of 10 for an essay on the medieval town and I put the book proudly in front of my father's place at the lunch table, expecting a verbal pat on the back. He didn't comment so I drew it to his attention. He grunted and went back to his food. Afterwards he retired to the living room with his coffee. I hissed aggrievedly at my mother 'He didn't say anything!' When he woke, I told him all over again and he looked at me steadily and said, 'Yes.'

'What do you mean – "yes"?' I asked heatedly.

'Well,' he said, teaching me a very important lesson, 'ten is perfect. You can't do better than that. So you'd better move on and try something else.' And there I expecting a bouquet.

I was better at some subjects than others, but maths, oh dear, maths. I was somewhat vindicated to read that it is arguably one of the worst taught subjects in our schools. And there is no question that I was one of its worst pupils. I think the trouble began in infants' school where our class teacher told us not to put up our hands unless we were *sure* we were right. Never sure, I never put up my hand.

I remain relatively reliable at simple arithmetic, but the very names of logarithms, trigonometry, algebra, geometry and calculus sound to this day like an incantation of doom. And I had to have a headmistress who had impressive maths qualifications and who was very keen on girls 'doing science'. Miss Muddle, Gertrude Emily Muddle (known as the Gem) was a gifted and sympathetic class teacher, a frighteningly nervous woman whose hands twitched and danced as she spoke as though they'd a life of their own. She spoke well on speech days, once or twice rose superbly to meet a very difficult occasion but was generally a prisoner of the administration inherent in the post of head teacher and this must have frustrated her sorely.

I was very accepting of school. It was there and so was I. When I look back at it now, I wonder what on earth was the value of those traced maps, the written exercises in French which didn't help you to read or speak the language, those essays on tropism and the Rump of Parliament? School did not teach me to learn. My family and home taught me that. School did not teach me to fit in. That took years of living. It taught me how to manage, how to keep the peace and if a teacher liked her subject, I was happy enough. But the end of my twelfth year produced a kind of watershed.

My sister Lesley was by now attached to the Air Ministry in London and that Christmas couldn't get leave to come home. Her fiance Terry could, so he flew home to spend a family Christmas with his mother – he and Lesley planned to marry the following February. The plane, a Stratocruiser, crashed on the runway at Prestwick. Christmas Day fell on a Saturday. Lesley was on duty and she kept silence. On Sunday morning my father picked the newspapers up from the door mat and told my mother.

It was the Christmas before I was 13 and I can see them now, caught in the half-light of our front hall, their voices thin and strained. It is only comparatively recently that I came to understand why the picture was always so clear and yet so blurred. I saw them through tears. That they didn't have the money immediately available to go to my sister didn't impress itself so much on me as the extremity of their distress. There's nothing worse than being a helpless witness to the pain of someone you love. That was the first time I ever saw my father weep and after that, if the roof had fallen in, I wouldn't have been surprised.

When the first awfulness had receded, the bruise lingered. My poor sister. I think she sleepwalked through the next 20 years of her life. And even then I only knew half the tale. I had always placed her on a pedestal. She was special. We were indissolubly different and somehow I always felt that she was more than me. I felt that nothing I could do was enough, that I wasn't enough to console them or her. And I didn't at that age know what else I could or should do. Years later in an abortive psycho-therapeutic relationship, my therapist commented, 'You know, when I hear you talk about your mother and father and Lesley, I have this picture of them dancing in a circle – and there's this puppy that keeps trying to break in and join in with the dance. You know how puppies try to please? The puppy is you.' I replied rather stiffly that I didn't think the image was fair. Actually, I can still sometimes hear myself jumping up on my fluffy hindlegs, barking and panting and pleading. Powerless to ameliorate the situation, I settled for being a diversion. This is when I remember consciously wanting to make people laugh more than ever before and when I couldn't raise that kind of response or dramatise the situation so that everyone was involved, I hid behind one kind of reading material or the other.

* * *

Ma was delighted that I enjoyed reading but she began to feel that my solitary existence wasn't ideal, trying to find me alternatives which would bring me into contact with other youngsters.

To begin with she tried to get me to go to a youth club. I went once. It was depressing. The boys wanted to smoke or drink (or talk about it) and make quick grabs at whatever bit of your anatomy was handy in passing. And all the girls wanted was the boys, wanted them with an unreasonable hunger. In those far-off days we had numbers for what you'd 'let' a boy do

– holding hands was number one, an arm round you was number two. Number three was kissing. Number four was (explosion of giggles) *proper* kissing – you know, with your tongue. Number five was (lowered voice) a hand on or in your blouse. And number six was – 'Oooooh, she never! Go on – tell us!' I thought the prurience and the competition between both sexes to exploit each other was repugnant. 'They don't even talk to each other,' I complained to my parents.

By now (I was 12) I knew about the facts of life as the essentials pertaining to sex are somewhat sweepingly called. Ma told me one afternoon in the depths of a deep discussion when the subject came up. We were walking the dog round what we called 'the Arty' – the artificial lake – at the time and my initial reaction was fascinated repulsion. But I couldn't see then, and still can't, why you would want to do all that if it wasn't interesting, if it wasn't with somebody you found interesting (and preferably with somebody you could talk to) so what he looked like or how shocking it was paled in my mind beside the all-important issue of doing it, if you were going to do it, with somebody who interested you. I never had any difficulty in accepting that my parents had a sexual life – something which repels a lot of youngsters – because there was a well-defined emotional context into which it fitted. But all the groping and scoring and telling my contemporaries revelled in repelled me. Still does. So charmless.

Ma tried again. Wouldn't I like to go to a dancing class? I'd always pirouetted round at home to the Overture to the Thieving Magpie and assorted bits of the more popular classics. The music derived from the radio – our record collection numbered two chirpy tunes from my parents' younger days, LPs of Paul Robeson, 45's of Lonnie Donegan, Cliff Richard and the Everly Brothers. I wondered briefly what all the girls would be like at ballet class. Interested in Baron's photographs of the ballet, in how people danced in the movies – or endlessly chewing over how far Dorothy let Ken go last week? I was pretty sure it would be the latter. I declined.

What about music lessons? The only instrument I wanted to play was the guitar and I was sure that would take loads of practice and who would teach me anyway? We sent away for a grey and white plastic ukulele and my interest was sustained just long enough to learn how to strum 'Little Brown Jug' and 'My Old Kentucky Home'. Then I went back to my books. The great thing about reading is that you don't have to put up with anybody else to do it and you don't have to practise.

Undaunted, mother played her trump card. Mrs Greet, the aunt of my first best friend Rosemary Buxton, worked in the wardrobe department of the Middlesbrough Little Theatre. Would I like to go and see what that was about. I would.

The Middlesbrough Little Theatre was the cultural jewel in the municipal diadem. It was built by public subscription, the first new theatre in the country after the Second World War, as the permanent home of a long established and very committed amateur dramatic society who played to high standards, working usually with a professional producer.

When I joined through the good offices of Mrs Greet and the tolerance of the Wardrobe Mistress, Zena Devine, Shaw's *Caesar and Cleopatra* was under way. I sorted buttons, slapped on a bit of gold paint here and there and tried to be unobtrusive. I couldn't and still can't sew.

After two or three evenings there, I discovered that the resident director, Raphael Jago, had announced auditions for a Junior Theatre production of *Alice in Wonderland*. Junior Theatre was a sort of club for the young who liked to play at theatre but who were liable for small parts in main theatre productions, by virtue of their declared interest.

Inspired by my mother's rendering of Kipling's *Cat-Who-Walked-By-Himself* I read for the part of the Cheshire Cat – and got it. That evening in the library, I met two boys, David Baume and Robert Peacock. David was cast as the Knave of Hearts and Robert (whom I christened Pete) as the March Hare. Pete lived miles away, David relatively nearby. We all went home together and talked for hours under the streetlight outside my house. We became inseparable. I knew Pete as a close friend for 13 years and David's still around.

Meeting two boys who became my friends at this juncture saved me from all sorts of adolescent gropings, literal and metaphorical, and I am eternally grateful to them both. Once again, people muttered – I don't know why friendship among the young is a subject of such prurient interest to others – but my parents and David's let it be known that they were happy with the way things were. Peter seemed more independent of his family, or was it just that he lived so much further away? He was the son of a working class family who'd made it to grammar school. Were there other pressures? He was certainly a workhorse. Anyway they didn't, as far as I know, attempt to disbar our relationship.

We must have made an odd trio. Peter was very good looking, compact and trim, not tall but well made. David was longer and softer in outline, more like a bear and facially resembled the young Winston Churchill. And I was thin and dark and toothy.

All we wanted to do was talk. We met at the theatre, spent the evening there and then they brought me home. We did not always want to go in and have something to drink. We just wanted to stand outside under our lamp and talk. Many mornings, most mornings, we met on the main road corner on the way to school, to talk there. In time we developed into telephone addicts and rang each other to talk for hours on Sunday afternoons. We discussed each other and ourselves and our friends and peers, the books we were reading, our schoolwork. Their interests were in some ways opposite to mine (Peter did PPE at Oxford, David went to Imperial College) so they explained what they were currently enthusiastic about. The theatre and in some cases films were common ground. None of us was going to stay in Middlesbrough. We went for walks together and with my parents, we went to tea at David's house or mine and my first Christmas present from them is *Gone With The Wind* in two volumes, inscribed to Scarlett from the Tarleton twins.

* * *

At school I did averagely well in most things, shiningly well in my declared favourites. I sang in the choir, I read the lesson when our form presented assembly and my father found me prone and weeping when I wasn't asked to do it the second year running. 'Why,' he asked, 'are you so upset?' 'Because I've got a good voice and I read well and – why haven't I been chosen?' I wailed. 'Darling,' said my philosophical papa, 'you haven't been chosen because it's somebody else's turn. Somebody has to give way and somebody else has to have a go.

Everything you say about yourself is true – but it's not your turn.'

I was terribly excited when the theatre decided to mount a production of Arthur Miller's play *The Crucible*. I auditioned for and got a small part as the Reverend Parris's daughter Betty, whom we first meet lying in bed, overcome with her so-called intoxication with the Devil. In due course, backed up by others equally hysterical, she rises from the bed and screams. I got the role because I was a great screamer.

I read everything I could find by Arthur Miller. What was then called the Third Programme, the serious and consciously (if not self-consciously) 'cultured' part of the radio, broadcast *Death of a Salesman*. My father, deaf in one ear and normally dismissive of radio, listened with interest as rapt as my own. But neither Miller nor the atmospherics of the play made for sound sleep.

At this time my mother was working partly during the day and still putting in a number of evening sessions per week. Pop formed the habit of taking her one or two evenings a week after she finished at 9.00 to a country pub, where they'd have a quiet chat and relax a bit. During the rehearsals of *Crucible*, I was taken with them, once a week. I was encouraged to sit on (I can't say I rode him) the landlord's enormous bay hunter Nimrod, a horse of dulcet nature who ambled round the village causing me no more effort than the comfortable disposition of my legs. Then, towards the end of pub hours, I was allowed into the quiet back bar where I was fed fresh goat's milk.

All this helped but one night when I still couldn't sleep, my father taught me to smoke. He appeared with a pack of the mildest filter-tipped cigarettes he could buy and taught me. It helped. It still does about twice a year when, in moments of great stress, I reward myself with a single cigarette – though I'm sure that the memory of what it's supposed to do is more important than the tobacco.

As I progressed through the school, it was clear that I was not maths or science oriented and I was allowed to take a second language. I had to choose between German and Latin, and remarked to my father that I was thinking of taking German. 'Why?' he said, storm clouds gathering about the brow.

'Well, at least it's a living language.'

My father walked purposefully into the front room where the *Radio Times* lay and opened it to the page which showed the vocabulary to be used in a current 'teach yourself German' programme. 'Look at this,' he pointed, 'and this. And this. Look at the word for stewed apple. How can you want to know anything about a people with such tortuous minds?' I took Latin.

A year later I asked him why he was so adamant about my not studying German. He explained that although civilian suffering in the Second World War had been so much greater than in the First, what really horrified him was that it was the second time with the same people. He was the least blimpish man but he felt, as did many of his contemporaries, that the 'War to End Wars', as they'd hopefully called the 1914-18 War, only set the stage for the Second. And he regretted, sometimes bitterly, that the campaigns he fought were forgotten. Years later I saw a book on the war in India and Mesopotamia, paying tribute to the soldiers of a forgotten war, and I was sad it was too late to rush to the telephone and tell him about it. He was wise about the cost of war, was my old man, and he'd have broken his heart over Vietnam and Northern Ireland.

In the year that I was 14 I played a Japanese girl in *The Teahouse of the August Moon* and Dunois' page in Shaw's *Saint Joan*. It was then that I fatefully decided (I blush as I write!) to use a speech of *Saint Joan* for auditions When The Time Came.

Then the next year a new producer watched me and told me that he had decided to put on *The Diary of Anne Frank* next season and that I should audition for the leading role. At the time I was preparing for my prelims – the mock exams which, in our school anyway, decided what subjects you were going to be allowed to take at 'O' level. When I told my mother what had been said, she told me I must choose. So I decided I wouldn't audition, and then I pined all summer.

One night my father went to collect my mother from work. She had said they were going on out so I made cocoa and went to bed. When they came in, they came straight upstairs and my father asked if I was awake. I said yes, sat up and put on the light.

33

My mother sat on my bed, Pop stood at the end of it and they told me that they'd watched me all summer and that they thought I should have a go at Anne Frank. Exams weren't the be-all and end-all of everything – and after all, I'd done exams through the runs of two other plays and flourished. Typically I burst into tears of joy and gratitude. If I'd gone shopping for parents, I don't think I could have done much better than mine.

'I'll go and see Miss Muddle,' offered Ma, 'so that she knows what's happening.' We agreed that she would not do this until after I'd auditioned. I might not get the part. But I did. And mother's conversation with the headmistress ran thus: having been informed that both my mother and my father supported my decision, Miss Muddle commented that she had never expected me to be academically distinguished. Blue eyes blazing, Ma retorted at her most steely that 'if that means sitting on her bottom and passing exams, I'm not sure I want her to be.' More of this conversation is not reported. I began a programme of rehearsing five nights a week from 7.00 till 10.00. Homework and revision fitted in, some late at night, some early in the morning. I don't remember anything except being determined to do it. I thought my parents' faith in me was wonderful and I wasn't going to let them down if I could help it.

Anne Frank remains very special to me. We sort of share a name but more extraordinarily my father and hers shared a nickname – Pim. Because of that role, I began a journey into being and not being Jewish about which I have only just begun to speak, but, as a result of playing this role, I discovered that my father's mother, adored by both my parents, was born Julie Rosenbaum in Whitechapel. My grandparents were all dead before I was born and my father can only have guessed at what a chunk of myself he gave me when he told me about her.

Because of playing Anne Frank, I was invited to the Festival of Lights, *Hannukah*, at the local synagogue. I'd never heard a cantor and the music moved me. I was given a most emotional welcome to tea afterwards and for the first time, having become accustomed to being an outsider for so long, I found a reason for my colouring, my features, my emotionality, my gestures. The room was full of dark, emotional, excitable people. I was 15. It is a very impressionable age. I cannot say that all the Jews I've met have been lovely people. I'm not a Jew because in their tradition, being a practical people, the line travels through the mother so my father was and I am not a Jew. I'll never convert because my father taught me that you can only be born a Jew. I'll never be an Zionist. But I've only had three serious relationships with non-Jewish men in my life (one of those is the super goy I married!), and part of the responsibility for that preference rests with my mother.

When I went out into the world two years later, she said, 'Listen, if you're going to get mixed up with somebody, remember the Jews. They're clean, they have a strong sense of family, they don't want trouble so they take care of you. And if you do get into trouble, any trouble, they probably know somebody who'll fix it.' By and large, I've found her advice good – that I can say from a distance. But for years I hadn't got that distance. Take me to a party of five hundred people where there was one preferably Middle European Jew and I would be drawn as though by a magnet. I've read and talked and read some more and those qualities which my mother and I loved best in my father are among the most admirable of all that is aspired to in the Jewish personality. All this because of a play. Oh yes. And I got 8 'O' levels. And the man who played the father of Anne Frank's friend Peter in the play was the lovely Frank Bough, who was just about to embark on his television career and whom I did not see again until we met in the doorway of Kensington House 20 years later.

Chapter 4

I think I've said that the school I went to was very academically oriented. Out of just under one hundred girls in my year, 12
did not go on to university, teacher training colleges or some
other form of further education. I was by now totally serious
about acting and what my mother had accepted, my father
came gradually to confront. But the depth of my conviction
was more to do with playing at being an actress than doing it
properly. I was so green that, although I knew I needed
money for tuition and some sort of bursary to help me live
while I studied, I only really thought about one drama school,
RADA. And we agreed, my family and I, that there wasn't
much point in my getting money for tuition from the drama
school if the local education authority wouldn't make a
maintenance grant available to me for my living expenses.

Accordingly representations were made by my parents,
teachers and theatrical colleagues. I was summoned to the
education offices to be met by the assistant director, a friend of
my father's, who broke it to me as gently as he could that 'the
authority does not make such grants available on a regular
basis and the feeling of the committee is that such grants are
particularly inappropriately spent on girls because they always
get married (and give up the theatre).'

But of course all this just fired my romanticism. Training?
I'll show 'em. Actresses, my dear, are born, not made. So,
once again, my ever-practical (and stoical) Ma pushed me
firmly in the direction of a secretarial training because, that
way, I'd never starve.

Duly we went to see Miss Rowlands of Rowlands Secretarial
College, a tall grim building just behind a railway bridge. I
was to study Pitmans shorthand and typing – we thought we
would not tempt fate by letting me loose on bookkeeping. I

was bought a typing manual, a portable typewriter to do my exercises on and a shorthand textbook.

Most of the teaching was done by Miss Rowlands' star graduate who was, presumably, too good to be a secretary. She was doll-like, immaculately turned out and had beautiful legs. She even wrote beautiful shorthand outlines, but she was no teacher. When Miss Rowlands, who looked like a beaver with glasses, dark hair set round her head in those little stubborn bundles metal curlers used to effect, took a class, we felt we had to try harder and we learned a lot more. It was Miss Rowlands, bless her, who taught me the greatest piece of sense about secretarial work for anyone like me, who are at best just sensible, competent, middle-of-the-road office workers. We were called into a meeting to discuss our speeds, what we had and hadn't achieved and how this affected our job opportunities. Miss Rowlands said, 'When you go out into the world of work, except in exceptional cases, you'll find that your prospective employers are much more interested in other things before they ask about your speeds. They want to know if you're polite, if you can spell, if you do clean work, if you're reliable, if you can take and remember to pass on telephone messages. They want to know if you'll file correctly, run an errand when it's necessary, learn how to handle the duplicating machine or the switchboard in your lunch hour. Only then do they want to know about your speeds.'

I stand as a testament to Miss Rowlands' wisdom, because I never held a job where typing speed was of the essence but I achieved credibility by fulfilling all the other criteria. Far from being the star of her establishment, I left after five months with a typing speed of 18 words a minute and a shorthand speed of 80. I have never used the shorthand and I was sure that once I stopped fiddling about trying not to look at the typewriter keys or struggling with my hands under an apron to hide them from me, I'd be all right. For now I was determined to go to London, backed up as ever by my Ma.

In the summer of the year before I came to London I went on holiday with my sister. She drove us in a large green Bedford van. I felt the whole enterprise was an acknowledgement of my advancing maturity and was happily honoured. We went off to Kent to a sympathetic sounding guesthouse which was in reality clearly the model for Railway Cuttings,

East Cheam, immortalised by Tony Hancock. Every available surface in the guest room was covered with glass and china ornaments and as the trains whistled by every few minutes, they and we slid sideways as the house shook from top to bottom. Weak with laughter and fatigue we moved on to Sussex where in a quiet seaside hotel we had a very important conversation.

Lesley was asking me about coming to London and inquired, without preamble, into my knowledge of contraception. Offended that she thought me so unsophisticated, I retorted that I thought I knew how to take care of myself.

'It's very important that you do,' she said. 'I didn't.'

I looked her uncomprehendingly. Her voice was level and patient.

'I had a baby when I was 21. It was adopted.' I was bewildered.

'Whose baby? Terry's?'

'No,' she said regretfully and then she told me the story.

She had fallen in love with Terry when she was very young. He was a few years older than her and anxious for her sake that they shouldn't rush things. She couldn't convince him that she knew her own mind. One night they had a terrible row. She went into the mess bar, drank rather a lot and went to bed with a married man. When she discovered she was pregnant, she drank gin, exercised furiously and took quinine until her ears rang. The baby flourished.

She rang my mother whose prime concern (which she regrets to this day) was for my father's public position. Ma told her to go to the man concerned and ask for money to see her through. Lesley did as she was told. My sister and my mother connived to keep the baby a secret from my father although my mother went up to Prestwick to see her on every possible occasion.

She spent the last weeks of her pregnancy in a kindly home for unmarried mothers and their children. Ma told my father who, typically, came to see Lesley and offer to adopt the child. Lesley refused. The adoptive parents were wealthy and Jewish. Lesley was allowed one picture of the child at any age. She had a boy. She has a picture of him aged two years old. He was fine and strong and she nicknamed him Buster.

I was shattered. It explained so much. It was after this, and in full knowledge of it, that she and Terry decided to marry. And then he was killed. It explained my parents' grief, the worry about her, the pouncing on letters, the nagging 'specialness' with which I always felt she was treated. My sister, my big sister up on the uncomfortable plinth where my adolescent idealisation of manners and morals put her. I wept all night. It was all so awful.

The next day Lesley forbade me to cry any more. I remember with great admiration and respect that she wasn't foolish enough to say it was over. She bought me a ring with an elephant on it and I thought that was right because elephants never forget and I didn't intend to. And we had a fine time.

Afterwards at home alone with my parents, when all the holiday tales were done, I asked them why they hadn't told me. My mother said almost angrily, 'You always knew.'

I protested that I didn't.

'Well,' she said unhappily, 'I always felt you did.'

I looked at my father.

'Maybe you're right,' he said. 'Maybe we should have told you.' There was a long silence and then we had a cup of tea, and talked of other things.

* * *

I arrived in London on my 17th birthday, April 3rd 1961, with a large suitcase full of beautiful clothes, promptly cashed in the return half of my ticket and decided that, barring holidays to see my parents, I'd never go home any more. So sure was I that Laurence Olivier would one day trip over my feet and proclaim me Britain's brightest young star, that I didn't work for the first three months I lived in London.

I fell in love with London. I still like it better than any other city I've ever been to. I like its size, the feeling that somewhere here, even if you have to look for it for a while, is anything you could ever want. I loved its neighbourhoods, how the character of the streets and shops changed from place to place, the noise of the traffic and the wonderful feeling that nobody knew who you were. The streets were full of people just waiting to be discovered. Nobody knew who they were and nobody knew who I was, which gave me a nice feeling of belonging without rupturing the wonderful sense of privacy. I was far too excited to be homesick.

The first two weeks were spent in the company of a delightful actress called Wendy McClure in a crisp little flat off Baker Street. From Baker Street, I walked everywhere or at least everywhere that interested me. I eventually mastered the appropriate bus routes to get me to the Victoria and Albert Museum and Chelsea, but initially I was far too scared to get on buses or tubes. I had met Wendy when she played the principal boy in a pantomime in Middlesbrough and she was everything I wanted to be but wasn't. I worshipped her as only a young girl can worship a grown up woman. I still admire people like her because I'm not one. For a start, she was tall and slender with very pretty legs. She had a complete 'look' which incorporated every aspect of her hair, makeup and wardrobe. She managed to be interested in other people as well as herself and she was able to disagree with you without altering the generally pleasant tone of the conversation. Her nails were always manicured, she folded her clothes and her tablecloths with equal precision. She arranged flowers beautifully. She had black hair and white skin like rose petals (Scarlett O'Hara again), so imagine this goddess waving aside my anxiety about the dark shadow on my upper lip with a pot of wax and the airy comment, 'Don't worry about that, I'll fix it the way I do mine!' She taught me two things thereby. First, that every good-looking man or woman has to work at it, though only the classy ones are prepared to admit it, and secondly, that knowing what to do is a wonderful thing. But I couldn't stay with her for long because there wasn't room, so I took up a lead from a very nice South African girl I'd known at secretarial school, and moved.

Sybarite and snob that I was, my eyes were on Knightsbridge, but I wound up in the heart of Kangaroo Valley, Penywern Road,\Earls Court, where I was the only Englishwoman in a flat full of colonial renegades in the form of ebullient South and East Africans. They were all golden girls, extravagantly untidy and undomesticated. Their friends, the boys they'd grown up with in Dar (es Salaam), Salisbury (Rhodesia) and Cape Town, were all over here studying at university or agricultural college so that the flat, designed to hold perhaps six, habitually contained some 16 to 20 noisy, lively young people all living together in amazing innocence. I suppose there were affairs from time to time but I don't remember them, probably because I wasn't having one myself. There were hugs and kisses and screams of excitement over mixed bathing but truly, cross my heart, not much else.

I made a deal with the girls. Whilst waiting to be 'discovered,' I would do all the housework and pay no rent. I could also be by the telephone all day for the calls which never came and sneak in a quick few in response to the ads in *The Stage* or to whatever agent I was trying to get to then. I never got past first base with agents – who wants to handle a 17-year-old with probationary Equity membership and only semi-pro experience? So I did a lot of housework. It was quite satisfying. And I lived on a diet of alternate mugs of milk and black coffee. I was far too frightened to take my meagre savings, made up of scrounged birthday money and my wages from working at a dry cleaners' on Saturdays, out of the bank, and too unrealistic to admit that discovery in a shabby flat in Earls Court, with no photographs, no track record, no skills and no agent, wasn't likely. Heroically I ignored the rumblings of my stomach – one must suffer for one's art – until one day I was straining to clean the top of a big window and the floor came up to meet me.

I came to in bed with Fay, an Anita Ekberg lookalike with the thickest Rhodesian accent I've ever heard, looking at me intently.

'What,' she demanded, 'have you eaten lately?'

'Not much,' I confessed.

She went on to tell me that she had taken my temperature, which was considerably raised. She had called the doctor attached to the (now defunct) Overseas Visitors' Club who had said that I probably had German measles, as there was an epidemic of it in the area. No he wasn't going to visit, it would run its course but I must stay in bed and drink lots of fluids. 'And eat,' said Fay. Thereupon with her own hands she made me an enormous plate of steak and vegetables and stood over me while I ate it. A rash began to come out. Another girl lent me her palest makeup to hide the spots, we put silver shadow on the holes where my eyes used to be and, swathed in somebody else's red shirt, I was propped up in bed and permitted visitors.

The hit show of the year was *King Kong* and one of the boys had the LP which we played over and over again. Everybody danced, there was a little hooch about in the form of beer or cider and altogether I can't remember a nicer start to an illness – but start was the key word. Undermined by lack of food, I really was quite ill. I passed the next two weeks in a stupor in which people were kind, cups of tea and Complan were brought in and I dozed and woke haphazardly, responding if I had to. I do remember being blanket bathed by one of the girls, so my fever must have run quite high. But the shock came when I didn't start feeling better. I suppose I was writing home, or even ringing occasionally but one day I got frightened, crawled out of bed to ring my sister who was then living near Portsmouth. If she could confide in me, I could confide in her. She arranged for me to be collected the next day.

I remember bathing because I felt so lightheaded that the bath didn't really seem to be there and every bone ached when I put on the clothes which hung off me. When the doorbell rang, I came face to face with the son of one of my sister's friends, a boy I knew quite well, who looked straight at me and asked for me. In dry-mouthed sleep I was transported to my sister's house, where I walked into the kitchen with the well-chosen line, 'Lesley, I don't think I'm very well,' and collapsed.

If I had lost some of the preceding two weeks, I lost the next two entirely. After that I was very afraid of London but felt that my experience of it was a bit like being thrown by a horse. I had to go back and try again. So back I went, paid my bills and got my first job for £7.10s working for Joseph Graves, Paper Merchants, at 39 Great Marlborough Street where I discovered that my typing speeds, so hard won a few months before, equipped me to be nothing more than a clerk/typist. This was a bit of a blow because secretaries earned more and at least they typed letters while I typed invoices and filed and answered the telephone and ran errands and was generally useful. But whatever dreams I had were not about being a superior form of office staff. I was very glad to do what I could do, collect the money and begin to take charge of my life instead of playing at it. I liked work. It made me feel dignified.

The offices were small, though I didn't often go anywhere except the one that I was working in. I shared this with a wonderful lady called Ellie, a tall, heavy-set Cockney who had trained as a secretary during the war. The man she was going to marry had been killed and she lived with and cared for her ageing parents. She belonged to that group of people who always inspire me because they are so good that it just shines out of them. I couldn't tell you whether she was pretty or plain, because any aesthetic judgement was suspended as irrelevant from the moment you'd looked into those true, blue eyes.

I remember her because she was kind and funny, super-efficient, patient and practical. She showed me how to type invoices, she encouraged me to learn how to handle the switchboard. She helped me to laugh off the tragedy of my first London salon hairdo, a long bob with flip ups at the sides and a teased top, the whole edifice lacquered to the consistency of gritty plastic and as enduring as teak. She listened to my talk about my dreams, my wishes, my family – did I say she was patient? She must have been a saint. For the eleven months I was there, during which time my salary rose by the princely sum of one pound, she encouraged me daily to do better – get my speed up, take a refresher course in shorthand, remember everything Miss Rowlands had said at secretarial college, do it neater, quicker, better, brighter.

Within a very few weeks of taking this job, I learned that even in those far off days when money went much further, what I was earning wasn't enough. I found a second job at Lavells, the confectioners next door to the London Palladium where I worked from 5.30 until 9.00 every evening during the week and either Saturday or Sunday, depending on how shortstaffed Molly the manageress was. To begin with I gorged myself but there's nothing like relentless exposure to sweets to make you long for a Marmite sandwich. The work was surprisingly tiring. Rushes of people came in on their way home from work and just before the curtain went up. You learned to rig cigarettes so that you could serve more people quicker, to weigh out and wrap quarters of the most popular sweets to have them ready (though there was always somebody who had to have his weighed again, just to make sure he hadn't been done). Boxes and jars of confectionery are quite heavy and ripping them open was harsh on the hands, but strangely satisfying.

The job didn't last long. Molly the manageress and I had a misunderstanding and eventually I went to see the film *Judgement at Nuremberg* instead of going to work. I found the fact that I could vanish into the crowd very exciting and very welcome. In those first years in London I think I surrendered to it and very nearly lost myself on more than one occasion. To begin with the values seemed quite different. I don't think it was so much the difference between Middlesbrough and London, as the difference between being a young person still living at home and being off on your own, answerable to no-one. I had never before messed up on a job. But the thinking was, it's hard work, not much money, she's been getting more and more unpleasant, it's been getting less and less fun. There are (there were then) other jobs. So I drifted. And moving from scene to scene, without having to explain to anybody, is feeling a sense of power for the first time in your life. And then there was the business of my name.

Somewhere right back at the beginning of my time in Penywern Road there had been another Sally in the flat. I was christened Sally Ann Taylor. We stuck three weeks of the confusion of both of us answering and both of us feeling a bit irritated by it, and a fair solution had to be reached. It was agreed on the principle of first come, first served, that Sally would remain Sally. My flatmates would call me by my second name but although I like the name Ann for other people, I recoiled from it for me. I asked them instead to call me Anna and so I chose another name, another beginning which, while it was very exciting, was also rather cutting myself adrift and often I felt as though I were making up a role as I went along. I think I was. Sometimes I think I still am.

Somewhere during the eleven months that I worked for the paper merchants, the happy band at Penywern Road disintegrated and as I couldn't afford a decent room on my own, I looked around for someone to share with. The only person that I could say I knew, though she epitomised quite a lot of the things I can't stand in women, was the original Sally. Not an ideal choice, but my attitude towards roommates was that as long as they paid their share of the rent, anything else was tolerable, short of snoring or stealing. Better the devil you know than the devil you don't. She came from a moneyed family in Kenya, went to a smart secretarial college in London for debutantes and dukes' daughters and was doing the world the greatest favour by working until she married a nice well-heeled young man. She was also what the French call an *allumeuse*, the worst kind of sexual tease, all talk and no do. She was always superficially smart but I never remember her cleaning her shoes or her handbag. Her nail polish and lipstick matched but as she rarely washed her face at night, she had an inclination to spots, duly covered in their turn by yet another liberal layer of makeup. She was giggly and charming in a way that makes me feel that underneath there is a harshness towards the human race – to women because they're rivals and to men because they're always finally unsatisfactory. However she was gainfully employed in the City and good for her half of the rent.

The rooms we shared varied from a filthy hotel in Holland Park where the plughole of the alarmingly communal bathroom was always blocked up with black hairs, to a cold water flat in Gower Street. As long as I was happy I didn't get homesick but as we dragged from one miserable place to another, bound together by nothing but the rent and tolerance, I fled into a telephone booth and rang Ma. 'Please, I want to come home,' I said tremulously. 'No, you don't,' she said. 'There's nothing for you here' and she went on to talk me round and up and over the next hurdle. It wasn't until years later that she told me she put down the receiver and howled.

Eventually Sally and I came to the good offices of 21 Cranleigh Gardens. This was a rooming house presided over by Reuben (known as Ruby) and Doris, their daughter whose name I've forgotten and a mynah bird called Charlie. Ruby was curved of spine, shrewd of mind and looked remarkably like his bird, but essentially he was as kind as Doris. Always good for a pint of milk or a shilling for the ravenous gas meter, they bore with the numerous telephone calls I received each evening by the most acceptable method yet. They answered and took the first half-dozen messages. Thereafter they simply said she's not here, call back, and kept that up till the callers desisted or I came home.

I was not aware of being fabulously popular but thought that the wider you cast your net, the better range of fish to choose from. I didn't know anybody and I wasn't going to be able to decide who I wanted to know unless I met as many people as possible and then made my selections. So there were always lots of calls and in those days I drank too much. It's pretty easy for me to drink too much because I have no head for liquor. Nowadays I could not sit and drink all evening, but then it seemed to be what one did in the group I was running with. The smart drink was whisky, which is now something I put in toddies when I have a cold and where it tastes so awful that I feel it must be doing me good. But what shocks me in looking back is how rarely I bought a drink. Bearing in mind that nowadays I am regularly regarded as a 'women's libber' (of which more anon), I look back and shudder to think what a cold-blooded little freeloader I was. I figured that men had more money than me so if they wanted my company, they could pay for it and frequently calculated whether or not I could afford to buy some garment or other against how many times I would be taken out to dinner that week, i.e. how much money I wouldn't have to spend on feeding myself. It wasn't until quite a lot later that I discovered that many of the young men I looked to for my food and entertainment were living on tick and pretence rather than admit that they were scraping by like most of the girls they knew.

With the loss of my secondary job, I decided it was time to change the primary one and accordingly got myself on the books of a small secretarial agency called Personal Services. To my now rather quizzical ears it sounds like the name of an escort agency but in truth it was strictly above board and I remember its proprietors with gratitude. My shorthand had died a terrible death for lack of use. My typing was mediocre. I still fulfilled all Miss Rowlands' other preconditions for being hired into an office but my speed was not speedy. Joe and Miss Barton obviously knew this, so they sent me out to jobs in which I would have to get up speed but wouldn't disgrace myself or them too much. It worked. A year later my speed was a reliable if unexciting 45 words a minute. Bless them.

But there was still never enough money and I was bitten by a bug which still nibbles me. I began to buy clothes. By all the laws of reason, I shouldn't have needed any new clothes for a couple of years at least, for when my mother took over the running of the evening school in Middlesbrough, she made friends with a wonderful sewing teacher called Jasmine Greenwell. You've heard of having an 'ear' for languages? Mrs Greenwell had an 'eye' for clothes. Remember that I was thin, wanted to look like a ballerina and was more interested in elegance than any of the other words so often attached to dressing. Remember too that my mother was no slouch when it came to fleshing out every dream she could. She had had to take my sister through an adolescence when there were acute clothing shortages, financial difficulties and my sister's weight to be taken into consideration. Now she had a bit more money, there was more in the shops and I was fortuitously slight. Bingo! I had a wardrobe. Sadly, having a wardrobe did not guarantee having a figure. My father commented that a square meal would stick out on me like an egg on a snake. I made up my mind that I would spend the rest of my life in black and dark grey, looking austere and so dashing that the question of measurement would never again raise its head. Measurements were nothing to do with elegance or art. I was, as you can see, a skinny little prig.

Chapter 5

The last part I played in the Middlesbrough Little Theatre before I came to London was Carol in *The Flowering Cherry*, a play by Robert Bolt about a man, who among other things, makes a fool of himself over a pert little art student. To play her we sprayed my hair dark red every night, painted the rest of me golden brown and I wore a white fluffy sweater, black drainpipe trousers and pointed boots. It looked all right. It was just that I couldn't quite handle whatever it was this girl was supposed to be doing. The director kept saying, 'Sexy, dear, do it sexy . . .' which sounded fine except that I didn't know what it meant.

In the course of a rather acrimonious evening with the aforementioned director, who claimed of course to be interested in my talent, I found out. It meant that I was palpably a virgin and it was getting in the way of my acting. He tried to get me drunk on gin and 'help' me himself, which I avoided. He then hissed at me that I would shrivel up and die if I didn't get on with being a woman soon. 'You're too much of a spectator,' he said. 'You're never involved, you're always outside with your nose pressed to the glass.'

It wasn't difficult to understand why he was being so waspish but it seemed that there was a certain truth in what he said. Certainly I didn't want anything I could do something about to get in my way. There were enough imponderables already. Roll on London, I thought, and then I can deal with that.

One night in Fulham (not as trendy then as it is now) I went to a party where, across a crowded room, I saw a very attractive man. I pranced over, spilled some of my drink on his shoe and got talking. One thing led to another, I think we met about four times, and my first sexual encounter changed

48

my shape. I do not mean to sound prissy or evasive by calling it that but I have an aversion to all this stuff about 'lost virginity'. Dogs get lost – physical sexual virginity is either taken or surrendered. In my case it was positively thrown away. I can't remember what part I was playing that evening. All I can remember is that I didn't say no (as a matter of honour, because I meant yes) and if I'd know how expensive it was going to be in terms of wardrobe, I might have reconsidered it. Few of the clothes I'd brought with me from home ever fitted me again. I went virtually overnight from having what my father had called the vital statistics of a snake (28-28-28) to having bust, waist and hips. Aren't hormones interesting? And I can't justify it in the name of love because I didn't love him at all. I just thought he was very beautiful and very romantic, being as he was of mixed French and Armenian extraction. He wasn't very bright but he was a dead ringer for John Keats as displayed in the National Portrait Gallery and he looked as if he might know what he was about sexually.

Upon reflection I think it's fair to say that he probably knew less than me, was much less affectionate in temperament and was frankly horrified to discover I was a virgin. He did the deed, largely because I clearly wished him to (I thought it would make me into a woman, you see!) but then he suggested I went and slept elsewhere because he never slept with anybody. As the location of this episode was the double room at Cranleigh Gardens, with belated apologies to my landlords, and Sally was away, I crept over to her bed to curl up, a bit sore and tearful.

The next morning he drove me to the tube, kissed me goodbye and vanished from my life.

To begin with I felt sad. I didn't think he'd been kind (any kind of pleasure was much further down on the shopping list) and I felt a bit let down. A mutual friend took me to his mother's cottage where we had a fraternal weekend which included him advising me that our absent friend was not somebody I should get involved with. But when I heard that my erstwhile swain (or do I mean swine?) had been hospitalised with appendicitis, I raced to his bedside, obviously hoping for tears of remorse and reconciliation. 'What on earth are you doing here?' he demanded crossly. I told him I'd come to see how he was. 'I'm fine,' he said impatiently, 'but my mother and my girlfriend are arriving soon so I'd be very grateful if you just hopped it.' I hopped.

Outside the hospital, I decided that everybody makes mistakes and I'd just made a lulu. Who wanted to make love with a rude boor even if he did have the face of an angel? It is said that you never forget the first time. It's not worth remembering unless you learn something from it. Mine was neither horrible nor wonderful, just a bit sad but there were two little sequels which keep it in the mind's eye.

Two years later in the Café des Artistes where the young would-be hip used to go, he stumbled upon me again and by now I was much more his cup of tea. I was dressed in black, escorted by a man who looked and sounded right and he apparently remembered nothing except my long-ago infatuation. He was charming, Lord yes, he was always charming. We danced and he muttered increasingly passionate nothings into my increasingly wrathful ear. My hair was long in those days and when he murmured, 'And your beautiful hair – how much more beautiful it would look spread out on a pillow' – not one of the most shiningly original lines, you'll agree, I kneed him as hard as I could before walking away, leaving him bruised and furious on the dance floor.

Nine years after this, I worked with some film students, one of whom had a curious name. I queried it and was told it was Armenian. The Armenian community is small and without thinking I asked, 'And do you know this name?'

He nodded, a bit surprised. 'How do you know him?' he asked.

'He was,' I said with all the aplomb I could muster, 'the first man I ever went to bed with.' He looked taken aback and I laughed. We all have to start somewhere.

* * *

I met my first love within a few months of this episode and I displayed no great judgement of character there either. But again, he was very beautiful. I suppose it's all this early experience of judging people by their externals which has made me so wary about doing just that as I get older.

It is true that you cannot help but be attracted or repelled by some people, that others make no impression and are

50

unmemorable, even faceless. It is true that there are people who appeal to you and others who make you wrinkle your nose. But as we live in an age dominated by all kinds of media and media make the darnedest people seem familiar, beware.

To build a relationship, you have to get to know the other person and he or she has to get to know you. If you spend as much of your life as I did skittering from one to another, it's not surprising that the relationships weren't worth much. Of course you can still have your favourites, your dream men and women, but until you spend some time with them, you know nothing about them.

I never knew Paul with whom I first fell in love. I fell in love with what I wanted him to be. He was a little like Nureyev, tall, muscular, blond, green eyes. His grandfather had made a fortune, his father lived on the remnants. He had been educated with his brother at Harrow and he was fitted for nothing so much as a life he could never lead.

He was kind to me when I was an unformed, farouche little thing of 17 and I saw him at intervals in other people's houses until I went off to the States two years later. He wrote me one or two inviting letters which made me homesick, a disease I never shook off anyway. If I'd been older – or maybe just wiser – I'd have known that his professional ability to string words together (he'd started as a journalist and gone into public relations) attracted me far more than anything he had to say.

He loomed about and I felt boneless and dizzy every time he hove into view but He Was Not For Me it seemed and anyway I was getting very tired of not doing what I really wanted to do, which was to act.

When lo and behold! I was invited to play a little Scots girl in a piece called *Lace on Her Petticoat* at York Repertory Theatre. This was several kinds of miracle. Firstly, it was an acting role. Secondly, it was for a whole month. Thirdly, it was in York, which is a good deal nearer to Middlesbrough than London and so I could look forward to seeing something of my parents. Fourthly, it got me away from this demi-god who didn't know I was there and fifthly, it was a chance.

Of course I should have smelled a rat. But I was so happy that even if I had done, I'd probably have sworn it was a rose. The play was a filler, the company not very distinguished, the director the same I'd had the run in with over the small matter of my body in Middlesbrough, so I prayed he would now take me seriously. He played it very shrewdly. He ignored me just enough to make me terribly nervous and took just enough notice of me to keep me permanently poised for flight with one eye on the door.

My mother came to see me and we had lunch. York is the home of a chocolate company whose product is my mother's favourite and in York they have a restaurant. We had three courses with ice-cream – a grown up lunch – and Ma stayed to see the play. Within a couple of weeks I was back in London. I had one further tiny acting job on television in *Dixon of Dock Green*, of which it can truly be said that if you sneezed you missed me. And I did one promotional job, being one of a bevy of young ladies sitting on the back of a large American car when Helen Shapiro opened a supermarket in Barkingside. I was still full of *Plays and Players*, Stanislawski and dreams, all of which took a terrible knock when I next looked round for a job.

There was a black spot in London, no temporary clerical jobs. I had promised myself I wouldn't take another permanent job, it would just take me further and further away from my chosen career. But after two weeks I'd have sworn on a stack of Bibles that I'd stay in the filing department of the Gas Board for 40 years if they'd have me. The jobs just weren't there. In desperation I rang Lavells the confectioners, praying they wouldn't send me to the Palladium shop or ask too many questions. They didn't do either and I worked at their branch in St. Pauls. In the evenings I tried to become a barmaid but I was no good and wound up as an usherette at the Academy cinema in Oxford Street. There I saw Godard's *Vivre sa Vie*, a Czechoslovakian cartoon called *The Happy Apple* and a short about the dancer/choreographer Maurice Bejart 56 times. Other people read books in the bad light at the side of the cinema or gossiped in the hall but I couldn't not watch that screen. I continued to think Bejart was wonderful until I went to one of his less reflective later works and emerged finally disillusioned. And I knew Godard must be special because I didn't understand his film at all.

* * *

My next birthday was my 19th and I felt that I'd blown whatever chances I might have had. The only option, I thought, was to start all over again. So I announced that I wanted to go abroad. My father mentioned the Dominions and I said I wanted to go to America. Pop loved Westerns. I said I was thinking of New York, he thought I meant New York State and when it became clear that the child of his old age was off to yet another city, he was not happy.

I expect my mother talked him round using the line she'd used when I went to London. She told me about it too and I thought it was generous and very farsighted. She said she always felt she had to give me a long lead in the hope that I'd come home when I'd had enough. If they (my parents) tried to hold me on a short one, she felt I'd kick up and rebel, breaking the tie and going off anyway, so that we'd all lose contact. No manacle could have bound me closer than what she told me.

It seems impossible to me that my parents, whom I valued as wise people even then, would ever have mishandled me in such a grave matter. Now, with a child of my own, I see my mother's wisdom and her courage and her foresight. It cost her emotionally far more to let me go to America than to London. London is only a train ride away. But once you've crossed the Atlantic, you don't hop on a bus and come back. I knew nobody in America, neither did my family. And had we known of its unreason, its violence, I might never have got there.

I got a job through an agency called Country Cousins. If you were over 21, you could apply for a secretarial job but under that age, you had to be employed to do domestic work by a family so that you had somewhere to live and older persons could keep an eye on your welfare. The family concerned advanced your airfare – $300 in those far off days – and the form required you to list the tasks you were prepared to do in the home. I blithely filled in everything I could think of and we paid a registration fee. We checked the contractual form with a solicitor friend of the family and he couldn't see anything amiss with it, though pointed out that once resident over there, it was their laws I should be worrying about, not ours.

It then became apparent that if I were to apply for a visa in the north of England, the port of exit would be Liverpool.

With apologies to all Liverpudlians, I didn't want my last sight of Blighty to be Merseyland, so I went and slept for a few days on a friend's floor while the American Embassy at Grosvenor Square did its stuff.

Even in those days there was no such thing as a temporary job in Middlesbrough and I didn't want to lie and then drop myself or someone else in it, by just walking out when the visa came through. My father suggested that as the educational authorities were desperately short of teachers, I might get a job as a supply teacher. He sensibly asked me not to apply to the North Riding Education Authority for whom he worked but to apply in the East Riding just across the River Tees. And I did.

I told a very pleasant man that I had 8 'O' levels, that both my parents were teachers and that my time was limited because I was applying for an American visa. He sent me off to Nunthorpe Primary School where the head teacher was a man slightly known to me from my acting days at the Little Theatre.

Mr Black asked me to spend a day with a different class every day for a week and then decide which age group I felt most comfortable with. I chose nine-year-olds. I took English, arithmetic and general activities classes and twice a week read a story to 98 kids, who then acted out sections of it, discussed it and wrote about it for a double session.

It wasn't so much teaching as performing and although it was utterly exhausting, I liked it very much indeed. It was a happy time for my father. He had wanted my sister Lesley to teach and she had declined. I was never interested in it and now here I was doing it with apparent enjoyment. He used to drive up to collect me from school and ask me how I felt. 'Tired,' I'd say. 'You'd better be,' he'd say. 'No good to anybody if you don't do it properly.'

After three months I still hadn't received any payment although I knew the rates. I was very much younger and more easily embarrassed about money then. So I just waited. But one morning my mother said, 'This is ridiculous. Stay at home. When they miss you, they'll ring and then we'll get somewhere.' In due course the telephone rang and the supervisor of the department I worked for at the education authority demanded, 'Mrs Taylor, where is your daughter?'

'She is at home,' retorted Ma, 'which is where she is staying until she gets paid.' There was a shocked silence. Our irate caller apologised, said there must be some mix-up and he'd call back. It transpired that I couldn't be paid until I had been seen at work by an inspector, questions would have been asked about my qualifications and my head master found me too useful to risk losing me to the inspector's critical eye. I had worked for nothing.

Then I sat in an office and scaled exam results for my father's employer – a job which left me with real distaste for 'places' in the streaming system, though I must say that at a cursory glance the alternatives don't work too satisfactorily either. But it did seem cynical to say well, you've got twelve suitable kids and there are five places, take in the first five, and send the other seven wherever you can fit them in, which is what we did.

All this time, I really wanted to go, but the American Embassy lost one set of forms and we had to start all over again. I think my parents hoped against hope that I would relinquish the project if it was delayed enough, but when they saw that I was determined, they gave me their support. Their friends criticised them very strongly for letting me go: what some thought was selfish, others thought was dangerous; and still my dear stubborn family smiled and smiled.

You cannot get into the United States the way I did any longer. Then there was a quota system, so many able-bodied Anglo-Saxons with visible means of support for specific kinds of work were admitted at regular intervals.

I spent a whole day at the embassy, clutching photographs and certificates of one kind or another and handing out money. Every time you passed through a section or were told, 'Just go to that window there –' you handed over money. Then there was a panic because the X-ray showed scars on my lungs. 'Can't give you a visa,' they said. 'Tuberculosis.' But I hadn't actually had TB, just the preparatory stages and it was ten years previously that I had been cleared. Could I prove it? Frantic calls to Middlesbrough General Hospital, records dug out of a frozen file – deep breath, that scare over. My last memory before being granted my visa was of having my feet examined. 'Why my feet?' I asked. They informed me with the utmost gravity that fallen arches or other difficulties could

55

preclude me from the domestic work I was applying to be allowed to enter to do. I have had considerable respect for the US Immigration Service ever since.

Chapter 6

My first impression of New York as I was driven smartly out to New Jersey by the agency representative was of some very tall black buildings. When I asked what they were, he replied drily, 'Harlem.'

The suburban home in Tenafly at which we arrived looked like a set for *The Graduate* or one of those later movies in the same vein which showed that the externals are gleaming over the decay within. My employers were a gynaecologist and his wife. He was civil, but preoccupied with work. He seemed to be from older money than she, so he could handle anything in the way of domestic fittings, even an English maid. His wife Reggie always made me think that she had married above herself and everybody within a five mile radius was going to pay for her insecurity as a result. The house was spacious, white and detached, comprising some 11 rooms. There were four children ranging from 6 to 14 and I was the only domestic help.

When I look back I like to think that Mrs Lincoln meant to be kind when she insisted that I didn't wear my own clothes for the housework in which I was everlastingly involved but at the same time it sounded as though she wanted me in a housedress to be sure I knew my place. Nowadays when I meet unhappy students or au pairs who say things like 'Yes, I eat with the family but . . .', I know something of what they mean. I ate with the family too, but not when the family had company and not until everything that had to be done on the day's domestic schedule and all preparations for that meal had been done. Thanking God that I couldn't cook and had said so firmly on the agency form, I did everything else. I had never shopped in a supermarket. Nowadays they're commonplace, but then the glittering rows of goods frightened me. I had been brought up to be particular and brand-loyal about what I bought. So was Mrs Lincoln and I was truly terrified of buying the wrong thing.

I had a rota of work which included thorough cleaning of one section of the house every day, fitting in the washing, ironing, silver cleaning, marketing, laying and clearing of tables round whatever the children may need. As I recall I had trouble from the outset with the eldest boy Donald. He thought I was there for him to mock. I was never very good at being mocked. The next child was the odd child out of the family, a nervous angry 12-year-old called Duncan. I got on well with 9-year-old Andrea who appreciated having another female around, but 6-year-old Geoffrey was my cross. He whined, he lied, he cajoled and I got thoroughly confused trying to keep him occupied and tackle the ironing. One day I hauled off and thwacked him whereupon he ran to tell his Mommy who was writing a letter at her desk in the master bedroom. She asked me if I needed to hit little children. Nowadays I'm afraid she'd have had a rather grittier response than the tearful and embarrassed recantation I gave her then.

Within three weeks of my arrival Dr and Mrs Lincoln decided to go away for a week. It was the longest week of my life until then. They seemed to see me as a sensible girl who could handle anything and it was only with difficulty that I convinced them that they must leave me the name and number of a neighbour, the doctor and the local police. They looked at me as if I were a bit odd. That was the last time I remember being frightened of responsibility.

They departed leaving me with a stock of things in the freezer to be heated for supper and dubious authority for getting the kids up and off to school, fed and into bed.

Within two days I discovered I could appeal to Andrea for help and get it. I could get the awful infant Geoffrey dealt with by sheer volume of sound (mine) which exceeded whatever he could produce. Getting any of them off to school was easier than getting them to bed. Duncan would procrastinate for a bit but then go to bed and read and I could only empathise with that. It was so wonderful to find that one of these aliens should do anything remotely comprehensible to me. But Donald really played up.

On the second day of his parents' absence he told me that he needed a note for school. 'But I can't write it,' I protested. 'Yeah, you can,' he insisted. 'You just sign Mom's name, they'll never check the handwriting.'

I refused. He threatened. I stuck to my guns, arguing that if we were discovered, we'd all look foolish. He went off to school in a sulk and avoided me as much as possible until the night before his parents came home when, upon my repeated requests that he please go to bed now, it was half past ten, etc., he picked up a kitchen knife and told me to shut up or he'd use it.

Donald was 5 feet 10 inches tall and I'm 5 feet 4. He was also a great deal stronger than me and I was psychologically disadvantaged by having no previous experience in dealing with bad tempered adolescents with knives. Just as I had decided to invoke my father's best sergeant major impersonation, Duncan appeared from nowhere and hurled himself between us shouting, 'No, no, you mustn't do that to Anna. It's wrong. Don't, Don, don't.' Donald looked a bit sheepish and went to bed. Duncan looked at me and I looked at Duncan. I said 'Thank you.' He said 'G'night.' The next morning Donald asked me not to mention the incident to his father or he'd be in serious trouble. I stared. But he gave me better advice than I knew. Because, like a fool, I mentioned it to his mother who said, 'Well, you managed, didn't you? What's all the fuss about? Young people get a bit excited sometimes, that's all.' Pure brick from the knees up, that one.

The terms of the agency contract were that the family who wanted my services advanced my airfare – and that once I had successfully gained entrance to the States, I must pay this back at $30 per month. I was paid $100 per month. In fairness, 20 years ago $25 a week meant £8 and if you had been living with a family who really took you to their hearts in Britain, £8 a week wouldn't have been a fortune but you would have managed. However there was more than a currency difference between here and the States and even 20 years ago $25 a week was bad news. As the laundress from a neighbouring establishment I met at the bus stop commented, 'Honey, they're paying me $25 a day and I'm black!' On top of that I had landed with the sort of people who paid my $100 over with the $30 already subtracted and submitted a bill accompanying my miserable $70 which asked that I pay for my housedresses, my telephone calls (all local, inquiring about drama classes) and the extra oranges I consumed.

Down the years I've been able to rationalise everything except the oranges. I thought it was mean to charge me for clothes I didn't need to buy and none of my telephone calls had been long distance but I could see the logic of those items if I tried. To charge me for eating extra fruit seemed and seems pathetic.

My day off was Thursday but I soon discovered that if I wanted to have a day off rather than a few hours break, I had to fight for it. Mrs Lincoln could always find something for me to do. The oven needed cleaning, Geoffrey's toys were all over the basement (how I wished he was!), couldn't I just do this or that before I left? After the first few weeks, I summoned up the courage to say no.

As I saw it, I rose, made six beds, assisted with breakfast, loaded the dishwasher or washed up by hand which I preferred (how to you tell Mrs House Immaculate of 1963 that her dishwasher smells bad?) and then having checked that we had everything necessary for a snack lunch for the kids, I left. She goggled at me and I descended to my basement bedroom, picked up my handbag and marched with righteous dignity to the bus stand. Two weeks previously I had auditioned successfully for a place in drama classes taught by Gene Frankel in the city.

When I look back at all the people with whom I could have studied drama in New York City, I wonder how I came to Mr Frankel. But I know. I was probably awed by his direction of Jean Genet's play *The Blacks* and proceeded on the same principle as with Godard – if I didn't understand it, it must be marvellous.

I had already made friends with Ellen Brody who shared a nice little apartment in a beautiful brownstone with her sister-who-was-hardly-ever-there. Ellen, daughter of rich Jewish parents, currently in rebellion and therapy, lent me a black linen coat dress. Don't laugh. It was then the epitome of how to dress. It still is – for Ascot.

Frankel had hypnotic eyes and a beard; he looked just like an unconventional intellectual should look. I humbly sought entry to his beginners class. After my reading (I think I actually had the gall to use St. Joan!) he announced that I could join his intermediate scene study class. I should have known then, but no. I was thrilled. As I walked down McDougal and into Bleeker, these two streets being the arteries of Greenwich Village, I met a man called Edward Gordon.

He was quite tall and dressed from head to toe in black. The dramatic impact he made was increased by the fortunate possession of a craggily aristocratic face and shoulder length flaming red hair. And I shall say of him as I say of all sorts of other people: I don't know what he was to anybody else, he was wonderfully kind to me. I started to smile at this vision and then changed my mind, this being New York, Greenwich Village even, and he a strange man. He said, 'Hey, if you're going to smile, you might at least do it properly!' Irresistible. I blushingly obliged. 'So what are you smiling about?' Poor man. Nobody should ever ask me a question who doesn't have a half an hour to spare. I told him about Frankel, the class and wanting to be an actess. He asked what I was doing now. I told him, including some of my employers' less delightful be-haviour and he remarked, 'You know, that's a bad deal you've got yourself into. If you want to get out, I'll help you.' I thanked him but declined. I owed the people money, I couldn't leave until it was paid and I had that very morning handed over all my savings to Mr Frankel for his class. He looked at me patiently. 'If you get fed up and you want out, just come and tell me. Anyway, you can always come in and have coffee.'

I met him several more times after that. My classes were from 9.00 pm until midnight on Mondays and Thursdays. Thursday was fine because it was my day off but getting away from Tenafly, New Jersey where my gaolers lived to get a bus into the city for 9.00 on Monday evenings became a work of art. Significantly, neither of my employers ever thought that I might have been gypped out of money or in danger, they never asked where I'd been or evinced any interest. I could have been making bombs or dealing dope for all they knew.

My friendship with Ellen Brody flourished. She showed me around New York and I could always come back to her apartment for a bath or a rest. It was the first place in the continent of North America where I ever felt at home and as she loved the city, I fell in love with it too.

I've written about the difference between being in love with and loving – to my mind, they're worlds apart – but the feelings unite when I think of New York. Recently I did some work there and understood for the first time why some people don't like it. It was always hard and frenetic. When you're young, with boundless hope and energy, you think that's romantic. It was always grubby and glamorous. Contrary to the myth New Yorkers love to build about their city, it is never easy to be poor in any city if you aspire to acquire anything more tangible than knowledge and experience. But in New York, even when it was cold and you were broke, there was always the possibility of immediate wonderful change. Anything could happen and often did. But it takes courage and energy and self-knowledge (or a synthesis of all three) to deal with New York. Last time I went back I saw only the conspicuous consumption of midtown and it repelled me. It was like having to look at 16 visual Christmas dinners when all you really wanted was a boiled egg and brown toast. But in 1963 it was the City of the American Dream, it was better than Hollywood could ever have made me think it was and I loved it.

Ellen took me to meet her mother, an imposing woman who offered us coffee and cake. The cake was heavy with chocolate and cream and we were offered mocha ice cream to put in our coffee. Her mother approved of me. I've spent most of my life being approved of by other people's parents. So now I could answer the telephone in the apartment without apologies. Ellen's mother knew I had keys.

Elena (my nickname for her) was the first person I ever met with an analyst. He seemed to dominate her waking life to the extent that she couldn't buy a hat without consulting him. She was funny and elegant, she cooked well and she knew some interesting men. One such was a Graeco-Armenian Jew called Allan Garboos who convulsed me by explaining how he grew marijuana plants among his mother's tomatoes in Brooklyn. And it was he who thoughtfully insisted that I should at least try smoking dope. I should say that quite a lot of other people who lived around and visited Elena did and I was usually happily contact high (from inhaling their smoke) on the bus back to terrible Tenafly.

Another man I liked very much was a pianist called Jerry

Tannenbaum who seemed to know the composer Aaron Copeland or maybe I just thought he did because he loved his music so much. Anyway one night I decided that, as I didn't have to be on duty until 7.00 am, I would give up racing for the late train to Port Authority and the last bus home, and Jerry very kindly offered to drive me out to suburbia with the dawn. Elena cooked chicken parmigiana, we drank wine, smoked and listened to Jerry and other music. It wasn't much more daring than a gathering of friends, like a transatlantic edition of Penywern Road. I wound up in Elena's sister's bed after everybody but Jerry had gone home. He dozed and played his way through the night and in due course I roused him, we drank some coffee and set off to take me back to New Jersey.

He dropped me from his rather grand car and said he'd give me a call some time. I let myself into the house, showered, dressed appropriately and went up to the kitchen where Mrs Lincoln was starting breakfast. I greeted her and though her reply was chilly, I just went on doing the necessary for breakfast. It was only after Dr Lincoln had left for hospital and the children for school that I asked her was something wrong. 'Wrong!' she exploded. 'I should say there is! Turning up here at some ungodly hour in the morning, so all the neighbours can see. And don't think I don't know what you've been up to!' To which I replied in the accents of a junior Lady Bracknell, 'Madam, with what you're paying me, you should be glad I'm not running a call girl service from the house.' And I went about my many tasks.

I was angry. They'd never asked anything about what I did or where I went. They'd never showed the slightest concern for my welfare. Several times the local police (yes, even in bloody old America) had picked me up, walking up the hill from the bus at 3 or 4 in the morning, and driven me home. I gathered from the glances they exchanged that they didn't think much of the Lincolns' casual attitude. And then she presumed that I was whoring around because that's what young servants let off the leash did!

The day passed in prickly silence. When Mrs Lincoln went out to play golf, I rang the man at the agency who had collected me at Idlewild Airport when I flew in. He was not interested. Why became clearer when the telephone rang later in the afternoon and I picked up the kitchen extension, crossing with Mrs Lincoln answering in her room. 'Are you,' asked the man at the agency, 'having trouble with that girl?' I put the receiver gently back and stood and thought.

The next day I rang my friend Clayton Ruby in Toronto. Well, I hoped he was my friend. We'd met in the lift at South Kensington tube station and he had offered help if I ever needed it. Clayton was studying law and I asked him about the wording of my contract with the Lincolns. He wrote me a most detailed letter which arrived a few days later and which said that, as far as he could discover, the terms of my contract were invalid under a United States Supreme Court ruling of 1944 with reference to 'bond service'. My obligation to return the money the Lincolns' had advanced for my airfare was moral, not legal.

The next time I went to my class in the city, I went to see Ed Gordon and told him that I did want his help, all $300 worth of it. It seemed to me the most enormous sum in the world and he sensed that I was appalled by what I was doing. He took me for a walk and pointed out various buildings which he said either he or his family owned. To this day I'm not sure if I believed him but if he owned even one of the pieces of real estate he showed me, then he could afford $300 worth of whim. He asked me when I was next coming to the city and said he'd have the money ready for me. If he wasn't there, he'd brief his manager Steve and Steve would tell me where to find him.

I don't remember much about my acting classes from that time on. It was all along the lines of 'think deeply and relate to the ashtray' and I was deeply disappointed in the guru Mr Frankel. Perhaps the denouement was the night of the performance of the scenes we had variously been studying. One boy had ill advisedly chosen to perform the 'To be or not to be' soliloquy from *Hamlet*. He chose wrongly because it's famously difficult and as if this was not enough, he had a heavy Oklahoman accent. There are plays and parts in plays where this might have been an advantage. Shakespeare's *Hamlet* is not one of them. And he wasn't confident enough to let the accent be and concentrate on interpretation. He flattened his voice into an awful mock-English through which his drawl escaped at intervals like smoke under a dirty door. When he finished, Frankel destroyed him in a verbal tirade reminiscent of Attila the Hun. Criticism is something actors have to learn to accept (who doesn't?) but this was overkill. The boy began to cry. Frankel surveyed his students. We were aghast.

'Any questions?' he asked.

I sounded terribly British asking 'Mr Frankel, do you think your criticism is justified?'

He smiled at me knowingly, 'Anna,' he began, 'that's not the point . . .'

'You're damn right it's the point' I said, surprised that anger had not destroyed my power of speech. 'That could be me down there. How dare you?' He started to bluster, then cut his losses and asked me to work next. When I was done, he praised me fulsomely and when he'd done I thanked him still trembling with rage, and pointed out that I had not come 3,000 miles to find out how good I was, but to get better. With that episode, my idol fell into a thousand pieces. I didn't care to finish the course.

When I came in to the city to meet Ed Gordon, I was frightened. I thought of everything that could go wrong. I thought about the white slave trade, dope rings, the Mafia. I reminded myself that Ed Gordon probably couldn't remember my surname and didn't know my address. Maybe I'd been followed. To Tenafly? Unlikely. What it came down to was that if the price for $300 which would buy my freedom with honour from the Lincolns was going to bed with Ed Gordon, he could have me gift-wrapped.

But Ed Gordon, bless his red beard, just wanted to do me a kindness. He wasn't in the cafe, so I nervously asked for Steve. A cheerful young man with black curls said, 'You Anna? Oh fine, he's expecting you, go on up.' Every alarm rang at full volume. Here it comes. I rang the bell to his flat and he let me in. I followed him up some stairs and it looked as if he was expecting a witches' convention. The place was draped in black, very clean and neat with lots of books everywhere. Once I'd seen the books I felt better. I don't know why but I thought that seduction and literature didn't go together. I asked him what he did when he wasn't running the cafe and he showed me into another little room, full of guitars of all sizes, bits and pieces of them lying on a bench. 'I make

65

guitars,' he said. So, 15 minutes later, unrumpled and breathing a little more easily, I re-emerged into the street, having met his cat (black of course), named Shakespear (no 'e'), and clutching an envelope containing $270. 'We'll just take the rest out of the till,' said my unlikely rescuer and we did. I thanked him, refused a coffee and went off to think for a bit.

I went to see a man called Jimmy who owned a shop called 'Si Como No?' (which means 'Why not?' in Spanish, I think). There were three boys my own age sitting there and one was just going into the army. Of the other two, one was introvert to the point of silence and the third was black. We sat in a bar on Sixth Avenue for an hour or so, having one of those 'this is quite nice but it isn't going anywhere' conversations and I made my way back to Port Authority at 42nd Street, which is where the bus depot is. The New York subway was never my favourite mode of travel and that night the carriage I travelled in was completely empty until two stops before I got out, when I was joined by a very large drunken man. He sat down unnecessarily close to me and I was too frightened to move, reasoning that if I did and he followed me, I'd be caught off balance by the train. He stood in front of me, grabbed the front of my dress and between extreme good fortune and the madly swaying train, I managed to floor him with a boxing feint of my father's (left fist to gut brings head forward, right hook into chin) plus a knee in the essentials. Clutching my dress, I belted up the steps and very quickly aboard a bus where I sat and shook. Somebody would try to mug me the only night I had enough money on me to make it worthwhile.

I didn't mind walking up the hill from the bus stop that night because at least I could see the end of this chapter. But somehow I couldn't believe I'd got that magical, wonderful $300. I kept it in a drawer and counted it every night for a week, until I was sure it was there and I wasn't dreaming. Then I rang my Canadian friend Clayton and told him I was going to resign and go to work in the city. He immediately offered to come and spend a long weekend with me, his father having offered to finance the spree as I was new to New York. Delighted, I agreed. I then wrote a formal letter of resignation complete with one month's notice, stuck it on Mrs Lincoln's desk and got on with cleaning the bathrooms out.

She was so angry she declined to speak to me further. Dr Lincoln said he regretted it all very much, felt I was letting them down, after all they'd waited all those months while the American Embassy lost my papers and it did seem . . . I let him ramble on. All I knew was that this might have been a wonderful job for a masochistic dogsbody but it wasn't for me. However, it did have two advantages. It taught me that whatever you get yourself into, you can get out of it, if you want to hard enough. And it taught me to make hospital corners on beds.

I left Tenafly never to return in a grey imported Jaguar – the housemaid's revenge. I gave Andrea my pearl and marcasite earrings because they were little and pretty and I thought she'd like them but saying goodbye to Duncan was painful. 'Are you really going?' he asked. I said I was. 'Don't you like us?'

'Well,' I said, 'let's just say I like some of you better than others.'

He looked at me, hungry brown eyes and hunched shoulders. 'Good,' he said. 'Liked you too.'

Chapter 7

How can I explain what living in New York meant to me? As a starting point, it was totally unlike anywhere else.

In London, it had been made perfectly clear to me that without further education or a handy fairy godmother, I would have to wait until I was about 30 before I qualified for an interesting, let alone worthwhile, job. In New York, all they wanted to know was if you could deliver what you promised and if you could, your birth certificate didn't enter into it.

In London people were always asking me to calm down, slow down. In New York, everybody was wound just that much tighter. They expected to play as hard as they worked and my alleged high energy level was quite unexceptional.

In London I'd been going the round of theatrical agencies being told I was plain, hard to cast. At one memorable open audition Brian Rix described my face as 'a little hard for farce'. Why, agents kept asking, didn't I dye my hair, straighten my nose, inflate my bosom? I'd been in New York for six weeks when I exchanged smiles with an elderly couple as I walked down Fifth Avenue. Breathlessly the woman caught my elbow a few blocks further along. 'He won't say it,' she panted, her shyer husband nodding in agreement, 'but we think you're the most beautiful girl we've ever seen and I think we should tell you so!' To put such a tribute in proportion, this was around the time that Barbra Streisand stopped the show in 'I Can Get It For You Wholesale'. But still . . . And if London was a centre of activity, then New York was the intergalactic capital of the new. In New York, anything could happen.

I went to New York in the July of one year and left the Christmas of the following one. It was a sort of abbreviated course in life as it was lived in the early sixties on the eastern seaboard of the richest nation on earth. Not that I saw much of the wealth except in shop windows, but being poor in a city is a particular way of coming to know something of it. And the something was very different from the movies I'd seen.

I had to get a job. As New York has the biggest Jewish population outside Tel Aviv and was allegedly at the height of its affair with the British secretary, and since I looked Semitic and sounded BBC, how could I lose? Secretarial agencies may vary one from another, but the ones I visited were not the cosy or comfortably disinterested organisations I was used to in London. They were cold and cryptic and unnerving.

Struggling through questionnaires clearly designed along the lines of enrolment forms for some law enforcement agency, I made another unpleasant discovery. At that time the policy of British employment agencies was to charge you one week's earnings if they placed you in a job. The New York version involved a frightening percentage of your first month's earnings so that even if I did get a job, I didn't know how I was going to live for the first month.

I couldn't stay at Elena's flat because her sister-who-was-never-there had decided that she wanted to make use of her share of it for a while. An abortive attempt at rooming with a girl I'd met at my ill-fated drama classes ended when she chased me round her flat, bombed out of her mind on pills and vodka and waving a carving knife, just because I dared to disagree with her. My next stop was at a brownstone on Lower Fifth Avenue. The elegance of the address was somewhat marred by the discovery that the flat hadn't been cleaned for about 20 years. I made little inroads with disinfectant through the muck and forebore to draw the curtains in case they disintegrated. Because it was so neglected, it was cheap, but still it strained my resources.

I became a receptionist for the Beneficial National Insurance Company on the 26th floor of the Chapin Building on 42nd Street and Lexington Avenue. The office manager took pity on me and I still think of her with gratitude every time I see an advertisement for her perfume – Replique – which I disliked about as much as I liked her. I was shown how to work an enormous Key-Lite switchboard and introduced to American office life. They gave me a pet name which I was very excited about because I'd never had one before. They called me English – short for English Muffin – and they kindly waited for me to settle in.

According to Miss Rowlands' Golden Rules, I did well but I never belonged there or anywhere else. My fault entirely – I was so busy keeping the door of alternatives open, I nearly perished in the draught. It's not as simple as saying I'm ashamed of the next few months but the way I saw things then and the way I see them now has inevitably changed with the passage of time. Heaven knows if ever that quip about 'What qualifies you to be an agony aunt?' has an answer, then 'Agony!' must be apt.

I don't think I was so much intensely curious about sex as intrigued as to why so many people got excited at the mere thought or mention of it. So I tried men the way nicer girls tried hats. I was not promiscuous. I was never anybody's. Either I chose somebody or he chose me – with a bit of luck it was mutual. Some I got to know, some I never saw again. Some were friends to begin with and stayed so. Others I made it my business to lose. Certainly I tried men out, just as they did me. Sometimes I felt that what I was about was the only way to be and other times I longed for it to be different. The one thing I didn't do was 'have sex'. I made love and like pastry sometimes it was good and sometimes it was better. And what about something practical like contraception, you ask? Well, it makes me sick to record that I used none, which makes me living proof of that profoundly silly and all too common belief clung to by others as much at risk as I – 'the longer I get away with it, the less likely it is to happen'.

I was embarrassed and ambivalent about my conventionality. It wasn't the stuff that any sort of stars were made of and although I'd given up the dream of being discovered, I still longed to be recognised for something. And all these years later if you asked me what I want, I'd say, 'To be really good at something.' The trouble was then, that I thought that if I only could be 'successful', at least I'd leave a mark. Now I know that the only thing I'm really good at is intangible. I like to think I've accepted this but when I talk into my mirror, the dreams I spin are not so different from what they ever were.

But I couldn't shed myself. How much of a personality is innate and how much is formed by what goes on round it? I went to New York in the sixties when you could feel the cries of change in the air even when you couldn't hear them. All over the world, people were reassessing what was on offer and trying to find new ways to live, through new and old philosophies, through music and drugs and politics and art. I didn't share all of their convictions but I could sympathise with their search for an alternative to what the various establishments proffered. And yet, here was I, 19 years old, holding down an unambitious little job five days a week, answering to some stubborn practical streak which reasoned that the money I earned bought me the freedom to choose. I chose to spend some of my evenings and most of my weekends in thrall to the so-called bohemian/beat/hippie life I'd already glimpsed in Greenwich Village. I don't think I was ever fool enough to think it was glamorous – it was too genuinely tense and grubby for that – but it was the furthest away from anything I'd ever known before. In that life, everything seemed higher, harder, more extreme, nearer some sort of edge and I fell into the romantic kid's trap of thinking that that made it more valid.

In that other New York I was one of four people I knew who worked. One was a doorman, one had a factory job upstate and Martin was trying to be an agent. Nowadays he has his own record label. Everybody else I knew 'got by'. Although I had heard of drugs and had prostitutes pointed out to me in London, it took me months to work out that one of the pack I ran with was off but mostly on heroin, that another became a hooker to support her drug habit and that a third went on the game because she couldn't think any further. Everybody I knew was a misfit in one way or another and I was happier with them than with anybody else, though I made commitments to nobody. I think I succeeded in feeling comfortable with them because none of them were any more at ease with themselves than I was. We were all on the road to somewhere but nobody knew where or if we'd ever get there. We all suffered from the same feeling of exclusion and they were very protective of me. I was around hard drugs but nobody tried to give me a shot. I was around hookers but nobody suggested I turn a trick. They were rather proud that I was different, a foreigner in more ways than one.

It was one or other of these amiable losers who showed me the different areas of Manhattan, who took me riding on the

Staten Island ferry at 5.00 in the morning, when the skyscrapers glisten like sugar towers and you can't see how furious and filthy the city really is. It was they who took me to the Apollo, the big theatre in Harlem where all the class black acts play for the brothers. It was they who showed me people who were every bit as interesting as books and who accepted without question my double life, uptown and Village, plain and purl. And they gave me my one Christmas away from home. We hocked a television, had fried chicken, bad wine and a fine time until I decided to ring my mother to ask my birthweight. The sound of her voice, quite unflustered (don't your offspring call over 3,000 miles with such trivia? – and a Happy Christmas to you too darling), turned the freedom I thought I was celebrating into something as cold and unfriendly as freezing fog.

A short time after this Martin the agent who was, I should explain, a sort of link between this world and the straighter one I inhabited during working hours, got a job at *Billboard*, the bible of the music industry. Martin was at heart a nice Jewish boy and I was probably the only person who ever called him Martin. He was Marty (pronounced Mardy) to everyone else. He thought that perhaps if I had a more interesting job, I wouldn't continue my flirtation with what he considered unsavoury characters. Grubby dealings in Greenwich Village could only enhance his aggressive virility while they sullied my female opposite but equivalent, was the way he reasoned it. So he arranged for me to work a little more remuneratively for a man who had his own record distribution outlet. I bought copies of Italian knit suits, very high heeled shoes and took to smoking untipped Gitanes in a short bamboo cigarette holder. How could I ever mock anyone else's prolonged adolescence or sense of unreality? Until comparatively recently I approached every new phase of my life as if it were a role. Learn the lines, change the make up and wardrobe and for heaven's sake, get the props right. Will the real Sally Taylor please stand up? Who's she?

My job lasted only a couple of months before the poor man went bust and Martin slipped me into *Billboard*. It was a fascinating place to work, although my typing speed had once again seriously declined because I'd never seen an electric typewriter before and *Billboard* owned to nothing else. The magazine was printed in Cincinnati, which is a long way from New York. The company had secured a concession from the Bell Telephone Company for so much time each day long distance at a reduced rate. Each department had to use this time quite literally to the minute to assemble their section of the publication over the telephone.

One day in the offices of *Billboard* I was telephoned by Capucine. She was then involved with William Holden whose secretary, Hella Loeffler, had asked her to make sure I was all right in the wilds of NYC. To trace the connection, I had met Hella while I was working for an eccentric Greek in Highgate who was supposedly financing a new musical. I was sent to him by the heiress to a sugar fortune whom I'd met at a nasty party given by a man who frequented the same pubs as me and who was looking for what was then described as 'fresh fruit'. The moral of this part of the story is – you don't have to turn down the invitation, but always make sure you don't drink too much and that you've enough money to get home!

It is not every day that a movie star invites you to lunch. Many of the details of this event remain on the photographic files at the back of my eyes. No, she did not make a pass at me. No, I do not remember what we ate. But I do remember that her colouring was exquisite and never appeared to advantage on films. In life her hair and skin were the same exotic tone, a mixture of milk chocolate and silver nail polish. She looked like La Belle Dame Sans Merci in black jersey trousers. She was immensely kind to me, even indulgent, to the extent of encouraging me to sing her some of the songs I was then trying to write. And, for a clothes freak like me, she brought our afternoon to the most wonderful conclusion by having to go out and changing into the first couture clothes I'd ever seen close to. I'd clocked the Balenciaga bra and stockings in the bathroom but she topped that with a charcoal St. Laurent suit, dark brown suede turban, croc shoes and a vast liquorice coloured mink.

What Capucine did for me is the story of how not to grab an opportunity. When I'm feeling phlosophical, I shrug my shoulders and say, 'Ah well, it wasn't to be.' Most of the time I think I was just too green and silly and scared to seize the chance. And the lesson is – why bother being scared? You can only fail and it isn't the worst thing in the world. Not trying is far worse. As I've grown older, I've learned to turn that fear inside out into a kind of energy which propels me forward but then, if anything unexpected happened, I was drawn speedily backwards, as though into forceful retirement.

Through Capucine I met the cousin of one of Broadway's most prestigious producers, who was also Harry Belafonte's manager. Impressed by my gullibility (I can't think of anything else which could have impressed him) he took me and the songs I'd written to meet Belafonte. Mr B. liked the stuff so he paid a guitarist to sit with me in a loft and make lead sheets out of the songs I could hear in my head. (I couldn't and cannot write music.) I was then sent to see Jac Holtzman of Elektra Records who was very encouraging and wanted me to work on them.

But I didn't know what he meant. I thought works of art fell perfectly formed like pearls from the brain. I couldn't ask him for an explanation. I felt I ought to understand and that asking such a question would make me lose face with him. All I could think was that work meant 8 hours a day at least and how could you work like that if nobody was talking about money? And how could I bring the subject up because it would be so crass if it was the wrong thing to do?

When we parted Mr Holtzman asked me to ring him. I never did. I kept the music sheets to prove I didn't dream the whole thing and recently I gave them to Linda Thompson, the only professional musician I know, who was looking for new material and temporarily stuck in the writing of her own songs. There isn't one of them worth a bean in their present form but I wanted to help her if I could and I knew she'd understand. They are still my progeny and I stammer when I talk about them.

Life continued with rather more routine highs and lows. My first job at *Billboard* involved endless filing. My second had me working for six of the most delightful, harried, overweight Jewish men it has ever been my good fortune to meet. They sold record advertising space and they didn't even question that I was Jewish too. They flung Yiddish slang (Ameridish, according to Leo Rosten) backwards and forwards across my seemingly impeccable nose. I learned most of what they meant by intonation or context until the day I had to ask, 'What does that mean?'

74

'Whaddya mean, what's it mean?'

'Look,' I said, 'I'm sorry, I'm not Jewish.'

Silence, round eyes. 'Migod,' they exclaimed 'a shiksa!' and they teased me about it forever. As far as I can remember, I was fired from *Billboard* – reduction of staff, most recent arrivals being the most vulnerable – but not before I'd learned to listen to what makes up a record, not before I'd been to some record promotion parties where there was so much to drink, it made me want to sign the pledge and not before I'd moved in with Martin.

When I did this, he changed. What was formerly European eccentricity, like mixing with what he called bums in the Village, was now a major no-go area. Nobody needed to spend more than a few months getting all that out of their system and my time was up. Eating wasn't a no-go area, thank heavens, because at that time I was going for gold as a trencherman. (At my all-time high I weighed 156 lbs, a great deal too much on my 5ft 4ins frame). But pizzas and sandwiches were vetoed in favour of broiled hamburgers and cottage cheese. Martin erred towards the chunky and wanted to slim so I did too and we were aided by spansules of Dexhedrine and vitamins, which increased my nervousness and made me very uncertain tempered.

I liked Martin. Sometimes I thought I felt even more than that for him and I'm sure that part of his mission was to save me from the dangerous ground on which I often walked. But I could sense a little reforming zeal in there too. I was bright, relatively attractive and, with a quick makeover, I was just the kind of girl you took home to mum. Once that happened, I could see suburbia beckoning and I wasn't interested. So we argued about all sorts of silly things.

One night he removed me from a bar because I was getting 'too excited' and once we got home, stuck out his chin and said, 'Go on, you're so mad at me, hit me. Go on, hit me!' I socked his jaw (too big to miss), he overbalanced, hit his head on the wall, the table and the iron bedstead on the way down and came to with me weeping on his chest, 'Martin, I've killed you. Speak to me!' It was the nearest I ever came to behaving like a heroine. He left with dignity. Outmanoeuvred, I smashed the bedside table in rage and he went to stay with his family in the Bronx for a few days.

We came to the crunch in a way I couldn't have anticipated.

He had among his friends a couple called Peter and Eloise. One evening we were getting on each other's nerves when he announced, 'I don't know, Anna, maybe the problem is you're really a dyke.' I stared at him. I asked very quietly what gave him that idea, being aware, even then, that there are large numbers of men in the world who, if they aren't getting what they want of you are quick to allege that you reject not only them, but all men and are really One of Those. 'There's that ring,' he said, tapping one of my proudest possessions, a silver ring I wore on the third finger of my right hand. 'That's a dyke ring.' I digested this. 'And then there's the way you kiss Eloise, every time we say hello, every time we say goodbye.' I looked at him very carefully. This man was somebody I'd had real affection for. Was he mad or was I? 'Eloise has noticed it. She's commented on it.' Part of me was hurt. Part of me was curious. He wasn't the first person to comment on my physically comfortable rapport with women. I was more hurt by Eloise than him. What I said was, 'Martin, one of the things you liked best about me was bed. If you think I'm a dyke, it's your balls we should be worrying about, not mine.' Goodbye Martin.

I moved and I moved again. I lived with two other girls briefly and discovered that it was too late to play the flatmate game. I lived alone and shared the apartment with various friends, including David and Pete from Middlesbrough who came over for several weeks that summer. I began to understand that just because I lived in New York, it didn't follow that I had to run all day and all night every day. I began to work for a PR company with an out of work modern dancer from Texas called Sally and a wonderful fat lady who'd changed her name from Ida Crumstein (or something equally unappealing) to Moselle Meanders, which she'd read on a wine bottle in a stupor and thought had a certain ring to it. I had ceased to go to the Village except to look at it and I had begun to be able to bear my own company. Suddenly I became ill.

I had thrush, the dreaded pain and itch, but I'd never had it before and didn't know what it was. All I knew was that, if it was down there, you took it seriously. Sally sent me to see her doctor. He wrote out a prescription for a boiling water douche with white vinegar. Boiling is what he wrote. And antifungal pessaries. I couldn't believe my eyes, I thought he meant 'boiled', so I asked him. 'Well yes,' he said. 'As hot as you can bear.' There's a jokey saying about not knocking it till you've tried it. Well I tried it and it hurt.

For a week or so I alternately inflamed and semi-soothed my long-suffering private parts. The day I stopped, I began to feel very odd, lightheaded and feverish. By midday I couldn't sit down or cross my legs without discomfort and an hour later I couldn't pass water. I remembered a friend telling me about a wonderful new doctor she'd found so I rang her at work and got his number. When I called his receptionist said he was out but would ring me. I put the receiver down and began to feel very frightened. Within minutes of the call being returned I was edging down the five flights of stairs into the street. The journey took 20 minutes. I crawled into Dr. Waye's office. He took a history and asked me to slip into a hospital gown so that he could examine me. For some reason he couldn't give me any pain-killers and I bit through my lower lip trying not to scream. He wrote me a prescription and I went home to bed. He visited me frequently, trying out one drug after another to try and get the infection under control. Matters were made much worse by the additional moisture I'd been pumping in by douching and the internal scalding I'd given myself. He fed me tranquillisers to keep me lulled, and I edged from the bed to the loo, holding on to the wall, very grateful when I was at least able to do that for myself. Dr Waye was gentle, competent and furious about what had happened to me.

I hallucinated and dreamed, significantly about my father's mother and my mother's father, their respectively favourite parents. I was too scared to think about my own parents in case they discovered what kind of a mess I was in. I had to resign from my job, but gradually I got better. Then one crisp late autumn day I went for a walk in Central Park, got carried away with the freedom of it all and walked too far. The scar tissue broke and then ulcerated. Dr Waye sent me to a gynaecologist, a plain gingery man with a charming voice and a much needed sense of humour. Squelching with gentian violet, I still didn't heal. When Dr Waye discovered what I was eating – lemon tea, fruit and yogurt – he ordered me to ring my friends and tell them I needed red wine, steak and white bread. It worked.

Of course I thought I could just get up after all that and be my usual energised self immediately. I couldn't. My knees gave way and the room swam four or five times every morning between rising and leaving for my last job in America – as secretary to a small engineering office. Thoroughly scared by what had happened to me and what might have happened, I was chastened in demeanour when I went for this job. The boss, whitehaired, vigorous and gentlemanly, considered me rather carefully before giving me a month's trial.

Dr Waye kept an eye on me until one day he finally pronounced me discharged. Very gently he asked me what I intended to do about his bills. I told him the truth, I'd have to pay him back at so much a month. He asked me about the fainting to which I'd admitted after having collapsed in public a couple of times.

'Have you got the bills with you?' he inquired.

'Yes,' I said, 'I have, but I know how much I–'

He asked for them quite firmly. Silenced, I handed them over. He tore them up. 'Thank God you're all right,' he said. 'I'll tell you now there were a couple of times when I was really worried. Now, I want you to do something for me.'

I gulped. 'Anything.'

'Right. Call your parents and ask them to fly you home. You aren't going to be able to work or run around for a while. You should sue the bastard who got you into this mess through the American Medical Association but you haven't got the time or the money so I'm paying for his mistakes. Now please, go home.'

From my high of 156 lbs, I now weighed 94 lbs. That night I rang my mother and tried to tell her what had happened without frightening her too much. They flew me home on the money they'd got from insurance after my father was hit by a car. Had he not been, the money would not have been there.

Chapter 8

While I was in America, my parents retired to St. Peters, the village in Kent in which my father was born. I think I probably looked most unwell, and I certainly felt distinctly ropey but I was longing to get back to London. However my parents weren't happy about this and I didn't see how I could come home dependent upon them and then go back to London against their wishes. Accordingly I got a job as a hotel receptionist in Margate. Pa drove me to and from work while I tried to acclimatise myself to England and my parents tried to acclimatise themselves to me.

I felt I was living in a beloved but constricting dolls' house, except that the whole landscape was small, not just the house, and that depressed me. That area of Kent is known locally as 'the elephants' graveyard' because the air is so pure that people retire to spend their last years there and then go on living for ever. There wasn't much companionship for me. And I drove my poor mother up the wall with the violence of my language and the constant translation of all significant prices into dollars or 'real money' as I called it.

It is never easy to come home in defeat and I hadn't planned to come home at all. I had emigrated to the US, determined to make a success of myself, if not to achieve international stardom, and all I had to show for it was a collection of adventures. But my parents were so glad to see me and I to see them that somehow or other we muddled through the first few months.

But really I wanted to go back to London and soon began to point out that I had not much chance of social life or job opportunity where I was. My parents hesitated but I per-suaded them that, as they loved the country, so I loved the city. And I couldn't (and can't) imagine being tired of London.

Accordingly I began applying for jobs through the then *Evening Standard* and *The Times*. Of course there were companies who regarded living in New York as enterprising and those who thought it indicated irresponsibility, rather more of the latter than the former, sad to say. I was beginning to be rather discouraged when I answered an advertisement for secretary to a doctor. Dr Kildare, eat your heart out. He was a plastic surgeon and he looked like a Jewish James Bond, tall and elegant in a peerless grey suit with discreet but expensive cufflinks. He was blunt but courteous, I didn't attempt to make myself sound more than I was and he didn't seem to want a commitment for life. The interview was half enchantment, half cold shower. Towards the end he said that though he was desperately looking for a secretary, my lack of shorthand was a deciding factor against me. And although I thought he was a fascinating and appealing man, I was so intimidated by the suite on Harley Street, the attractive nurse Judy with the shortest mini I'd ever seen and a glimpse of the soigné clientele, that I was almost relieved I hadn't got the job.

That afternoon I was interviewed by a man who was, under one hat, an investment consultant and under another, an executive at Oxfam. He was dull and ratfaced but he offered me the job.

That evening at home Mr P the plastic surgeon rang and asked if I'd reconsider because, shorthand or not, he'd be willing to give me a try. I said I was sorry but I had that afternoon accepted a job. 'Blast,' he said. 'Oh well, if you're not going to work for me, I suppose the least I can do is invite you to dinner.'

I can't remember where I stayed for the first few months in London. There were all sorts of acquaintances old and new, so I lived out of a suitcase while I got to know Mr P a bit better. He was divorced, unhappy and very gifted. He had enviable professional credentials and the charm of seven devils. He was a serious gambler with a uniquely silver voice, part cockney, part toff and part American. He traded on his partial deafness by making you say things you were shy about louder and louder, over and over again. And although to my knowledge he spoke no other languages, he could communicate with anybody once he'd decided that he wanted to. He was a perfect hero for a worldly waif, a bit above my touch really but lovely to dream about.

And then I met Paul again, Paul who would never notice me before I went to America. I didn't get the chance to flatter myself I was going to have to choose between them because Mr P rang and asked me if I'd like to do some part-time work for him. He was behind on a paper, he'd pay handsomely – 'There's just one thing,' he said. 'If you work for me, that's it, you understand? I don't think you can mix the personal with the professional.' That seemed fair and I accepted.

Paul was the Nureyev lookalike I'd imagined myself in love with before, but now, desperately wanting to belong somewhere (or do I mean to someone?), I was sure I was in love with him. Presumably the two years that had elapsed had enhanced me sufficiently for him to feel that he wanted to bother. He borrowed his brother's flat for our first tryst. The next morning, wearing his shirt and all the worldliness I could muster, I asked him how he liked his eggs. It was humiliating to confess that I didn't know how to scramble them and he had to demonstrate.

During that day, he said very properly and seriously that if this was going anywhere, meaning him and me, we should be thinking about precautions. When we next went to bed, I assured him that I was taking the Pill. Three weeks later my period did not arrive. Deeply ashamed that I had lied to him, I fled to a friend's flat in Tufnell Park. If he rang my office, I cut him off. My friends lied for me and covered the telephone at home. After a few days he turned up at my office, took me for a very civilised drink in Sloane Street and asked me what was the matter. I remember playing some scene about 'giving it time' and 'it was so lovely, I didn't want to rush it.' Recalling this makes me very uncomfortable because it was so phoney and because it was and is the kind of verbal outmanoeuvring game women play with men. What could the poor man do but bite the bullet and wait? I refused to give him the number of the flat where I was staying ('I need time to think') and I went on running and hiding until a few days later when I fainted on the tube. I knew, before I hit the floor, that it was not because the carriage was hot and crowded.

How could I have a baby? Emotional immaturity was my middle name. I had nowhere to live. I had no financial resources. My parents weren't young, I couldn't embroil them in this mess and ask them to go through all that. It never occurred to me to have the baby and give it up for adoption because it is the hardest thing to do and the damage that is done to the mother is probably irreparable. In any case, I wasn't any good at real suffering. I just liked attitudinising. It was my fault. I'd got myself into this corner and I had to get myself out. I had no well thought out rationalisation about 'blobs of jelly' or it 'not being a real baby'. I can cry no mercy. I knew what I was doing and I clung very hard to what my father had always taught me, that the mercy of God far exceeds the mercy of man.

Before the 1967 Abortion Act, if you could raise the funds you went to certain private doctors in Harley Street or its environs who, in turn, referred you for two psychiatric opinions. If the latter opinions concurred that your mental health would suffer if the pregnancy were allowed to continue, you were whisked away for an 'appendicitis operation' at a cost of £150 at a selected nursing home. Vacuum curettage was not common, the 'scrape' (as the d and c is called) was most frequently used and more complicated procedures later in the pregnancy were not always successfully undertaken.

If you had no money, you asked around. A friend introduced me to a man who said he could do it at home for £40. The grimmest preparation was covering the bed with newspapers and polythene bags. In furnished accommodation, you were always wary of stains on the mattress. The man arrived. His hands and his instruments were clean. He examined me and then passed a mixture of soap, water and quinine into my womb. The pain was memorable, like a kick with a cobbler's awl on the end of it. I was sick. He gave me some soluble aspirin, told me to go to casualty at the local hospital if there were any complications and left. My girlfriends cleaned me up and sat with me, talking quietly by the gasfire. I became light headed and their murmured conversation made me feel more lonely than silence. They went away for a bit. I went to the loo. Are you supposed to look? What are you supposed to see? I walked up and down the corridor between the bedroom and the lavatory, gagging against the wall, instinctively knowing that I had to keep walking. There was an expulsion and a lot of blood. I cried myself to sleep.

Two days later Paul rang in the evening. I couldn't imagine where he'd got the number from. He had obviously been drinking, just to get his courage up, and he asked if I'd been doing what he feared. When I said yes, he asked, 'But Anna, why didn't you tell me? Why didn't you let me help you?' I explained that I had lied to him, that it was really my fault and anyway it was women's work. It was years before I could let anyone help me. I was always asking for help but never knew how to take it. I might add, with some asperity, that there are many people who offer it but few who know how to give it. Anyway, he asked when he could see me. I told him soon, I'd ring him. And at this point Mr P the plastic surgeon asked me if I'd work for him full time because he decided that, even without shorthand, I couldn't be worse that the temporaries he'd been having. I grabbed the job with both hands, began seeing Paul simultaneously and once again embarked on a divisive double life, being at that stage aware that Paul and I were not going anywhere and sublimating my affections for Mr P into his typewriter!

I continued to bleed for six weeks, not enough to worry about but enough to preclude going anywhere without spare pants and STs. Paul fed me Guinness and held my hands, literally, while I wept and slept. One morning I woke up knowing, the way you do, that something had happened. I looked down at myself and the bed was black with blood. I woke Paul apologetically and he helped me to the bathroom. I felt weak but I felt better. I don't know what he did with the sheets – threw them away I think, they were ruined.

Upon examination by a doctor, I was told that I'd probably had a retention, some foetal material left over in the womb, and now that that had come away, things would probably go back to normal – did I know I was lucky to be alive? – and that they'd take a blood sample. The lab technician was quite aggrieved to report that, bleeding or no, I wasn't remotely anaemic, a testimonial to the health-giving properties of porter.

Although Paul and I endured a couple of years after that, I don't remember anything else about him as kind or loving as his attitude towards me up to and after the abortion. I don't recall feeling guiltily that I must live with him because he was the father of my child but I suspect that somewhere in there I felt obligated to at least try and make a go of it. It didn't work. We were, I think, burned out before we began, In any case, my job was much more interesting than my life,

Mr P. had three children and he was a good father. He fought for his children in the teeth of his wife's vagaries and her remarriage. He had debts everywhere, he lived very high off the hog, he had just completed seven years of formal Freudian analysis and had not inconsiderable emotional problems of his own. He was, in short, a great deal more inspiring as a love object (being besides all else an Older Man) than a young unsuccessful journalist, even if he did have green eyes. The deciding factor was that Mr P.'s work was fascinating. He could and did explain operations, motivations and techniques and more than once handed me a mask so that I could watch. I remember he had a new form of prosthesis for breast augmentation and he shouted excitedly 'Hey Anna, come and see this!' I rushed into the little operating theatre, just in time to see him pumping dextrose solution into an aperture in the patient's breast (the silicone balloon designed to hold the fluid was already inside). 'Look,' he said enthusiastically. 'You can get the dimensions exactly right. And feel – just like real boob!' Such tactics did not endear him to all his colleagues but his patients thought he was wonderful. They were right. He would do anything for them and his assumption that Judy, his nurse and I would do the same was what brought me a cropper.

It was Paul's birthday. I'd warned Mr P. that this was one night I'd have to go on time. He had agreed. A very unhappy woman had a car accident. She was a patient who'd earlier presented herself for surgery but on whom Mr P. declined to operate, because he felt that her problems were unlikely to be assuaged by anything he could do, as he put it, 'with a knife'. Whether the door of the car flew open or whether she had tried to throw herself out is unanswerable. She had the misfortune to fall on a patch of gravel which, with the impact, was driven into her face. Somehow she got into a taxi and came to the one person she felt she could trust. Everything swung into action on the spot the way it does in medical circles on those occasions. Troubled, I did everything I could and left.

When I came in the next morning, the patient was bedded down in the spare room and Judy said she'd been up half the night. Mr P. had got every piece of stone out of the poor woman's face and he was grey with fatigue when he left. When Mr P. arrived that day, he stood in the reception area and told me in tones of ice, 'What you did last night was unforgivable, just not on. You've got a month's notice.' And I was too frightened of what I might hear to ask him what I had done so to this day I don't know. I think I was supposed to stay on hand in case I was needed, whether to make tea or run an errand, just to be there, to be part of the team. And I'd left. I'd gone off home because I'd arranged that that was what I was going to do that night. And I hadn't wanted a row about being late. It was my bid for independence but I couldn't have chosen a worse time or a worse occasion for it. What I said was, 'What do you want me to do about getting you a secretary?' He avoided the question. Then he went on a working trip abroad. When he came back, I tried again. He yelled at me. I desperately wanted to understand what I'd done wrong, to ask for an explanation, to apologise and be forgiven but fear of what I might hear stopped me from asking. I've spent large portions of my life in fear the way other people are in want. God knows why, I've had more advantages than many.

So because of my inability to take my medicine and try and sort it out, I left the one job in the world I'd had at that point that really mattered to me. I was caught between my two lives again and it wasn't comfortable. I got another job to force him into replacing me. The practice couldn't run without some-body to answer the telephone at least. Eventually we had an agonising conversation in which he talked himself into asking me to reconsider. I didn't understand the look on his face but it was painful to see. Nowadays if I witnessed such an expression, I'd ask about it. Then, I was too busy being appalled at what I'd wrought. I refused to continue in the job, found him a temporary and left.

Shortly after all that, Paul proposed. I accepted without thinking. I'd just been on a bender, utterly miserable about the loss of the job with Mr P, an almost acceptable sublimation for the man himself, and here's the other man in my life offering marriage. Our relationship was entirely back to front so this ran true to form. He bought me an antique coral engagement ring which I disliked but wore amid appropriate comment and we planned to be married in the church in St. Peters. When Paul had to go away on a job, I promptly developed nephritis (inflammation of the kidneys) through which ghastliness I was devotedly nursed by Monica Flynn, a large and elegant lady I'd first met as one of Mr P.'s more dramatically overweight patients. (It's nice to see that she now has the dress shop she's always wanted, for large and elegant ladies.) Between the reading of the banns and the fever, I panicked.

'I can't go through with it,' I appealed to my mother.

'Then don't,' she said. It sounded like a benediction. When I told Paul, he drank warm champagne, was mildly abusive and violently sick. We parted acrimoniously but without regret.

* * *

I went to work briefly for an advertising agency in Knightbridge and hated it. Right area, wrong business. And I intensified, having already begun, a passionate friendship with a beautiful, troubled girl who took herself nearly as seriously as I do. I call it a passionate friendship because I don't know what else to call it. I had begun to be frightened by my track record with men. That I was desirable didn't seem to be a problem. But I just didn't seem to be very good with them. I was always living a divided life, divide and rule being the only way I could see to control some part of it, to have some territory which I could have private, secret, ultimately mine. Perhaps all those people who'd hinted darkly were right. Perhaps I should be with a woman. I still liked men, was still drawn to them but for emotional sustenance, I preferred to come to home to Nat.

It's not surprising that we didn't have many friends. For a start, we were very 'love me, love my dog' and whoever took on one of us, soon had to take on the other. And then we were so involved with ourselves that we probably sent anyone else to sleep. We painted and shopped and argued and wrote poetry. She made me clothes, bullied me about colour (I was now 23 and I'd been wearing black and beige for about five years by then), saw me as a creative person. This was a good deal more rewarding than being commended for housekeep-

ing, sitting in pubs or surviving bad dinners at boring dinner
parties. Perhaps from the outside the relationship was cloying
and unhealthy. But it was safe. A great deal of the time it was
unquestioned. We were just two enthusiastic young women on
an endless window shopping spree who obviously enjoyed
each other's company. The rest of the time was spent in her
flat or mine, in each other's company.

She had been very hurt by a romantic Polish engineer she'd
met while she was working for an oil company in North
Africa. I don't remember the details. I will never forget the
shock when she first showed me his photograph. I still had
long hair in those days and I hope I hid my doubletake behind
it. I was so like him, it was unnerving. However I successfully
put that out of my mind. It remained out of my mind until I
recalled recently that she called me Anya or Annuska, Slavo-
nic diminutives. And she changed her name by deed poll from
Bridget Mary Susan to Natasha Marie, because I had begun to
call her Natasha or more often Nat as a nickname. She had the
colouring of a girl of that name in a novel I was reading about
revolutionary Russia, green eyes, white skin and lion coloured
hair. She had a little white mini and I've been scared of white
cars ever since.

For Nat was all give and no give. One night we'd stayed up
very late and she was too tired to drive home. I had a double
bed and no inhibitions about sharing it. So we slept together
and held hands and talked and she told me all about her
horrific family and I told her all about my marvellous one.
And the sexual attraction grew and was diffused and finally
there was a day when I was doing something in the kitchen of
my flat. She came and stood in the doorway and looked at me.
I could feel her eyes. I turned round, slowly, not to frighten
her. We stood there looking at each other for so long that I
began to shake and just as I had decided that I must say
something and knew what I would say, she said, 'I think I'll
have a bath now' and rushed away into the bathroom.

She was not a happy lady and had begun to see a psychiatrist who treated her with alternate sessions of LSD (this was in
the days when the drug was still licensed for therapeutic
purposes) and Ritalin, a very heavy tranquilliser. At that stage
she depended on me and I didn't want to push her into
anything she didn't want. In time the ambiguity of all that

intensity leading nowhere unsettled me so we saw less of each other while I threw myself into the arms of the first man who was consistently kind to me. And, for the enlightenment of all students of second year psychology, he was impotent.

Peace be to Masters and Johnson, Kinsey and Ellis, Hertzog, Krafft-Ebbing and all, what I knew about the workings of sex was fairly straightforward. Impotence was something that most men experienced temporarily, as far as I knew, because they were tired or drunk or the income tax demand had just come in. Danny had never been potent in his life. He had had recourse to the ladies of the night with whom he could presumably experience some sort of pleasure in other ways but full intercourse with a girl he was fond of was not possible.

He was tall, Jewish of course, funny and delightfully direct after the ambivalence of Nat. We sat up all one night, hugged each other, talked and kissed and he told me that was it. I had the sense not to say anything very much more than 'Oh, I see,' and frankly, I could think of worse things. He had his own business, worked very hard and ate like a horse. The first time we went out to dinner, he said, 'Now please don't be embarrassed. I eat two helpings of almost everything.' He wasn't a pig and he wasn't fat. He just liked food. His cry when I went out shopping was, 'Don't forget – buy Jewish!' meaning large portions. My happiest nights with him were spent watching Robert Culp and Bill Cosby in *I-Spy* on television, eating chopped liver and drinking Hine brandy. There is no disparagement intended in this remark – he was kind, warm, funny, attentive, boyish but not a little boy. He was the second man in my entire life to buy me perfume and typically he found the only place in London which then stocked the new Yves St. Laurent and bought me the biggest bottle I'd ever seen. I'd come home from work and find all my clothes had been meticulously cleaned and pressed and put in plastic bags. 'Thought it would be nice for you,' he'd say grinning. He's the only man I've ever known who found out what size and colour tights I wore and bought me a dozen pairs. Impotence be damned, he was a prince. He also encouraged me to write and believed in my ability to do anything I wanted to do.

Within three months I had proved that his impotence could be alleviated if not dismissed. Five days after that, he asked me to leave. I didn't argue very much. I knew enough about fear from the inside to recognise when I saw it in somebody else. I didn't have anywhere to go, I was always moving from one place to another, with somebody or not. That night I thanked God that the PR company for whom I was working at the time had a very thick carpet and a nice warm office to which I had keys. Wandering down Park Lane, everything seemed wrong. To plan was wrong and not to plan was wrong. To love was wrong and not love was wrong. I wasn't 18 any more, I was nearly 24. It was too late to be tall or blonde or good at anything. There was one car coming very fast and I moved in front of it. The driver came so close that I was knocked over. I got up shakily and he came steaming out of the car towards me. When he saw my face he just said very gently, 'Oh my dear, go home. Go home.' That was the one place I couldn't go this time.

Chapter 9

I still saw something of Nat, the girl I'd been so tied up with, and various escorts, but life was becalmed. Working for the PR company wasn't particularly exciting – most of their accounts were for food rather than fashion or cosmetics – but it was demanding. The bosses worked, the executives worked and the secretaries slaved. Anyone who thinks PR is a doddle should try it. The trouble is that no matter how hard you work, the end product is usually insubstantial. All that talk, those lunches and dinners, those endless policy documents and press releases and phone calls can only produce, at their most concrete, column inches whose life is limited by the life of the publication in which they appear. At the other end of the spectrum, where public relations is at its most amorphous, all that effort produces is a momentary thought, a passing glance – or a direct hit into the wastepaper basket.

One Thursday I rang my mother to see how my parents were and say that I'd be down that weekend. My father was not keen on the telephone because he was deaf in one ear and in any case still regarded any call from either of his children as a sign of alarm. 'Hello daddy,' I'd say cheerfully. 'What's the matter?' was his standard reply.

On this occasion, however, I got Ma, which was more usual, and she sounded subdued. Pop hadn't been feeling well, he was in bed and seemed to have angina. I tried to resaure her and said I'd come down on Friday night. When I arrived, she grabbed my shoulders and said, 'Now, keep calm. Daddy's in hospital. We'll go and see him tomorrow.'

His face was leaden. He looked terribly tired and he never took his eyes from my mother's face. His big frame wasn't comfortable in the bed and, indignity to end all, they made him use a bedpan. We tried to be cheerful but at the end of the

90

visiting hour, Ma went to speak to sister about something and he reached for my lapel and drew my face down, right on top of his. 'You know,' he said. 'You know'. I nodded. I did know, but Lord, I didn't want to.

From what my mother said, both to me and my sister on the telephone, I went through the next week on automatic pilot, secure in the belief that Lesley would go down and visit them the next weekend. It was December and come the end of the week, my mother's voice seemed to be sinking with every call. 'Lesley isn't coming. She can't. You know she's over in Hampshire and to get to Kent means coming to London and then taking a train down here. It's too much.' Why doesn't she drive? My sister could drive. I still can't. 'Sally,' reasoned my mother. 'It's starting to snow, there's fog about, black ice on the roads . . .' I didn't hear. In midst of all that loving, my mother felt my father had wasted his life, that Lesley was unhappy and was wasting hers, that she herself hadn't got her act together until much later, maybe too late. I was the little white hope. All I heard was what I seemed to have heard for years. Be more, be more, be more. And I couldn't. I didn't think I measured up to anything that anyone wanted of me, including what I wanted of myself, but this was frightening. In my family the phrase 'not fair' was forbidden. It was a serious business to accuse somebody of being unfair. Life was, often, that you couldn't fix, but it was not a complaint we were encouraged to use of people in personal situations.

In this anguished corner, I snapped and bit at everyone. I knew I should just get on the train and go. Heaven knows, I owed my parents. I shall owe them till I die, and they needed me. I was selfish. I was also angry. My sister's life, which is a whole story by itself, had often overshadowed mine. I have always loved her but at that time I didn't like her very much and to be fair, I think it was mutual. And now when the chips were down, even when I thought she was in the wrong, she managed to make it sound like being in the right by being 'practical'. Eventually I took a bag of change and went to the telephone box on the corner and rang her. Half an hour later, the money mostly spent, the walls of the booth were dripping with bile and I felt as though every bone in my body was splintered. It is entirely possible that the gratitude in my mother's voice was because *somebody* was coming. At the time it sounded like delight that it was my big sister, though I don't flatter myself that I made her make the decision. And it was then I first thought that perhaps I couldn't make it on my own and was going to need professional help.

Pa was better that weekend. His appetite improved, he had more colour and he bullied his nurses into letting him use the commode. What was initially thought to be angina turned out to have been a heart attack. He'd had one eleven years before at school, sat, rested, gone round to the doctor and sworn him to secrecy. But it showed up on the cardiogram. He and Mummy began to plan for his homecoming.

Four or five days later my mother rang me first thing at the office. 'They've asked me to go to the hospital,' she said. 'I think this is it.' I'd come in early to type something and I was afraid to stop typing. If I pretended it wasn't happening, then it wouldn't. Two hours later, the girl I shared the office with said (with poignancy as her father had died before she was born), 'Anna, that's your father in that hospital and he's dying.' The words penetrated. I went to see my boss. He was wonderfully kind, so were his partners. I fled home, collected things, went to the station.

In the hospital I was shown into a room in which my father lay in an oxygen tent, his magnificent chest bare as were his enormous feet, his colour unimpaired in spite of being hooked up to all sorts of machines. My mother sat at the foot of the bed, my sister at the side. Every so often the heart would stop. We would turn to the monitor, then back to the bed. As if gathering itself for effort, my father's body would push and the heart would start again. It lasted for about twelve hours and remains one of the most moving sights I've ever seen. At one point my mother said, 'Oh dear, I do wish it would be over. Poor old darling, he's so tired.' When the monitor fizzled out, the resuscitation team appeared from nowhere. Ma's hands flew to her ears to block out the sound of the punch the doctor delivered to start the heart again. We were ushered into a room and given tea. Ma was in agony. 'I'm sorry –' said the doctor. 'Can we see him?' she asked.

He didn't look as big as he usually did but he was still my lovely father. My mother and sister kissed him and said goodbye. I kissed him and said hello. Just because I can't see him any more, it doesn't mean he's gone.

92

A nurse came to offer my mother a sedative and put her hand on Mother's arm. Ma whipped it away and fled. There was a sort of alley at the back of the hospital with old bracket lamps to light it. Lesley tried to explain to the nurse that she hadn't done anything wrong, this was just Mother's way while I approached her like a wild animal in a snare. My poor Ma. We sat in the car holding on to one another unseeingly while my sister drove back to St. Peters. And we talked and talked, remembering. At one point my mother said, 'You know, grief is just like being pregnant. I have so much inside and it's got to come out.' And she began to rock the way people all over the world do when they mourn. I went to the pub, bought the bottle of brandy I thought the occasion merited and methodically pumped it into them. When the doctor arrived, I told him what I'd done. He said, 'Good idea. Have one yourself.' But I didn't want it. That night we lay (I can't say we slept) all three in my mother's big bed. My sister arranged the funeral, I cleaned the house. When my mother asked me why, I replied that Pop's sisters were coming. She nodded and shrugged. I know Lesley wept and mourned and had her own special griefs but I was not interested in them at the time. I felt as though some inner pulse had stopped and I did not know how I could continue to breathe without it marking time.

The church service was awful. If I'd nurtured any secret hope of consolation through Anglican Christianity, it was lost at that funeral. My mother was beyond herself, supported by my sister and my uncle. I had asked David Baume who's known us for so long and he stood beside me. The cart that carried the coffin was like a gun carriage. Daddy would have liked that. He's buried in his adored mother's grave. Her stone says, 'And her children shall rise up and call her name blessed.' His says, 'He fought the good fight.' And when we came up the churchyard, there were two rows of old men, my father's comrades from the First War. Everybody came back for a drink and a bite and I shall never forget those dear men, shaking my mother's hand and gently, every so gently, saluting her cheek.

* * *

For the next few months I hated God. I walked round London

railing at him. 'All the people you could have taken, you had to take him. I need him. We all need him. Why? In the name of all that's merciful, why?' And a desperate descent into beds and booze and bitterness. As usual, of course, I stayed afloat by being ever so efficient during the day and desperately rusticated all night. I spent weekends with my mother when we hardly spoke, just hugged each other every time we passed, sat and held hands. She was being brave and wonderful, too brave and too wonderful. Pop hadn't left a cent, she went back to work. At the time we were all very shaken about that, but looking back my mother reckons that's what got her through.

I grew increasingly numb. You know how a chicken feels when it's defrosting? Well, I felt the reverse, as if I'd been submerged in cold water for too long and it was all turning to ice. Nothing tasted of anything, no action produced sensation. There was a passage from the directors' office down to the kitchen at work. It was painted white with a red carpet and I remember literally bumping from shoulder to shoulder along it. Nothing was real. Day after day, I trapped my fingers in my desk drawers, burnt my wrists on the grill, banged my hip bones on the filing cabinets. I took to carrying a mirror. If I could see her, she must be there but I was damned if I could feel her. Everything was happening through mist and at a distance from me. One night I rang my sister to tell her that I had decided to seek psychiatric help. She was supportive and encouraging. The next day I saw Nat's doctor who declined to treat me because of our relationship and referred me to a colleague of his.

Dr Fox asked me what I'd come for. I said shyly that I thought my friend's psych., who had referred me, had explained. He looked at me very gently and said, 'I have a note here which says that your father died recently, you have some depression and in the past have made suicide gestures.'

'Thank you for calling them gestures,' I said, thinking for the first time that they were just that. The cut wrist at 13 stung too much for me to proceed so I said the carving knife I'd used slipped when I was trying to sharpen a pencil (it was the sharpest knife in the house and I'd been told before not to use it on my pencils). Trying to jump off a bridge or hurl myself under a car seemed rather half-hearted in the cool clinical light of a psychiatrist's office. After our first meeting

Dr Fox sent me away to think about whether I wanted to come to him for treatment. I did. We then discussed how I should pay him. He would see me at 6.00 on Thursdays so I had to break it to my boss that Thursday was the one day I couldn't leave late. When I told him I was seeing a doctor, he nodded understandingly.

'For your back?' he asked.

'I'm seeing a psychiatrist,' I explained.

He looked at me as if I'd dropped my drawers in church. 'You're what? But Anna, you're the sanest person I know!'

'Thanks,' I said, 'but I don't feel so.' He proceeded to examine me very carefully every Friday morning, as if I should look different after meeting with a mind doctor. It wasn't a bit offensive, just curious.

Fox worked very hard with me. He gave me no pills but, as I was then writing poetry, encouraged me to show him what I was writing. We pulled out and examined bits of my life and when I asked him about the burns and cuts and bruises I had inflicted on myself after my father's death, he came up with a wonderful description. 'Subconscious hysterical masochism,' he said grinning. Thanks, doc.

Within one month I'd met a nice young man who was a medical student. Talk about unconscious selection . . . I was relieved to have found somebody with every evidence of respectability until Fox asked me drily if I really saw myself as a suburban doctor's wife. I didn't like that question. I produced panic attacks rather than face Mark with any serious disagreements about his behaviour. He was a warm affectionate young man and I think the only thing he loved in his life was medicine. I have a weakness for people who are enthusiastic about what they do and at least part of medicine is observing people. We had therefore plenty to talk about, a comfortable relationship, periodically unsettled by my emotional upheavals and his habitual drinking. In the year we were together I think we spent less than six evenings other than in a bar. I must have been more long-suffering in those days. Or do I just mean more dishonest?

When Dr Fox decided I was free to go, I was terrified.

'What happens if I can't manage?' I asked worriedly.

'You'll get in touch and I'll see you again,' he said calmly.

I went back once, two weeks after that. We cut the session

short and parted laughing. Mark the medic and I parted three months after and I changed my job again. Heart high and full of hope as ever, I went to work for a film company. At first I thought I was going to be all right but then I discovered that the time with the PR company had conditioned me to typing not very well, correcting immaculately and copying everything while my new boss expected me to type long screeds perfectly at first go. His request was reasonable enough except that I thought that only secretaries did that and at our two interviews, there had been a lot of talk about being a 'really imaginative PA' and 'making the contribution you can'. In other words, it's the old con which happens when you're an intelligent person who happens to be a secretary. Bosses have sensors like bats and they find out very quickly what you want to hear, tell it to you and hope that, thus captured, you'll provide them with what they want.

I also discovered that being a secretary in a film company was a lot more problematical for me than working in a business I wasn't interested in being part of. I was mad about movies and all I wanted to do was talk to the various directors, read scripts and be there. Typing, dictation, filing and so on were irrelevant.

Within a very short time of my being there, a young man appeared and began to work as we were leaving the office. He looked like the photographs of the writer Maxim Gorky, with an immense brow crowned with unruly reddish hair, deepset hazel eyes and a small arrogant nose. He dressed like a brigand with an elephant hide waistcoat and medieval looking boots. I was told he was from Rhodesia. Thereafter I avoided him. I'd had my colonial phase upon first arriving in London and I don't believe in going backwards. Then one day I heard him speaking on the telephone. Perfect French. I was bewildered. When he came off the telephone I asked him where he learned to speak French. 'I lived there,' he said. I couldn't make the bits add up. He asked me to lunch and I refused.

'Why?' he asked.

'Because I'm scared of you.' When he tried to argue with me, I explained a bit about therapy and funny reactions.

One morning I went in early and he had just finished working all night. The man who owned the company would let him cut his film there if he worked at night instead of during the day. What was the film? 'About Rhodesia.' I asked again about the French. It transpired that his mother was an Italian Jew, born in Cairo when Egypt was an Italian Territory. His father, a British army colonel when he met his mother, was now headmaster of a very select public school. Michael's maternal grandmother whom he adored spoke only Italian and French. He learned French to speak to her, got an honours degree, a bursary for further study in France. There he fell in love with films, taught English in Paris, raised money and went back to make a film against the white regime in Southern Africa. 'And now,' he said, 'if you've finished being scared of me, do you think we might have lunch?'

Two weeks later we went to see *Citizen Kane* and decided we were made for each other. Three weeks after that I had a new job as the chairman's secretary in a management consultancy and took two days off to get married. I wore a tweed trouser suit and he gave me a silver ring so wide that the registrar asked, 'Madam, is this a ring or half a shell case?' The transformation of my name was complete. I was now Anna Raeburn.

Chapter 10

When Michael's books arrived from home, I sat on the floor of
our shabby flat in Kilburn and wondered what I'd got myself
into this time. There were books on art, aesthetics, cinema,
politics and philosophy. There were texts in English, French,
Italian and Portuguese. Michael had very little money, was
still finishing the Rhodesia film and we lived mostly off my
salary. I wanted to play house and take care of him. I did the
best I could with the flat but it wasn't much to write home
about. I learned to cook and I tried to do as much as I could
for him because I was so impressed by his talent.

Because I hardly knew him I kept discovering things about
him. He liked opera. He liked whisky. Sometimes we'd buy a
bottle and he'd ration himself to a nip every night. He lived,
ate, breathed and slept films. When we went out it was to the
movies. He knew very few people in London. Although he
was used to a far higher standard of living than me, he almost
seemed to flourish his poverty. I was a nice little bourgeoise,
brought up to clean up when company or the doctor called.
Entertaining was an excuse for effort and something nice to
eat. He shrugged. In that one room I fed the Czech and Soviet
cultural attachés (not at the same time) on stew. Michael had
lived with a Swedish girl in Paris. She remained a close friend.
His home life had been unhappy. His parents were always
rowing, his father hit the bottle. After their divorce, his
mother, dominating, possessor of a vindictive temper, became
ever more possessive. He knew a lot about politics in France
and Africa but if you cut him, he bled not blood but celluloid.

I did not see how I could hold this obsessively determined,
alienated man. He went abroad, to promote the first film or
raise money for another, five times in the first year we were
married and each time I was quite sure I'd never see him

again. His first film, *Rhodesia Countdown*, won the Mannheim Peace Prize and attention at other festivals. The only film festival I'd heard of was Cannes. In Paris it was taken up by the Fédération Jean Vigo who subtitled it and we had to go to Paris to introduce it to the press. That was when I first understood why he complained so bitterly about England's attitude to film.

At 10.00 on a Sunday morning, the cinema was full. The film was shown and he was kept on his feet for two hours in debate. This is more likely (just) in London now. Then it was amazing. I was so happy to be there, to meet his friends, to learn a bit more about him. I had by now of course adopted the uniform of the group – trousers, boots, ancient fur coat. This made me feel a bit less of a lemon and as everyone spoke French, I tried too. But the trouble was that like every other person who is attached to a section of the city, I couldn't get Michael to do what I love to do, which is wander and look. I pleaded for the Louvre, Versailles, the shops. He laughed and went back to arguing about film.

Michael and I talked about marriage. It was, we decided, a partnership based on mutual growth and honesty. If it was a real friendship, it should be able to contain other relationships. Fidelity was to do with the mind, not the body. Gosh, we were grown up and progressive and modern.

Things were less pleasant when Michael and I talked about my work. I can remember walking across St. James's Park to go to the Institute of Contemporary Art to see a festival of underground American filmmakers or new French filmmakers or South American films – I had so much to learn – when he commented that my work was a waste of time. I agreed.

'But I'm not trained for anything else,' I said.

'Everybody I know either teaches or writes,' he said. 'You could do either of those.'

I was nearly in tears. 'I can't,' I said. 'I would if I could but I can't.'

'Well, it's a damn silly job,' he grumbled.

'Look,' I said. 'Your work doesn't bring in very much. Somebody has to be practical. It has to be me.' I suppose, in the least delightful way, I always have to test everything and so, feeling second rate and a bit bewildered that the ring on my wedding finger had not produced a beneficial magic to make everything right, six months into the marriage I embarked on an affair.

The office in which I worked was a small one with some very nice men attached to it. The man in question was a long lean lurcher type with bold brown eyes and a lot of charm. He was a good deal older than me, married with a son and an adored daughter. We fell to talking and went out for a drink. Over the next six months, we talked a lot. He encouraged me to confide in him about Michael, the difficulties I felt in the marriage, my past and his. Most importantly, he encouraged me to stick to it. In turn he talked about the habit of matrimony he was in with his wife and didn't quite know how to break. He was fun, he was comfortable. In terms of time and energy I was much more unfaithful in my head than bodily but there's no doubt that bodily counts for a lot. We saw each other only as and when we could, no special arrangements or lies until the big one when he stayed in town for some quite proper reason and less properly, I stayed with him. My head wasn't blown off by a thunderbolt on the way home but I did rather now feel that I was back where I started. If the magic of marriage doesn't exorcise all the demons, what will? Shortly afterwards he wrote me a very nice note explaining that he and his wife had got themselves sorted out, he was very happy and didn't want to make my life untidy, so thanks for the memory. I was glad for him, pleased he was so straightforward and like a fool, kept the letter. Which Michael found.

Our salvation, consumed with guilt as I was, was to work together on a film Michael made in Southern Ireland. Off we went to Dublin on the mail boat on the coldest night the Irish had seen for 40 years with the wind blowing shards of ice off the Liffey. We had a Portuguese sound recordist and camera man, I was production secretary, chief cook and bottle washer. The film was made on the tightest budget you can imagine and poor Michael discovered that, in spite of the depth of their shared revolutionary views, when you're the boss, you're the boss and you are treated like one. Those two men made his life hell with demands for what he saw as luxuries and they regarded as necessities. As we all lived together in a rented flat, the atmosphere was enough to flatten anybody and I was beginning to be concerned about what was already established as Michael's 'nervous stomach'. What I learned on the film was that filming is exciting and boring and tiring, and after the first week, work like any other work, except that you can't ever say 'Oh go away and get on with it!' because if you want to have a say in the finished product, you have to stay with the damned thing all the way through.

When we came back to London, we passed through one of those terrible limbos, common to all freelance directors, where the producer hesitates and he may be changing his mind but you're not sure. You can't do anything and every day nerves are wound tighter. It was a most unhappy few months. Then Michael got the go ahead and we moved to Wimbledon and I secured the first not entirely secretarial job I'd ever had.

The project was to research secondary school education for the non-academic child. The sponsors were the Dulverton Trust, a charitable organisation largely financed by the Wills tobacco company, Rio-Tinto Zinc and IBM. It was handled through a public relations company in Green Park and I got the job by bluffing about my parents' teaching and administrative experience and sounding tremendously authoritative.

In the year I was there (working with a delightful old man called Colin Whittle, who made me feel like a human) I had the very real pleasure of sending out letters over my own name, compiling a research document into all the youth voluntary organisations and meeting Kenneth Kaunda's friend, the churchman Colin Morris. On the debit side I had to fight to be allowed to wear trousers which I now preferred after Michael had made me self-conscious about my 'funny little legs'. I did not wear a day length skirt for five years. And I had to face the fact that, called upon to type for longer than a page to my own preferred standard, I had to wind myself up till I was a shaking wreck by the time it was over. The strain of home on work and work on home was beginning to tell.

Michael wrote scripts, synopses for scripts, outlines and more scripts. Little Wifey-Helpmeet offered to type them and then felt naked resentment at so doing. Hadn't he told me, not once but several times that my 'work' was worthless? It appeared that my skills, limited as they were, were useful to him. And the material was never ending. The man in charge of the copier at work was a former film technician from the brief bloom in British filmdom. Sympathetically, he used to fiddle the meter for me so I didn't pay for all, just some, of the copies we made. I used to come in at six in the morning, smile efficiently at the cleaners and rip off pages and pages of stuff. I'm sure Michael did thank me but I never felt recognised for my efforts. He was unhappy in England. It was cold both physically and psychologically. His former love Gorel (pronounced Yorrel to rhyme with sorrel) told me that he had grumbled just the same way about Paris when they were there and he longed to go to England. By now we had established that he had the early stages of a duodenal ulcer and the medicine chest in the bathroom looked like Boots. He woke up in pain night after night and in the midst of all this, I was having great trouble with the Pill, tried a spermicidal foam and promptly became pregnant.

Michael's exact words were 'I'm very sorry, I can't handle that right now.' I went to see the lovely GP who'd put me together after the backstreet abortion six years before. All he knew was that I was married and living in Wimbledon. Putting two and two together, he rose, smiling, as I came in. 'Congratulations!' he beamed. I said I thought not. Within an hour he said he would arrange for it all to be done properly (by now it was 1970 and legal) and I left with an appointment to see a distinguished gynaecologist in South London early the following week.

I know now looking back that there were so many things wrong with that marriage, but at the time I had no thought except that these were teething troubles, must try harder. In my mind there was at least as great a stigma attached to divorce as there was to abortion. I wasn't against it in principle – it just wasn't going to happen to me. I felt I'd waited so long for a husband and I could always have another child. It was a no-win position: if I kept the baby, the marriage would go to the wall. I forfeited the baby and the marriage went to the wall.

Michael was working when I went to hospital for my appointment with Mr Pinker. He was very tough without being in the least unfair. He was quiet and patient but he questioned me very thoroughly and I responded wholeheartedly to this rather authoritarian approach. My answers must have satisfied him because he sent me to the Samaritan Hospital for Women a week later.

I checked in with a dragon of a sister whose heart was made of some substance far more precious than gold. Two hours before I was to go down to the operating theatre, my GP appeared at my bedside to point out very gently that I still had time to change my mind. I couldn't. Whenever I think of it, I think of a song Edith Piaf made famous called *Je ne regrette rien* and I think what a proud boast that is. I have prayed and wept and wept and prayed and I do regret, I do indeed.

When I came out, Michael bought me one of the few presents he ever bought me, something I'd wanted for a long time, a pine trunk. It reposed in the middle of the living room and I kept walking towards it up the passage saying 'Oh, how lovely' and 'What a surprise' and thinking, *No, no, it's a coffin. He's bought me a coffin for the baby*.

A few weeks later, one of Michael's oldest friends was extradited from Rhodesia. His wife was then eight months pregnant. Although her parents were wealthy, she and her husband adopted the attitude so prevalent among moneyed people and decided to save money on the birth. She was a nervous girl, understandably distressed by being driven from her family and her friends in such a way. If there was ever a case for every amenity surrounding a birth, this was it. But no. She went into the notorious local hospital where she became disoriented because she never saw the same personnel twice. She had a protracted labour with a lot of complications, promptly rejected the baby and was hospitalised with acute depression. Visiting her in the sight and sound of all those babies was difficult. Neither Michael nor her husband made any comment about it but the second time I went, from the depths of some hell of her own, she pressed my hand and told me not to come again. 'I know, you see,' she said. 'Michael told us and you mustn't. It's bad for you.'

Michael never discussed the abortion with me. I went on getting angrier and angrier until one day when I wept and screamed and he said he understood. I don't think he ever did.

* * *

We had let one room in the flat to a charming hippie – I hate the label but it saves longwinded descriptions. Rosie was kind, clean, honest, amusing and made the biggest joints I've ever

103

seen. Unfortunately her friends weren't all so desirable and after a while we were never sure whether the police were watching the house to check on Michael or them. At this stage Michael seemed to be doing much as I did in America. He was fascinated by anybody who seemed to dissent and or smoke dope. I didn't mind the dissent or the dope, I minded that we hadn't very much money, that these people always came in groups and ate like locusts. I also minded very much that many of them were physically dirty. The division between us widened bit by bit each day.

Michael hated shopping so I shopped. Michael hated cooking so I cooked. He did bits of housework occasionally, more in the spirit of reproof than contribution. I went out first, worked all day, came home and worked at night. He couldn't understand why I wanted to get up and get on on Saturdays and in vain I explained that, if I got all the chores done on Saturday, at least I had Sunday free. This focus on maintaining everything to keep life running round Michael was draining. At the time I did it. Now I'm outraged just to think of it. He went abroad to raise money for films or recce (look for locations). We never had a holiday. At the same time let anyone criticise him and I'd rush to his defence. When he was away, he lived his life and I lived mine. The difference was that I was never jealous of his peccadillos. I could envy women he was involved with, because they were brighter or better looking than me, but I didn't mind that he took them to bed. I took the easy way out and lied about my amusements.

* * *

When the boss of the PR company I'd been working for asked me to stay on next year as a secretary, I said no thank you and began to search the personal columns of *The Times* for a job. There I found the following advertisement: 'Wanted, attractive, articulate, native English speaking women, aged 18 to 30, medical, sociological or psychological background, for appearances. American radio and TV' and a telephone number. When I rang, I discovered it was *Forum* magazine. I was interviewed by an American woman and the interview was a perfect example of happening to hit a home run on interests and vocabulary, or in other words, telling the interviewer what she wants to hear.

104

I was taken to meet the then editor of *Forum*, a small American called Albert Z. Freeman with overdeveloped thighs and a voile shirt. He approved of me. They'd be in touch. I was asked to join the others members of the short list at the Penthouse Club. I didn't even know that Penthouse was the publishing company of *Forum*. Sitting in the half light I nervously sipped orange juice. In swept a handsome expensively dressed and emaciated girl who announced with a dazzling smile, 'Hello, I'm Susana Duncan. I've got a first in social anthropology. What's your degree?' I was so upset I spilt the orange juice all over myself.

Five of us were seen by Robert Guccione, the owner of the Penthouse operation. I shall never forget Mr Guccione's Thai silk checked shirt, open to the navel, nor his white boots, nor the bags under his eyes. It took a lot of self-control not to laugh. Bob (or Baahb, as his assistants seem to call him) may indeed be a hell of a sensitive fella. All I can say is he's hiding it pretty well. He believes that you should be thrilled to work for the company and money is way down on the list of priorities. We five were vetted by Edward Ernest, Albert Z., Guccione and Molly McKellar, a diminutive and long-suffering Scot who was the PR woman. We were asked the sort of questions it was reasonably felt the American press might want to ask young English women coming from swinging London to the States to launch a new sex magazine with an upfront approach. Among the questions was one about how we would each respond confronted with the opportunity for group sex. I said my only concern was who I was getting involved with, that on balance I preferred sex with friends. 'You fuck your friends?' asked Mr Ernest incredulously. In due course we were asked to go and be photographed. One girl withdrew, you should pardon the expression, another was found wanting. That left Susana Duncan, Susan Capel and I to run with the ball.

They paid us £50 a week for each week we were in the States, all expenses while we were there and £50 towards clothes for the trip. Michael thought it would be good for me. I thought it was better than thumping a typewriter on somebody else's behalf. The trip was planned for 6 weeks, 6 weeks in which I learned a great deal. I worked for *Forum* for 3 years.

Chapter 11

Three of us were chosen to launch *Forum* in the United States and we were given a two week induction course which involved meeting *Forum*'s 'experts', reading a required book-list which included various tomes by so-called sexologist Robert Chartham, Germaine Greer's *The Female Eunuch* and *The XYZ of Love* by Inge and Stan Hegeler – Scandinavians, need I say more? Plus 25 back numbers of the magazine itself so that we would be familiar with its layout, content and ethos. Reading 25 editions of *Forum* cover to cover in a short time is a crash course in continence.

When we flew to New York the British editor, himself an American, announced halfway across the Atlantic that a television crew would be coming to the hotel to film me with a girl who'd volunteered to do a 'sexuality study'. This was a regular feature of the magazine at the time, an anonymous interview in which the subject was asked to recall memories of his/her sexual development.

'Why me?' I asked.

'Why not?' he replied.

When we arrived at the plush Plaza Hotel, I went off to meet the girl. Sandy was tall, thin and rather thoughtful but it rapidly became clear that what she was prepared to tell me and indeed have printed anonymously or pseudonymously in *Forum* was not what she was prepared to discuss in front of the camera. Just to complicate matters, I had calls from the television station, which was worried about 'going too far' and 'being offensive'. The idea, cherished in the heart of the Brits, that America is the land of letting it all hang out, is only true of its stereotypes, not when it comes to real people. Eventually their instructions boiled down to 'keeping it cool' and not mentioning masturbation. My overall impression is that the

American media male does not believe that women masturbate, except in *his* fantasies.

Some time that night, jetlagged to fragments, what would and would not be said was agreed and I fell into bed in a room swathed with almond green velvet and a view of Central Park. The next morning the crew arrived. The presenter was small, sweaty and harried, the attitudes of the rest varied from cagey to contemptuous. The sound man Milt was in his fifties and about 7 feet tall. He leered as he fixed the microphone to my sweater and made a great play with my left breast. 'You married?' he inquired.

'Yes,' I said firmly.

'And how big is your husband?'

'Very big,' I replied with unwise emphasis. Nasty laughter. Openly hostile men are hard enough to dismiss individually. In clumps, they are harder to ignore.

The presenter kicked off, and Sandy and I launched into our carefully amended version of the frank interview on which the camera was allegedly eavesdropping. The loaded atmosphere of the room eased perceptibly when she made a remark about hoping that feminism would make men's lives easier too. When it was all over, Milt approached me rather more courteously to remove the microphone. 'That was OK,' he said grudgingly, 'but I suppose you do that sort of thing every day of your life.'

I looked at him. 'I have never done anything like that in my life before,' I said.

Before my eyes he became a big fatherly schmooze. 'Hey,' he called to his colleagues, 'you know this kid never did this before, not the interview, TV, nothin'. Give the girl a cup of coffee.' I was now his protégée. 'Tell her she did good.' Over and over in the next weeks I was to discover that you were expected to be a floozie or a doctor if you talked about sex and the general opinion was that Penthouse would not have risked us on this sort of promotion were we not all very experienced in sex or media or both. And I'm not sure what our reception would have been had they known how green we were.

The idea of keeping us in the Plaza was to keep tabs on us. We had no money but could take advantage of whatever the hotel had to offer on our accounts. This may have kept us under one roof but it cost a fortune. We guested on various television and radio shows and presided over the launch of the American edition of the magazine at a breakfast on the roof of the St. Regis Hotel. The invitation read '*Forum* invites you to come and discuss sex with these three attractive young Englishwomen.' The effrontery of it appalled me. The New York press dealt with children dying of rat bite, political payola and race riots. I could only suppose that we were the light relief. When we walked into that great big room, they eyed us and we eyed them. They didn't know what we were doing and neither did we. They could tell at a glance we weren't your conventional sex kittens, there wasn't a cleavage in sight and anyway we were all brunette. Gradually the message got through. Oh, we were going to *talk* about sex. . . .

The British editor introduced us and while he was doing that, the poised Susana reached for my hand under the table. Without taking my eyes off the lions in this lion's den, I wondered what the . . . 'Anna,' she whispered, her aquamarine eyes gazing soulfully into some unsuspecting journalist's camera, 'hold my hand, I'm scared.' I shot a quick look at Susan Capel on the other side. She (former air stewardess, currently teacher of liberal arts and one of the last Europeans to travel through China before the Cultural Revolution) was sitting there, her features composed into a beautiful smile but it kept slithering off her cheekbones like butter off a hot dish. Fear is contagious. I couldn't afford to catch it. I removed my glasses. What you can't see you can't worry about. The address finished, there was a pause and into that silence I heard A. Raeburn speak. I don't remember a word except that it got the ball rolling and even raised a couple of laughs. Then Susan and Susana chipped in and as the questions began, we managed. When it was all over and I'd been given a pat on the back, I tried to stand and discovered I couldn't, so I sat and cried into the friendly shoulder of the professor of psychiatric medicine from California. This was the beginning of a pattern that still pertains. I can do anything I have to do but I pay for it later in one way or another.

After New York we visited Philadelphia, Chicago, Los Angeles, Washington, San Diego, Boston and then came back to New York. The trip lasted five weeks: five weeks of press interviews, appearances on radio and television, informal guest lectures at International College, California, Washington's Georgetown University and New York University (known affectionately as NYJew). We talked about everything sexual or vaguely sexual you can think of, for breakfast, lunch, dinner and tea. And I learned that part of my mother's ambition for me had come true. I could always talk. I wasn't any kind of an expert or pretending to be one, I certainly wasn't a trained public relations person but I could always opine and with greater clarity and speed than most. I did not think of more than one day at a time then, still less of where such an experience might lead me.

In Chicago I received a letter from Michael. Delightedly I opened it. It described an affair he was having with a Belgian girl and I sat in a nasty pebbledash tweed chair and felt sort of glad he'd told me and sort of sad he'd told me and sorry for myself and that there must be another way to live without becoming an emotional fascist. That night I collapsed with a mystery fever and though one of *Forum*'s local contributors told me it was all in the mind, I still had a very high temperature and felt most odd. Like a fool (I was obviously working for my A-level in suffering at the time) I read a book about Zelda and Scott Fitzgerald, identified excessively and wound up determined that, talent or no, no man was worth such discomfort. The next day I went back to work, all sweet smiles and debate about the refractory period.

Authors who set out to promote their work (as they must in America) on such coast to coast trips, incorporating every kind of media coverage with particular reference to TV, have named the experience 'the circus'. Travelling like this is disorienting, all contacts are superficial and after a while you begin to wonder who you are. If you're alone you can impose some private discipline, whether it's endless bouts of aerobics or, as Judith Rossner, the author of *Looking for Mr Goodbar* told me she did, going back to her hotel room and working on her current book. When there are three of you you feel obliged to spend some social time together even though you're fed to the teeth with each other. But there were things much less pleasant than that to bear.

All this upfront, swinging London approach was all very well as long as we were escorted by a man or had some control over the situation but once in Los Angeles, for example,

109

we were sent along to a distributors' convention. Convention time in America is notoriously when the booze flows and the girls are ripe for the plucking. It was quite clear as we entered the room without our protector – Al Freeman had arranged to collect us later – that we were the evening's entertainment and the sooner they split us up and got us into the sack practising what we preached, the better. I spent all evening speaking in my most cutglass voice, taking hands out of my shirt front and off my lower back. Somehow we found out where Al was and rang him. He arrived and guiltily shepherded us away, by which time the atmosphere was overwrought and frankly frightening.

But the trip was invaluable. It taught me that the secret of taking care of your looks is (like Beau Brummell) to do everything you can before you leave your room for the round of the day's engagements and not to think about them again. It taught me that appearing on radio and television is a job. Nobody cares what it costs you, they just want you to be good. Going from one show to another all the time is a great way of demystifying the media, and the exposure to the consumer side of radio and television helped me to see it for what it is. In America there is a great deal of air time and it has to be filled. If you are fast, funny, have strong opinions, are interesting, learn to fix your own face, dress well for the camera, get on in there whether it's five in the morning or eleven at night – you're a good filler and they like you. Being liked is always infinitely preferable to being disliked. And fulfilling all those criteria was a challenge. I found that I liked it and I still do.

Back in New York it was decided that Al Freeman and Susan Capel would fly home, leaving Susana Duncan and I to pick up one or two more bits of exposure. This we did and I met some of her friends, one of whom took us to the Algonquin (former haunt of Dorothy Parker, Robert Benchley and other assorted wits) where I was introduced to a real live British book publisher. I was impressed especially when, apart from being dashingly greyhaired, he turned out to be interested in my 'career'. (How I hate that word.) He asked me what my future plans were and said we should stay in touch. Even I knew that the latter phrase could mean something or nothing but my passion for books made me think positively. I would, I vowed to myself, look him up in London.

Susana stayed on with other friends, all apparently as rich as Croesus and a great deal more bored, while I flew back to London, tired, cold and coming down. If this was the end of the present, what did the future hold? Michael met me at the airport and once the greetings were over, we sat in the van while I confessed to a one night stand in New York, the burden of my intent being that if he could confide in me (as per his letter to me in Chicago), I could confide in him. It was the last time I made that mistake. Three weeks of haranguing, blaming and sulking followed – it wasn't worth it. A week after that, Al Freeman hired me to work for *Forum*. And if sex wasn't a subject Michael felt strongly about, at least now I was an assistant editor instead of a secretary, which sounded better even if the money was the same – £35 a week for the first year, £45 thereafter.

Forum was housed in a converted pie factory just off the North End Road in Fulham. The building surrounded three sides of a courtyard dominated by a lumpy plaster cherub standing in a fountain with no water. As you stood just inside the metal gates, there was distribution and sex aids on your right, reception on your left, *Penthouse* editorial offices upstairs, *Forum* editorial downstairs. It is only in fiction and the higher echelons of power that offices are glamorous. These contained the usual beat-up typewriters, battered office furniture, filing cabinets and telephones.

When I began to work there the deputy editor was Jane Firbank, a journalist doing an extramural degree in psychology at Birkbeck. I joined the editor's secretary and three other assistant editors to make an all-female staff. The public line on this was 'that woman are so much more understanding and broadminded about sexual matters.' Be that as it may, the real reason we were there was that, for whatever reason, we were all prepared to work for a pittance.

Our main job as assistant editors was to edit readers' letters for publication – they comprised half the magazine. This involved putting everything in the letter into chronological order and rewriting it in the house style. Every publication has a style of writing peculiar to it which, depending on your point of view, is more or less acceptable. The basic principle of *Forum*'s house style was, as I recall it, that you never used one word where you could use two – three was even better – and you used a careful admixture of the vernacular with the over-correct Latin or Greek derived terms for the various parts and activities. The resulting uniformity made the letters read a good deal more falsely than they might had they simply been tidied up and allowed to run. However, contrary to the myth dear to the hearts of some of the press, I did not spend my days composing letters. They arrived every day in legitimate postal sacks, in proper envelopes, with stamps and addresses and joined up writing. And precious few deceits there were among them in terms of their writers' names and where they lived. As to whether they did what they said they did, the magazine took the view that if they wrote about it, it was real to them and so should be treated as gospel. My own view is better summed up by the old saying 'There's nowt so queer as folk.' When next you stand in a pleasant suburban street at dusk, looking at those neatly drawn curtains and rosy windows, don't imagine that all the couples inside do it once a week in the missionary position. Many of them are rather more imaginative and for some of them talking about it is as much of a hobby as cookery or fretwork is to you or me.

Within three months or so I had made Al Freeman aware of how strongly I felt about his approach to readers' letters. So he gave me another title and a different job. I was called the projects editor, which sounds grand but really meant 'if you haven't got time, give the whole thing to Anna and she'll make time because that's what she's paid for.' My first task was to try and bring *Forum* to the attention of all sorts of people who either ignored it or refused to take it seriously. Most of them were slightly surprised to discover that somebody who worked for *Forum* (under the umbrella of the bare and bosomy *Penthouse*) was bespectacled, married and could string two words together.

I arranged meetings for libertarian vicars chaired by Chad Varah, the founder of The Samaritans and a great supporter of *Forum*, under the heading (may we be forgiven!) of Christian Lib. Then we had a group therapy session for GPs led by a consultant psychiatrist which I sat in on and made notes, deciding that if the press were sexually the most ultraconservative bunch, the medical profession ran them a close second. Then I was asked to run the Personal Adviser, an informal counselling clinic held every other week at *Forum*'s offices.

Each therapist gave us three hours of his/her time and the arrangements as to who should see whom were made via the post by the administrator (me), except for a last minute ring around to make sure people would be keeping their appointments or fill in a cancellation, should one occur at the last minute. Each therapist was paid a token fee of £10, each client paid £2.50 per hour and *Forum* paid the overheads and my overtime.

When I first had anything to do with the Personal Adviser, I found it was staffed by some excellent therapists, there more out of curiosity than any desire to make money, as is evident, and some friends of the editor. Gently but inexorably I moved the latter to one side so that I could go hunting for a better class of help. Once we got them, we could point to the Adviser with justifiable pride. It was at about the same time that I decided that as far as I could I would reply to any letters too 'ordinary' (i.e. low-key) to merit publication, or whose writers specifically asked that they should not be published. When my boss the editor asked how I was spending my time, I pointed out that the magazine gave an undertaking in print that any correspondence would receive a reply. If that's what we'd said we'd do, we must be seen to do it. There was little enough to recommend *Forum* to the British press, it was not a mainstream publication, but if we could point with confidence to the way we handled mail, it seemed to me a reliable if not very speedy way of establishing some credibility. And I did all the other things my boss asked of me to justify the hours I spent ringing and writing to people who would otherwise have been ignored by the magazine they had confided in.

Typically he called me in one day to check what I was about and said, in concluding the meeting, 'You'll have to take my place on such-and-such a day because I have to go to the States for Bob.' When I tried to find out more, he waved me away with the name of the contact saying something about Round Table. Round Table? King Arthur and his knights? When I rang the number he'd given me, the man on the other end didn't sound a bit put out that Mr Freeman wouldn't be coming. You could say he accepted a replacement with alacrity. 'It's just an after dinner speech,' he said reassuringly. 'Maybe a few questions. We'd like to know about the magazine.' From this conversation I learned that Round Table is an association of men between the ages of 18 and 40, which meets once a month with the dual aim of raising money for charity and having as much fun as possible. I stuck my head back round AZF's door.

'It's after dinner speaking,' I said nervously. 'I've never done that.' (I couldn't very well tell him that eating in a room full of complete strangers was every bit as frightening as wondering what I was going to say).

'Oh you'll be fine,' he said. 'They just want a few laughs. Take a Pet.'

On the appointed day, I met Julie, a tiny little girl with a beautiful figure, who was carrying her full Penthouse Pet regalia in a suitbag over her arm. I had my most dressy, my only dressy outfit similarly packed. At Gravesend we were met and whisked into a hotel to change. Our street clothes safely stowed, our escort took us to the banqueting room and flung wide the doors. The room was full of men, 97 of them to be exact, and only three of them knew what was coming. Amid a great clinking of beer mugs and the British equivalent of a Bronx cheer, we walked to our places. We got through the meal and the chat and the notices and by now I was pumping so much adrenalin, my glasses were steamed up. What on earth was I going to say? I was introduced and amid roars of goodnatured laughter, I stood up. I took off my glasses, turned to Julie and said, 'Stand on your chair.' She looked at me. 'Please, on your chair!' She climbed up, all abbreviated frills and curves, and posed. I turned to my first after dinner audience. 'Good evening, gentlemen,' I said. 'For the next twenty minutes, you can look at her and listen to me.'

I talked about every facet of the magazine, the letters, the tour in the States, my own feelings about it all and I sat down, legs shaking, devoutly hoping I hadn't made a fool of myself amid generous applause. Some further 20 minutes into a 'few questions', I was asked if I was really a woman. Smilingly I replied that I had men on each side of me who'd be delighted to endorse my chromosome construction. 'And now you've had your laugh,' I went on, 'let's look at what your question is really about' and I plunged into some heartfelt exposition about the alleged differences between men and women, the real ones and the dreaded double standards which clutter up so much of our waking lives. And got applause. Hours later, the man who drove me home that night was the man who had asked the question that started it all. When we had dropped Julie off, we sat outside my flat while he talked about himself and his marriage and shook my hand warmly at parting. I'll always remember him. That was my first public speaking engagement for *Forum* and they paid me £1 an hour for every hour after 6.00 pm.

Word went out on the grapevine that if you wanted a good speaker for free, call Anna Raeburn at *Forum*. I soon discovered that I couldn't manage more than two such functions a week, it was too tiring and I got stale. But sometimes I could make as much as £14 extra cash and one magical week I bought my first gold earrings from a smart jewellers in Knightsbridge, for the grand sum of £9.

I have great warm feelings for Round Table because they reinforced my belief that the British male is nicer *en masse* than his transatlantic counterpart and it was fascinating how different the meetings were. Sometimes there'd be a resident joker or two and I'd spend all evening exchanging sallies. Another would have two factions and I'd be the bridge between the two. And a third would be much more serious and I'd spend all evening talking about the menopause or contraception.

I went to two at which it was obvious from the outset that I was the evening's entertainment in the worst way, one of which reduced me to tears. I remember a third where the body of the meeting was on the ball but the chairman was a bit blue and distinctly unfunny. At the end of the evening when he announced they'd a little keepsake for me, I nerved myself to accept split crotch panties with a suitable *bon mot* but they gave me a Dalkon shield (coil to you) dipped in silver, were fascinated that I knew all about it and I stayed another half-hour. But I'll always have a soft spot for the two guys who came back from the lavatory laughing uncontrollably. When I asked them what was so funny, the more coherent replied, 'Well we're standing in the gents and there's another of our number a bit further up with his mate. "What's she going to do?" says the first one. "I dunno," says his mate, "but the way I look at it, she's got to be better than the last speaker. He talked about reinforced concrete!" '

What I learned after some fifty Tables was that they had

two distinct visions of what I would be like. They thought I would either be blonde with thigh-high boots and a miniskirt or they thought I'd be tall and sharp and a bit equine. I treasured the comment of one man after my last *Table* appearance. 'You know, I saw you from behind in the bar before we started,' he said, 'and I thought you were too small for us.'

It was while I was at *Forum* that I made my British TV debut on *Late Night Lineup* with Dr Phillip Cauthery, a Marriage Guidance Counsellor and a family doctor. I took part in an ATV programme on Women's Liberation, a summer debate chaired by Austin Mitchell, a *Panorama* programme called 'Sex Can Be A Problem'. All this gave the illusion that something was happening. I already had six or seven ten minute snippets under my belt from Radio London and they weren't all about sex. They were about community problems and they were the most exciting things I'd done to date. I was paid £7 per programme so I used to rush out to buy *Time Out* first thing on Thursday mornings, turn to the AgitProp and Meetings pages, find out what interested me most, make frantic telephone calls to those involved explaining that I couldn't pay them but that I could offer them a drink and whatever they said would go out live and unedited. I was astonished at how many of these devoted people, struggling with small endeavours outside the machinery of the institutions could not communicate why they felt what they were doing was so important. But they responded wonderfully well once they found that what they said wouldn't be cut or shaped. The programme controller wasn't too keen, however, and in due course I was 'let go'.

Apart from learning all the time and getting my typing speed up to its highest ever because of all those letters I had a conviction should be answered, I was very glad that *Forum* was conveniently situated for food shopping with more elegant shop gazing only a bus ride away. Eating with total strangers had made eating in public easier so I spent happy lunchtimes in the local 'caff' with Jan, the editor's secretary, Genevieve Cooper her successor and then Rosemary Davies. Jan went into the hotel business and then became an executive in import/export, Genevieve went to *Cosmopolitan* as the editor's secretary, wrote a column there and is now deputy editor on *You Magazine* at the *Mail on Sunday* while Rosemary is Beauty Editor at *Company* magazine. *Forum* seems to have fired us all with something.

So that side of my life was fine. But home wasn't. Michael was still putting packages together only to have them fall apart, still travelling whenever possible, still eating, breathing, sleeping film. People still arrived five at a time, out of the blue, and I usually found them intimidating. At one point there was a break in the clouds while he made a documentary about golf and was briefly but beautifully solvent. He was only really happy when he was filming and there wasn't much work about. We went on for lack of an alternative. I suppose the situation was covered by the stock phrase 'he went his way and I went mine' except of course that only really works when you've both agreed on what you'll do and we hadn't agreed on anything. We did a lot of talking but increasingly the words bounced back like water off the back of a spoon and the atmosphere was cluttered with all sorts of thoughts, lying untidily about and not doing either of us much good.

Chapter 12

One morning *Forum*'s editor announced that he wanted me to leave in a week for New York to embark on the kind of promotional tour which had first brought me to *Forum*. Apparently the magazine wasn't selling as well as they'd hoped and it needed somebody to give it a bit of a push. I told Michael, got ready and flew.

In New York I paid my first visit to the then new Penthouse offices, all shag carpet, stale air conditioning and paranoia. I met the circulation director who told me what he thought the problem was. I met the vice president who was plainly – and understandably – unimpressed about letting me loose on this trip and I went to see the cashier. Armed with $600 and a list of stops along the way masquerading as an itinerary, I left the next morning for Philadelphia, Washington, San Diego, St. Louis, Miami, Birmingham Alabama, Atlanta, Chicago and New York again.

In order for the next section of my story to ring true, I must tell you that Anna Raeburn as she is now did not at that time exist. It's not that the outside changed – we all change on the outside. It's that the inside changed. It had not occurred to me, for example, that I would be quite justified in asking *Forum* to pay me extra for the inconvenience of this trip. I had no real idea of what a promotional tour was. I thought I was going to get on and off planes and be shepherded from place to place, as I had been when Al Freeman toured with 'les girls' in the beginning of my association with *Forum*. My faith was touching. But in mitigation there are no shortcuts to learning about life, love or anything else worth a damn, so the following weeks must be seen as part of that learning process. Nothing's for nothing. You have to remind yourself of that often, especially when things go wrong.

I was given the impression that hotel and flight reservations had been made for me. They had not. I spent my time asking people to call the circulation director in New York to verify that I was a Penthouse employee and that they should bill the company. I spent a good deal of time hoping that my panic and humiliation did not show. It was hard to learn that most appeals for mercy fall on deaf ears. People are busy. They want facts, not pleas for clemency. I learned to insist and smile and keep on insisting. The $600 which had seemed like a lot of money when it was handed to me began to dwindle rapidly. I didn't know the towns I was going to so I took cabs everywhere, into the city from the airport, from the hotel to meet the people I thought were going to come and meet me. Today I would not travel without a cheque card and at least two credit cards. In those days credit cards, in my vocabulary, were something belonging to other people. And I discovered that, although they were without exception civil in person, as far as the sales reps in the various areas were concerned, my presence was just one more wrinkle in their already pressured lives. Unmanaged and unguided, they did their best but they also did the minimum. Some took me to radio and television stations in the hope that the relevant personnel would like me and we'd get an opportunity to talk about *Forum* on air. One kept me in a town for three days without doing anything.

In the meantime, I who have always been frightened of aeroplanes, learned to get on and off them as if they were buses. There wasn't any point in making a fuss about it because there wasn't anybody to listen and I got pretty canny about preferring loneliness to company with the wrong stranger. I was also intensely intimidated by waiters, bartenders, receptionists – just about anybody you meet when you travel as I was travelling. I feared asking the wrong questions, too many questions, thus showing my ignorance, being a nuisance and above all, sounding dumb. I sweated profusely and looked even more nervous and travel-stained than I already was. But there were so many really insurmountable problems – like no contacts, nowhere to sleep, no seat on the plane, none of the work I'd been expecting to do – that very soon all these minor irritations like not liking to fly or to deal with people became unimportant. All problems are relative and you must never shrink in everyday terms from the value of Scarlett O'Hara's motto – 'I'll think about that tomorrow.' Shelve what you can't do and do what you can. It's called baptism by fire.

Not surprisingly I've blocked most of the details of the trip out of my mind. But I do remember flying into Atlanta. I'd been talking to a man on the plane, against my better judgement but sometimes you've just got to have a bit of human company which has nothing to do with work. The temperature in Atlanta was in the high 80s with about 70 degrees of humidity – like walking into a wet oven. I had a period. My hair was still long, and it felt heavy and sticky. The man on the plane was a soldier and we'd said our farewells and parted as I raced for the nearest loo but we met again in the baggage reclaim.

I don't know what I said or did or whether it was just a grimace in passing. Anyway he reappeared at my elbow. 'You really don't know anybody in this town do you?' he asked. I shook my head. He picked up my bag and walked me towards a cab. 'Come on, the least I can do is to see you safely to your hotel. Where d'you say you were going?' Of course I hadn't said – no point in courting trouble – so when I told him, he frowned. 'That's a motel,' he said. 'Why would they put you in a motel?' He made it sound really redlight and rowdy. I shrugged. I didn't know, what did it matter? We drove to the offending building, where the staff were nice enough but once again, I didn't have a confirmed booking. And I remember this pleasant young man regarding the floor, the ceiling, his fingernails, my suitcase while I persuaded the desk clerk to call New York and verify my credit so that I could get into a room for the night. I was so embarrassed I couldn't look at him and he was too well mannered to leave. Eventually, it was done, I was checked in and he departed.

My room contained two double beds so I commandeered one as a work top to try and sort myself out. There were no valet services, dry-cleaning was too slow so I hung everything that was creased over the hottest bath I could run and wrapped in a cotton robe, I slumped in a chair. There was a knock at the door. When I answered it, there was the soldier with an alcoholic looking bottle in his hand. As visions of depravity and decadence chased across my brow, he said, 'Seemed I should at least offer you a drink.' Feeling more and more as if I'd wandered into a 'B' movie out of Tennessee

Williams, I invited him in. (Please God don't let me die in Atlanta.) I went to get the tooth glass to share his gift. He was perfectly proper. We sat and talked and then I gradually became aware that when I gratefully stripped off my clothes, I had removed everything, including my tampon, the need for which was now making its presence felt on to the counterpane beneath me. Somehow or other, I covered the mark and edged my way back up the room, which seemed a hundred yards long at that moment, to the bathroom. There I shut the door and tried to rectify matters. So much for the glamour of travelling for *Forum*.

Apart from that I only remember fragments like thinking how easy it was to believe that the slow Alabama speech was always friendly until I recalled that all those Southern good-ol'-boys talk like that and some of them lynched blacks and killed civil rights workers on voter registration drives. And how unreal it was to arrive in St. Louis on Sunday and find a country and western programme on one TV channel with Laurence Olivier in *The Merchant of Venice* on the other. The relief of the kindness and intelligence shown me by students on the campus radio stations of the Universities of Maryland and Georgia. But most of all I remember being angry at the waste of time of all of this, thinking that if enough wasn't accomplished, I would be blamed for it and deciding that the Curtis Circulation Company (who handled the distribution of all Penthouse publications in the States) and the Penthouse head office (who were at least on the relevant side of the Atlantic) were not going to be spared. I flew home two days early and hid out in a hotel in Gloucester Road, kindly arranged by a friend of mine so that I could co-operate with a student film crew who were making a film about the employees of 'girlie' magazines, a golden opportunity to practise shooting my mouth off.

On my first day back in the office, I sat at my typewriter and drafted a long memo to Bob Guccione who owns the Penthouse Empire with copies to Al Freeman as my boss, Molly McKellar who was in charge of PR on our side of the pond and the circulation director in New York, just so that nobody should not know what was on my mind. I remain profoundly grateful that at this point the old lesson my father had told me about never arguing with anybody but the boss reasserted itself through the maelstrom of insecurity my life was at the time.

When Al heard that the document had already gone to Guccione, he looked worried and for the first time, some questions were asked about what had and had not happened in the States. Then he looked more worried. Mr Guccione took any possible sting out of the situation as only people with power can. He talked to me. I was summoned to his onyx, gilt and wolfskin lair and he told me how impressed he was with my thinking and my loyalty to the company. He offered me a job in the States. I explained that I had already lived in the States and anyway that wasn't the point. I wanted him to know that time and money had been wasted, my time and his money, that *Forum* was no better off than it had been, that it seemed to me that nobody was in charge in the New York office because nobody wanted to be and the victims of that attitude were me and the magazine I worked for. I forgot myself and got quite gritty and aggressive – something I'd previously only practised in the mirror when nobody was around – and *very* unfeminine, by the standards of Penthouse, where nobody minds if you think like Dow Jones as long as you look like Raquel Welch. And if you don't do either, for goodness' sake at least don't get emotional. Emotions are for dogs and mothers. When we parted, he having acknowledged my point and understood my justifiable anger, I was scared; scared of losing my job, tired of being scared, fed up with being patronised and patted on the head, sick of the whole deal but utterly unable to work out what to do next.

* * *

Then suddenly there was a man in the henhouse. Jane Firbank resigned as our deputy editor and went on to finer things while Freeman hired Phillip Ian Hodson, sweet of mouth, self-interested, all long curls and velvet jackets and so strenuously sixties' varsity that there is a story (unsubstantiated) that he even signed personal letters 'Phillip I. Hodson, M.A. (Oxon.)'. But he was a change and at the outset he was kind and I was very much in need of that kindness, it being a quality markedly lacking in my life at that time. Hodson initially changed the magazine for the better, both in content

122

and in terms of how it was run – of course he was given much more power to do that automatically, being the 'right' sex. He encouraged me to write the advertising blurbs for the magazine which went into various other publications, though at that time I found it difficult to put one word after another for fear of being wrong. There was no great debate about it. He insisted and I got on with it. He also encouraged my efforts to reply to those letters which weren't published and, more importantly, he increased the distance between the staff and Al. Somewhere along the line I'd been told that the reason I wasn't allowed to write for the magazine was that Al Freeman was of the opinion that I couldn't write. Consequently as of that date, the less I saw of him the better.

For writing was something I wanted to do somehow. One February morning the publisher I'd met at the end of my first US tour for *Forum* rang and asked, 'Is there anybody at your place who could write a serious book about group sex?' I replied that that was the nicest invitation I'd ever had. I asked a colleague from the office to come with me, we met in the John Snow pub in Broadwick Street, Soho where the publisher formally offered us £50 each for 60,000 words in a year. If ever there was an idea for a book which was passé before it started, this was it. In order to work at all, it should have been given to competent hacks who'd have knocked it out in half the time, except of course they wouldn't have taken the job because the money, even in those far-off days, was preposterous in proportion to the work involved.

In the ensuing year I tried to write and found that I couldn't. I was embarrassingly inept. We ran across London on all sorts of wildgoose chases to meet people who'd been to, or allegedly ran, 'sex parties'. We discovered that they were just one step more jumpy than the middle man in a drugs deal. We put ads in the *International Times* and *Time Out* to meet 'swingers'. We met and discussed and argued and gradually my friend grew disenchanted because I just wasn't producing the words. Her own life at this stage was far from happy but she managed to keep the pages coming, which was more than I did.

My painful lesson from this experience – which please note, doesn't end until eleven years later – is that it is always easier to talk about writing a book than it is to write one and that no matter what degree of trust you have for a publisher, sign nothing without being fully aware that what you sign is binding.

So, while I wasn't writing a book, I was introduced to Rosie Boycott and Marsha Rowe who were then credited with being the founders of *Spare Rib*, the alternative feminist magazine. Rosie terrified me from the first. She still does. Marsha was quieter, more understandable, but Rosie was a curious mixture of the colonel's daughter, writing talent, self-destruction (which is always fascinating, as long as it's someone else's self) and golden girl of the hip bit of the internationally entrepreneurial literary scene. And she was nine years younger than me. The first time she approached me, we crossed swords instantly and I withdrew. The second time she offered me a letters column in *Spare Rib*. So I poached letters from *Forum*, adjusted them to get the correspondence going and then wrote seven columns at £14 a go. Editing was minimal so I learned by seeing my mistakes in print.

Meantime at the flat in Wimbledon we had a new tenant, a slight and unprepossessing young man called Ian and hardly had he moved in than a young woman moved in too. He told me that she was in trouble and he felt sorry for her. She had no job, nowhere to go and considerable problems at home. Could she stay for a bit? Within ten days of moving in, Mary came out to the kitchen and said, 'I think you should know I use these.' I looked at the bottles and back at her. I asked what they were. 'Speed,' she said. I asked how she got them, on the street or by forging prescriptions. She told me both. I asked her how long she'd used it. A former nurse, she replied with precision, 'Sixteen months.' I thanked her for telling me and went off to work to bone up on amphetamines. That night Mary made the first of her suicide attempts.

In the weeks that followed, I learned about her family – dead mother, 'good' sister, forbidding stepmother, loving but ineffectual father. I learned that she had 'given up' nursing because nursing gave her up – she had been found out, stealing drugs. She was frightened of not being a nice person, of her appearance which she thought was plain, of her depression and lack of energy. She had exquisite taste and was as manipulative as a monkey. She made six suicide attempts altogether in less than two months, all of them dramatic gestures designed to get attention which they unfailingly did, while I tried to find out what was best for her and force her in that direction. I was reluctant to commit her to the local mental hospital, felt strongly that with help she could come through but eventually, backed up by a psychiatrist I knew through *Forum*, I told her she had to go and asked her father to come and get her. He arrived with the less than sympathetic stepmother, and Mary tried to throw herself first out of a window and secondly into my arms.

She went first to Phoenix House where she was frightened by her surroundings and the endless talk about heroin. Then she hit the bottle and wound up at the admirable Henderson Hospital, where the community admitted her only if she'd work at sorting herself out.

It stretches the imagination but somehow some time later she became an au pair for the columnist Jilly Cooper. She must have talked Jilly's ear off about me because one day the telephone rang and an unfamiliar voice asked, 'Are you Anna Raeburn?' I replied that I was. 'Well, I'm Jilly Cooper and Mary works for me. Do you remember Mary? Seems to think you're the next best thing to God and says you're interested in writing so I wondered, you know I work for the *Sunday Times*, if you'd like to meet the editor of the *Look!* pages.' I gulped. Yes I would, I said, very much. In due course I met him, he commissioned two pieces and left the paper. I was paid for both pieces but neither saw the light of day. The next time I saw Jilly Cooper she was standing in for the regular editor of the Atticus column and doing a puff on Hodson and me. At the time she was lending a certain something to commercials for Blue Band margarine so I had some giftwrapped for her in Harrods and tried to thank her for her help, which she brushed aside with typical generosity. I didn't know what to do about Mary. Should I ring her? Would she ring me? One morning I found on the doorstep a very Japanese-looking little pot she'd made accompanied by a note which said it all. 'Love, Mary.' I saw her a year or two ago, looking brown and healthy, riding a bike up the Edgware Road. I don't think she recognised me.

When Mary knew me my hair was very long, as it had been for twelve years, à la folksinger, hanging round and preferably over my face, occasionally pushed back by my glasses which served as an Alice band. 'I hope,' said my mother plaintively, 'that as you're coming up for 30, you'll do something about your hair.' Never one to pull a punch, my mother. I had had a good hairdresser for a long time and we had a running fight about cutting or not cutting my hair but on my 30th birthday, I did the deed. It was not anything like as short as it became subsequently but compared to the Afghan hound bob I'd worn for years, I was shorn.

Hardly was this done than Phillip Hodson and an artist friend of his told me that Evelyn Home was retiring from *Woman* magazine. 'Why don't you apply for the job?' said Hodson. 'I think you must.' I couldn't believe they were serious, John too (Phillip's friend) nodding sagely. They explained that *Woman* would be looking for either somebody in the same mould or very different and they'd vote for very different. Me. I began to laugh. I laughed so hard, I had to hang on to the desk. Here was I, 30 years old, marriage on the rocks, not respectable, not accomplished or even very experienced as a journalist, no white coat, no orthopaedic Oxfords, not a cardy or a degree in sight. Why on earth should an established publication like *Woman* even look twice at me? Hodson got sniffy as he always did when he felt he knew what he was about and you rejected his advice. I went back to my desk giggling.

That night there was a programme on television about the changes at *Woman*, how Evelyn Home was retiring and the new editor, a man and a man with a beard even, wanted the magazine to move with the times. And I began to think. I knew I had to get out of *Forum*. *Forum* was a specialist magazine and you can only go on being a big fish in a small pond for so long. Freelancing was out of the question. You can't run before you can walk. I had to have a job, ideally a job that paid instead of being on the treadmill with A for effort and no dough. I clearly wasn't going to get such a job at the *Sunday Times* or *Spare Rib*. There was a postgraduate course on journalism at Cardiff University. Maybe I should be aiming for that. Or perhaps I should be listening to my friend the educational psychologist who was urging me to apply for a grant and get on and work with him, assessing learning difficulties. 'You'll walk the degree,' he kept saying. 'They've got a place for you and you don't have to worry about money because I can and will employ you as soon as you know the ropes. Come on, what are you waiting for? I've spoken to the course director. What's the problem? What are you scared of?'

He'd asked me that so many times and finally I answered him slowly and painfully. 'I'm scared of hurting somebody more than I help them.'

He looked at me hard. 'In that case,' he said crisply, 'you'd better shut up for the rest of your days because that's the risk you take if you become involved in anything.'

So I asked myself, what was the worst that could happen if I applied for the job at *Woman*? IPC Magazines, the huge publishing group of which *Woman* is a part, would send me a polite note of refusal. What was the best that could happen? I'd be shortlisted, invited for interview and perhaps discover what it was I had or hadn't got, should or shouldn't do to move on from where I was. I wrote a very short, blunt letter explaining that I hadn't enclosed a curriculum vitae because I hadn't had that sort of a life, detailing my work for a doctor, for *Forum*, the educational research job, *Spare Rib* and enclosing my two best columns from there.

Against all this background, Michael and I had been talking about what we were going to do since the previous Christmas (the initial discussion engendered my first migraine attack which lasted four days) and it was now May or so.

I had tried to prepare my mother for our parting. She wasn't against it, she simply didn't know how to face it. I had wept and railed and wept some more. I had stayed with friends and thrown things and had some rather solid things like books and tables thrown at me, which reduced me to gibbering hysteria. I had been angry and frightened and frightened and angry for so long. Michael had gone to a therapist because he thought I wanted him to, but abandoned his treatment when it didn't persuade me to stay. And I had gone to a therapist who spent our first five sessions trying to push me back into the marriage until I decided between sessions five and six that if she wanted the marriage so badly, maybe she should have it, and saw her no more. When I'm asked why I left Michael, I can only reply that it was like being on one side of a pair of heavy swing doors. On the other side is a corridor with all sorts of other doors and I knew that if I stayed in that marriage, I'd never get through the swing doors into the passage, let alone discover where all those other interesting doors led.

Michael then made it clear that since I was the one with the job and the money, then I should move out. My cat ran away. I sorted the books. An acquaintance offered me a room in her flat. Michael assured me there was no hurry to move my things out, but suddenly there was, because he lost the flat, due to a very complicated subletting arrangement. I collected my clothes, my books, a mahogany plant-stand my mother had given me, an abstract painting by a friend of mine. I stored one half of my possessions on one side of London and kept the other with me on the other side. There was no word from *Woman*. One day I did what I still think is one of the bravest things I've ever done. I rang them. 'I'm pretty sure you're going to say no to me anyway,' I burbled, 'but it's the suspense I can't stand. I'd just like to know.'

There was a long silence, the silence of a sorely tried secretary raking through a big pile of papers. 'Oh Miss Raeburn, I thought so,' she said. 'You've been shortlisted.'

The one thing that would have driven me deeper into madness at that stage was time to think but God is good, Allah is merciful and Phillip Hodson told me that *Forum* wanted me to go to the States again almost immediately. He agreed to come with me while I confronted Al Freeman. It was the first and last time I asked for someone to hold my hand while I discussed money. I asked for £100 as a gesture of goodwill to equip myself for the journey and £100 per week payable in this country plus all expenses. Freeman asked Phillip what he thought. With rare lack of ambiguity, Hodson said, 'I think you should pay up, Al.' And so I began the best organised, best timed of my three tours for *Forum*. It began in Toronto with excursions to Montreal and Windsor, Ontario where there is a very powerful transmitter on what is called a clear channel, broadcasting into about fifteen states. I then went on to Dallas for four days of the National Supermarket Convention, continuing to Los Angeles, San Francisco, Washington, Chicago, Boston and back to New York.

It was a trip during which I began to discover that, however belatedly and for whatever reason, I had begun to grow up. There wasn't quite so much anguish about – mind you, there wasn't so much need for it. My itinerary read like a plan for war. There were names, telephone numbers, references and cross-references for every place. There was a detailed break-down of what shows on what stations, hosted by whom, with dates, times and the secretary's number. I was met at every turn, most notably by Fred Otash wearing a pale blue mohair cardigan on a frame resembling a mature version of the Magnificent Hulk. Otash talked like Ernest Borgnine, had worked as a bodyguard and gofer for the *National Enquirer* (arguably America's nastiest scandal sheet) and the Kennedys, among others. He was divorced, had a daughter my age he wasn't as close to as he'd have liked, and an Alsatian called Hooker. He was the first person to draw aside some of the veils of mystery which surrounded Penthouse and he explained that one of the difficulties in getting coverage for *Forum* was the Penthouse connection, because Guccione was liable to change his mind at the last minute and nobody liked that. Otash made the West Coast promotion work like never before, taking me for example to a radio station in the San Fernando Valley for a late appearance at 11.00 at night. I emerged at 4.20 the next morning. 'Great,' said my presenter, Allen Burton. 'Just great.'

Apart from that I remember the convention in Dallas, working the Penthouse stand with a Pet in full rig signing her centrefold for collectors at one end of the table while I in a fashionably long dress signed *Forum* at the other. I remember dining with Curtis Circulation's reps and their boss. I don't know if it was the haircut and the passing of time or I was just lucky with the men but nothing could have been further from the leering, groping past. And it is extraordinarily pleasant to be liked for yourself without having to argue about sex and gender. It also remains the only time I've ever drunk myself sober (on 14 margaritas) and I wouldn't do it again. I have a soft spot for Dallas because I'd watched the morning show and the blonde presenter two mornings running before I got there. It was really well put together and I was delighted to discover that the same person who had done such a good job with Peggy Lee yesterday would be serving me up for breakfast that day.

In Chicago I took my Penthouse boss and his deputy to dinner at the distinguished Pump Room and listened to them sing my praises. They'd been getting good feedback from the field and directly from the TV and radio stations. And because

I was European, they asked me to choose the wine, red and white. I acquitted myself well on the red but dropped a brick on the white, from which I was rescued with supreme tact by the *sommelier*. A year earlier the whole exercise would have been unthinkable.

But when I landed back in New York over the long weekend of Labour Day, I had to wait before continuing to Boston to finish the job and the sag in the tension flattened me. I developed a respiratory infection and I remember lying in bed, watching the Grammy awards on television because I couldn't sleep, wondering if I was ever going to do anything worthwhile in my life. Five days later when I walked back into *Forum*, the superbly discreet receptionist handed me my mail and said, 'Oh and will you call Miss Lambourn's secretary at IPC?'

Chapter 13

Patricia Lambourn was the publishing executive in charge of *Woman*, among other IPC magazines. When I rang her secretary, I was told that I would be sent several 'typical' readers' letters for which I should draft replies as if for publication and I should write a 1000 word piece on a related subject. The letters came, I did my best with them and then wrote about dependence, the underpinning of most relationships, healthy and otherwise, though not much discussed in women's magazines as far as I knew. They tend to concentrate on chase and discard, not continuum.

The only journalist I knew on conversational terms was the religious affairs correspondent of *The Times* so I rang him, explained what I was trying to do and asked if he'd have a professional look at what I'd done. He did so over dinner in an Italian restaurant in Old Brompton Road, commenting that he thought it was all rather good if a bit adventurous for *Woman*. I sent the papers off. In due course I was invited to come for an interview. I never allowed myself to think about whether I might get it or not except in the privacy of the bathroom and certainly nowhere near a mirror. All I knew was that I had hoped and prayed and dreamed I might be on the shortlist and I was. My guardian angel had once again done me proud and there didn't seem to be any point in suing for any more favours.

I went to the interview in a green aviator style suit from Wallis Shops. I had another in beige and I tended to wear them all the time. Retrospectively I'm not sure that they were at all becoming. The original premises of *Woman* at 189 High Holborn were not prepossessing – just as well, it was one thing less to worry about. Indeed, it all seemed remarkably familiar; the winding corridors, glassed-in offices, the familiar clack of the typewriters and smell of dust which gathers wherever there are masses of papers. I was left to sit in reception. To this day I don't know which is worse – fretting you won't arrive on time for an appointment or sitting there sweating, because everybody else is a bit late. On the table in front of me were some recent editions of *Woman*. I had seen *Woman* occasionally, but now it seemed as if I'd better give it close attention. So I turned to the back pages to look at the 'problems'. To my mind it isn't a compliment to say that it hadn't changed since I used to borrow it from the lady next door in Middlesbrough when I was about 12 or 14. And then I saw something which made me angry.

There was a letter from a girl of 16 saying that her parents didn't like her boyfriend, a year or two older, but that she really loved him and had commenced a sexual relationship with him. 'The only way out seems to be,' she wrote, 'to become pregnant by him because then they will have to accept him.' The answer began by sensibly pointing out that getting pregnant is no answer to a difficult situation, that it could only add to the bad feelings already engendered by this association and the poor innocent child might be just as much the victim as anybody else. Fine. But it went on to the effect that 'In any case, don't you think sixteen is a bit young for a sexual relationship with your boyfriend? There is plenty of time for that and wouldn't you be better off holding hands and being loving friends for a while longer?'

In defence of the writer I have paraphrased here, but the tone of what I've reproduced is accurate. Everything I've ever read or been told by parents, youth workers, doctors and any other useful adult I've met in all my life, everything I know, has left me with the very clear impression that the one thing young people embarked into sexual relationships don't do is stop and go back to holding hands. So where was the comment about responsibility towards yourself or your parents? Where was the contraceptive advice? Where was the advice about getting to grips with what the family took exception to and why? Where was the underscoring of what a disaster – not to put too fine a point on it – it would be to have a baby into such a set-up? Summoned to meet the editor and his deputy, I was still steaming.

Peter Lawrence was a thin man with a pointed beard who

would not have looked out of place in doublet and hose. Formerly an art editor, he didn't make any startling changes in the magazine but he moved it along in a more adventurous direction, running quite successfully along the knife edge of trying something new without alarming the old faithfuls. As far as his staff were concerned, his greatest merit was that you could always get in to see him. If he was busy when you stuck your head round the door, he'd ask you back and that accessibility stood him in good stead in running a complex magazine.

His deputy was Dee Remmington, an attractive woman, greying, charming, abrasive. She is of the generation of journalists who had to be as good as the boys at everything they did on the newspapers from which she'd come. Most importantly, she'd forgotten more about magazine journalism than I'll ever learn.

Between them these two interviewed me for 3½ hours, two hours in tandem and then Peter grilled me on his own. But we began with an eruption because, once the courtesies had been observed, Peter asked me what I'd do with the page if I got the job. I retorted with force, 'Well, I'll tell you what I wouldn't do' and told the story of the letter which had so enraged me while waiting to see him.

In the private part of my mind, away from listening, reasoning, wanting to be liked, this interview felt different from any I'd ever had before. I wasn't up in the clouds, sure I'd get the job but nor did I feel I should sneak away halfway through and drown my sorrows. For the first time in my life I felt I was in the running, not trying to be or wanting to be or knowing I couldn't be. I thought about a scene in one of my favourite films called *Queimada*, in which the manipulated leader of a revolt turns on the agent provocateur who's put him up to it and tells him, 'Nobody can give you freedom. You have to take it.' There are, I decided, two kinds of freedom. The first is when you own the whole shooting match and so can call every shot any way you like. It may not make you popular but you have the freedom to make those choices. The second kind of freedom is when you have nothing to lose. You forget all about being anyone but yourself because that's the best you have to offer and you just lay it all on the line in the way it seems to you. The second kind of freedom and its

133

possibilities hadn't occurred to me until then but as I was old enough at 30 to know that the chances of running the whole show were very limited, opting for the only real autonomy I could have became a real choice.

I said that I thought that problem pages in general were the consistency of cold porridge. I didn't like talking down to somebody who had a problem. I would want to write from the point of view of identifying with the correspondent as much as possible. The problem page as I saw it was a two way street. On the one hand there were all sorts of agencies and self-help groups and specialist disciplines. On the other hand there was the person with the problem. Acknowledging from the start the limitations of the medium and the individual's willingness to change, the column could introduce one to the other. I said I wanted a more direct approach, less diluted language. I said I wanted to be funny wherever I could, to tell stories, mention famous names, books and films. My listeners seemed to be taking this quite well. Towards the end, Peter said in an aside, 'I must stop talking about the shortlist. It's silly, there's only one name on the shortlist.' Now remember, arithmetic was not my strong point.

'You mean,' I said, my voice incredulous, 'there's only one person on the shortlist – and me?'

'No, dear,' said Peter Lawrence. 'You are the shortlist.'

I think I stopped breathing for a minute. Then I said very carefully, 'I don't know whether to laugh or cry' and discovered that my eyes were full of tears.

'Don't do either,' said my boss to be. 'Have a drink instead.'

I held the glass and looked at it. 'What happens now?' I asked.

'We have lunch with Patricia Lambourn and other interested parties,' he explained 'and then we write you a letter.'

I went into limbo until the lunch, but my worries were soon supplanted by the flow of liquor. Did they drink! Two or three shorts before, two wines with, brandies to follow – and this was lunch. And I, who couldn't drink, became rather flushed and forthright and did a bit of table pounding. Sobering on the way home, I panicked. I rang Peter. 'Peter, I'm sorry to bother you but have I blown it?'

'No, no, not at all,' he soothed. 'They liked your enthusiasm.'

When the letter of appointment was duly confirmed, I had to go and tell my erstwhile supremo, Al Freeman, that I was leaving. For a moment he looked taken aback. 'But Anna,' he exclaimed, 'where's your loyalty?'

I beamed him a lovely phoney smile. 'You've had it, Al,' I said. 'For three years it was all yours, and now I'm moving on.' And he gave me a hug and wished me luck. If I'd known how much I was going to need it, I'd have gone back and asked for seconds.

Had I known what I was taking on, I doubt if I would have attempted it. I have from time to time in my life been told how brave I am. I don't think this is true. The only kind of bravery I know anything about is the courage of ignorance. Don't prejudge. Don't let anybody else define your terms. Don't say you can't write till you've tried. Don't say you can't anything until you've tried. And if you've tried and you really can't, stick to your point and don't let anybody persuade you that your protestations are mock modesty. But if you've a shrewd idea that you've got some real ability plus the physical and emotional stamina to carry it through – get on with it. In other words, don't dream the impossible dream. Stick to the possible ones.

* * *

I joined IPC in August and my first column appeared in *Woman* in October. Perhaps the delay was just as well. I was very grateful for the offer of the room in which I was living but it was just about big enough to hold me, a bed and six coat hangers and while I don't have anything interesting or grand enough to be called claustrophobia, I'm not good at small rooms. Especially when I'd spent three out of the previous five years in a very spacious if shabby flat.

The separation from Michael was only a few weeks old. I jumped if anyone rattled a teaspoon in a saucer. I'd just got over the last of a series of menstrual problems which took the form of delayed periods followed by agonising pain and blood loss in the form of clots and prolonged heavy flow. Technically these may or may not have been very early stage miscarriages. I was fitted with the coil and if this fails as a contraceptive, it causes early stage abortion which is why the

Roman Catholic Church disapproves of it. Their disapproval mattered not one whit to me, I was so grateful to bring eight years of taking the birth control pill to an end. I am one of the exceptions that proves the rule, one of the women who really don't do well on the Pill. But after this last round of feeling as though somebody had put my pelvis through a washing machine, the gynaecologist had recommended a dose of ergometron to make sure that everything cleared out when the cycle ended. LSD is derived from ergometron and I certainly felt distinctly odd as I heaved about trying to carry on as usual. My face glistened with a film of grey sweat and I was so uncertain on my feet that I fell very badly, bruising my back and kidneys. I slept with the light on, about two or three hours at a time. Agony aunt? I should have been looking for one.

Although I had written letter columns before, they weren't as long as this. I found that my concentration wasn't what it might have been. I edited two letters complete with replies and walked round the block. Another one and went to the loo. Drank three cups of tea over a fourth. Wrote one more, made and received various phone calls and went off round the block again. Started another, put it aside and completed a sixth. That left at least four more to do. (It was more initially because I began with a double page spread which held twelve to fourteen and wound up with what is professionally known as six columns – a page and a half – which only held ten at the most, though it was always worth preparing spares.) The rest went home with me. I wrote before dinner, after dinner, at midnight and (once I'd ascertained that the typewriter's light click didn't disturb anybody) in the early hours of the morning. I tried to strike a balance between waiting for the Muse to kiss my brow and chasing her with a hatchet. The letters jumped in front of my eyes as much from nervousness as the side effects of the ergometron. I remember drinking coffee – it was before I developed my current allergy to it – crying into my brand new portable typewriter and then doing another letter. Now that I'd got the job, I had to survive three months' trial and I wasn't going to lose it.

Letters addressed to the problem page arrived at *Woman* in sacks. We may not have received as many as some others allege they do, but we had more than enough to be going on with thank you. In the golden past, when *Woman* sold millions of copies a week, and the problem department consisted of Evelyn Home and her minions, I'm sure they used form letters, but when I arrived, the problem page meant me, my secretary and two others. In the very first days they opened the mail and sent down to me only the anonymous letters of which the page is traditionally composed. Shortly after that, I went upstairs to meet them. They were somewhat taken aback because IPC reeks of hierarchy and they were not used to visits from the big wheels on the main floor. But I had some ideas of my own and I wanted their help. To begin with, we got round a union ruling that a member of NATSOPA, one of the clerical unions, had to open the mail by pointing out that my name was my real name, therefore all the mail was addressed to me personally and for anybody else to open it would be an offence. I decided that we could use for publication anything that didn't specifically request that we shouldn't publish. This would give me a much wider selection of raw material to draw from.

Problem pages generally set out to acknowledge and, if possible, reply helpfully to every letter they get. But I pointed out that as the style of the page was going to change, so the style of letters must. I didn't want any letters sent out signed 'pp Anna Raeburn'. They were to be signed by the person who wrote them, for and on behalf of AR. I couldn't possibly hope to read every letter before it went out and I didn't think the public was so dumb as to expect me to deal with everything that came in to *Woman*. What I did want was credit where credit was due for first two and latterly three 'repliers' but I also wanted them to co-operate in altering the tone of their letters to go with the page. The last thing I wanted was E. Home letters going out in tandem with an A. Raeburn page, signed by yet another name.

So I received the mail and went through it, selecting for use on the page whatever I could find, sometimes marking it 'reply and return for use on page' but more and more, tackling a significant portion of the mail myself, which was what I'd always wanted to do. My two repliers, Heather Walker and Jeanne Conn, did everything they could to help me and meet me halfway by changing their own approach. I was regularly sent copies of the letters they sent out and frequently went to see them bearing letters I thought one or the other was particularly well equipped to answer.

'But,' says a voice, 'how do you select a letter for publication? And how can you tell if it's a fake?' The way I found them was to see if they 'spoke' to me, if I could hear the person writing, imagine her set-up, feel her distress, get some sort of picture of what had caused her to write. (I say 'her' in deference to the millions of women who read women's magazines but there was always a proportion of letters from men and in the four years I was at *Woman*, the number increased. I was never sure whether that was because of the page I wrote, the kind of image I had, or just because I'd worked on a sex magazine! Whatever the reason, I included them on the page whenever I could.)

Sometimes 'hearing' a letter would work adversely. What you'd hear would be petulant, aggrieved, or otherwise unattractive. I'd have to work out whether it was unattractive enough to be illustrative or so unattractive it was just repellent. Apart from that, the only criterion was to publish as wide a range of predicaments as possible.

Whenever I speak in public, and I have done so a great deal down the years, there's usually one bright spark who says, 'But isn't it boring? I mean, you hear about the same things over and over again.' Well yes, I suppose that there are just so many problems and you do hear about them repeatedly. But you only get bored with a problem page if you get bored with people and with life itself. And I don't bore easily. Generally speaking I find people and what makes them tick fascinating. And in any case, people express themselves very differently. They may, if you were analysing the outline of each case, seem to have the same problem but they have different approaches to it, different backgrounds, different insights, different words to describe it. It might bore you but it doesn't bore me.

And then there's the business of fakes. Outright fakes are rare, usually couched in language that doesn't ring true, the jargon of contact mags, for example, with every four letter word put in to shock or a *True Confessions* special with an unformed hand on a sheet from a notebook. But assessing a fake is as much a matter of taste and personal experience as selecting letters for publication in the first place.

My rule of thumb is that the world is a great deal stranger

138

than fiction. Very few people would take the time and trouble to sit down and concoct pain or misery, particularly in the light of the fact that they're going to have to wait several weeks for a reply. Some people just want to 'get it off their chests' and for them, writing to a problem page is like writing to Santa Claus. Sealing it up in an envelope is symbolically getting rid of it. For others, writing it down is often the first time they see the problem from the outside and very often by the end of the letter, they're well on the way to sorting it out for themselves. They often end by saying that you needn't bother to reply to them because they feel so much better and they can see what they must do. Others write for information, like the girl who apparently really thought that masturbation weakened the eyesight and was very worried because she wanted to be a virgin on her wedding night but they weren't getting married for a year and both she and her boyfriend already wore glasses. (There's a fortune for somebody who wants to write a book on masturbation myths alone.) Some people write to have their view of a situation endorsed. They've already decided what to do, they just want you tell them what you think. And others again write because they love to moan. They need their problems to hang on to and if you resolved every one for them, they'd be off looking frantically for some more.

There are several approaches to a problem page and I can only tell you about mine. As far as I am concerned the validity of the page lies in reproducing the letters as nearly as possible in the form in which they were sent in. You may re-arrange the running order of the paragraphs, omit the repetitions, alter an all-too-recognisable detail in the interests of discretion, cut the length down overall, but you stick to the spirit and sense of the letter. I then set out to reply to that correspondent individually. Everyone else who reads the letter and its reply is a sort of eavesdropper and this is based again on personal conviction. I always saw the problem page as a vehicle for teaching. When you teach, you can offer information in general terms in the hope that it will filter down to the individual. Or you can appeal to the individual, knowing that others will become curious and give you their attention. I prefer the second approach

I don't know when I worked all this out. I don't remember

dark nights of soul-searching where I tried to work out my *raison d'être* as an agony aunt. But then I never thought of myself as an agony aunt. I know it's the 'in' term, used more or less affectionately or dismissively, depending on whose lips utter it, but I was trying to learn to be a writer and I began on a problem page. It was not the be-all and end-all of my life, though I quickly realised that it behoved me to have answers ready for those who would ask questions. The idea of admitting a problem, a loss of control, however temporary, is still a very threatening one for many people and the chief weapon against the serious consideration of somebody else's difficulty is to deprecate it, them and whoever else is involved. Problem pages are a perfect example of the 'us' and 'them' mentality. *They* write to problem pages, *we* solve problems. I always said that if we were going to talk in those terms, I was with what I more than once heard my bosses call 'them' 'our little ladies', a kind of belittling dismissal which made me try ever harder not to patronise them on my pages. So bitter did I become about this at one stage that I used to say that I spent the back pages of *Woman* trying to sort out the problems that had been created by the preceding ones. But to begin with I wasn't worrying about feminism versus women's magazines, I was just trying to keep up with an apparently insatiable demand for copy.

No sooner had I completed a column than it was spirited away. Under usual circumstances it would have been seen by the deputy editor in charge of that section of the magazine and the editor himself but as this was *my* copy, it seemed as if half of IPC had to see and approve it. I don't know what shocking things they thought I was going to be writing. But for the first three months, each column was seen by two senior executives, the editor, deputy and associate editors, plus comment from the legal and medical departments where necessary. And then would I please write my next column.

As I reached the hair-tearing stage of writing my fourth column in a row, I asked somebody why I was writing all this material, one column after another. She looked at me sympathetically. 'Publishing schedule,' she said. I didn't know what a publishing schedule was. Under the title *Woman* on the front cover is a caption which says 'the world's greatest weekly for women', so I naturally supposed that it was published

140

every week. My mentor explained that, although the magazine was released weekly, it was in fact put together nine weeks ahead because of the particular printing process we used. Which meant we could only use one press and had to fit in with their schedule. Years later my senior colleagues and I asked in the middle of an NUJ strike why the process couldn't be changed and were told effectively that it wouldn't be worth the upheaval it would cause. Such is the confidence the proprietors of publishing houses have in their journalistic staff.

But, these difficulties aside, I had what I had always longed for. I had a place to go, a job, a name. I had an office, access to telephones, paper, xeroxing. I also had a large outer office where my secretary worked. My first secretary was a thing of wonder. She looked like an escapee from the wilder shores of fashion and although in the long term she suffered from role-confusion (i.e. she couldn't make up her mind what she wanted to be) initially she was kind, helpful, and nice to have around. Between us we overhauled the bookshelves, the filing cabinets and the drawers. We found some clues about helpful references but most of the information I dished out on the page came from my memory, from sources I'd noted in my little black book and from assiduous reading. I left my successor with a fine set of alphabetised files on every subject which could be remotely thought of as relevant. I've always kept files. It's a kind of meanness, a way of resisting the disposability of newsprint. I keep files on things that interest me and update them at regular intervals so that when the subject comes up, I've always got somewhere to start. So my new office wasn't so very different from a lot of other places I'd worked. An office is an office is an office (with apologies to G. Stein). And although the idea of a secretary was a curiosity, I'd been a secretary for long enough, I knew how I would like to be treated if I were in her shoes and dealt accordingly.

The IPC tentacles would like to have drawn Peggy Makins (who was Evelyn Home for 37 years) into a lunch with her successor, but she declined and I was grateful. As the newly acquired flower in the buttonhole of IPC Magazines, I remember quite a lot of lunching in my first year. The purpose of killing three hours and more with an abundance of food and drink was not often clear to me and if I queried it, I was told, 'Oh but so-and-so would love to meet you.' What stopped whoever it was from dropping into my office for a cuppa I'll never know, but I did begin to understand that the business lunch is a symbol of power. You're not eating because you're hungry, not at all, nothing so prosaic. You're spending time and money (which just about equal each other in modern business) to show that you have enough status to do so. My curiosity about the people I'd meet soon became resignation. They talked shop and consumed large quantities of expensive food and drink. I think I was supposed to be flattered at my inclusion.

However one day while I was working, a head popped round the door of my office and a familiar face greeted me. I was momentarily embarrassed to be behind 'her' desk, but Peggy just shook my hand, wished me luck and put me at ease. She had come, she said, to make quite sure I knew she wasn't resisting lunch for any reason to do with me. I understood.

We met once or twice more and then I was reading an interview with her, which was partly because her memoirs had just been published, when I saw that she had been asked to comment on my taking over from her. She had answered favourably, adding, 'I wouldn't be ashamed to have her for a daughter and I daresay she wouldn't object to me for a mother.' I thought this was particularly gracious from a woman with no children for her own, so I wrote and thanked her.

Encouragement and support came from people I didn't know rather than people I did, but then that wasn't too surprising. Part of the price of leaving my marriage with Michael was the discovery that I had no friends. They were all Michael's friends. So it was very agreeable to have contact established by all sorts of new people in an outside business, to be wished well by Marje Proops and Claire Rayner, Betty Jerman and Anna Coote. I didn't have much difficulty in adapting to a whole new range of people (though few of them became intimate friends) but I couldn't get used to the fact that no matter how much I spent, I always had money.

I acquired objects for the home I was going to have. My mother never had enough storage space, vases, safety pins or sharpened pencils. So I bought with those in mind, and bits of china and a ring to replace my wedding ring. And clothes and books, and books and clothes. And as if that wasn't wonderful enough, not only could I afford to buy books (my salary having gone at one fell swoop from £1856 to £5548 per annum) but people actually sent me books for nothing. To begin with I was so green I actually rang up and offered to return them if they weren't of interest and although I don't do that any more (unless requested to do so), I still feel delighted at the arrival of a free book.

In my interview with Peter Lawrence we'd discussed the matter of my name. To begin with he asked me if I would use my own name. I replied that I preferred to. Then he said IPC wanted it exclusively. I thought fast and added a few noughts. 'That will cost you £25,000 a year,' I said calmly. They couldn't afford that so the agreement was that I could freelance under my own name provided I did nothing which would be detrimental to the magazine as a whole or to the role that I fulfilled in the magazine. He asked me how I felt about publicity. I said I wanted to work right across the media and I expected to co-operate with publicity as much as I could. Perhaps it was because my appointment was at the time of Watergate and we were all tired of President Nixon's face being thrust at us day after day. Or perhaps it was just the end of the silly season. But nothing prepared me for the amount of media 'noise' about Anna Raeburn succeeding Peggy Makins as Evelyn Home at *Woman*.

Once again, it's very hard to rehearse or prepare for that kind of experience. You just grab it, hang on tight and pick up as much and as fast as you can. You learn when to speak and when not to speak, you also learn when you can't win even if you don't speak. A skilful journalist can turn 17 minutes of repeating 'No comment' in an even tone into a very snide, not to say negative, paragraph about the end of your marriage, concluding with the time-honoured 'Miss Raeburn was not available for comment' which makes you sound guilty, defensive and not nice to know. You learn that what you say in life can look quite different in print. June Southworth did a very sane piece about me in the *Daily Mail* but one of my accurately quoted remarks landed me deservedly in Pseuds Corner in *Private Eye*. I didn't mean it like that but that's how it reads! Journalists have their own axes to grind, like the

143

photographer from *The Times* who went on and on at me to smile though I'm really afraid of my tiger grin, until he got me, fangs and all, at which point the paper published a paragraph headed 'The startling new face of the agony column' and startling it was. The most considered interview was in the *Church of England Times* but newspaper journalists don't want well thought out amenable dialogue – they want quotes. Years later Chris Hutchins of the *Sunday Mirror* told me, 'Anna you're a great talker, but you don't give good quotes!' And as if I had not been before, I became fascinated with images, how they are made, maintained, manipulated and broken and I decided that the one thing I wanted, as far as possible, was control of mine.

Chapter 14

The brass at *Woman* and IPC seemed quite happy to let me go on doing interviews with this person or that, speaking on such and such a radio programme and addressing various sorts of audiences, but three months into the job my media activities were momentarily called to a council of war when David Frost decided he would interview me. In the serious long term, I don't agree that two minutes of television is worth a thousand interviews but if you want to establish a name, there's nothing like a TV interview for doing it quickly. And in those days an interview with David Frost was big time.

The Frost Interview was David Frost's last series for BBC and it was produced for television by Iain Johnstone. It was he and a researcher called Helen Jay who took me to lunch at an unexpectedly subdued hotel near Broadcasting House. Between mouthfuls of whatever it was, they asked various questions which I tried to answer sensibly. Helen Jay had, I remember, a rather supercilious voice which she turned on me full wattage when I remarked that I was educated in state schools in the north of England. 'You must have worked frightfully hard on your voice,' she observed. I explained that both my parents had been born in the south of England and that I had not been allowed to develop a northern accent. 'Oh come on,' she said knowingly, 'no voice classes, no elocution lessons?' I thought firmly about cucumbers, as in 'as cool as a . . .' 'I have never had an elocution lesson in my life,' I replied quietly. We moved on.

In the last round of this preliminary bout, she suddenly asked, 'By the way, what do we call you?'

Now I know people think it's an affectation but I like being known as Anna Raeburn. If you like me, sooner or later, you'll call me Anna. If you don't you'll call me Raeburn. Either Miss or Mrs is correct if the formality makes you feel better and Ms is for envelopes. I replied, 'You call me Anna Raeburn.'

She pressed a little harder. 'No, I mean is it Miss or Mrs? You are divorced, aren't you?'

I said, trying to keep my temper, 'You call me Anna Raeburn because that is my name.' (Shades of cherished Arthur Miller.)

She shrugged: 'I'm merely trying to elucidate a line of questioning which David may wish to follow.'

'Now,' I said, 'you listen to me. If David Frost questions me about my marriage, I shall put my hand on his knee and look deep into his bloodshot eyes with my beautiful brown ones, saying David, look, we all know you too have your little problems in that direction, but perhaps you'd rather talk about it off camera?' Without missing a beat Iain Johnstone assured me that there would be no such questions. I thanked him.

So you can see that I wasn't sure I'd even passed muster for further investigation – but I did. Along came a second researcher who spent some three hours making notes on everything from how I voted to my favourite food and suddenly the interview was on, it was going to happen.

In order to go forward with this story I first have to go back a step or two. Some time earlier, before I joined *Woman* and probably at one of the lunches which were always being given at the Penthouse Club I had met a rather high-powered public relations man. Although I was initially attracted, he was such an operator, professionally and personally, that I couldn't keep up with him – nor was I interested in trying once he'd introduced his brother. Brother was doing very well in one of the fastest moving, widely diversified companies in the City and Brother Two did for me what would never have occurred to Brother One – he offered me a well-paid job with prospects while I was still at *Forum*. I knew it was no good to me because I'd drink away half my hard-earned substance just trying to come to terms with what I was really doing to earn all that money but the very fact that he offered it to me, apparently in good faith, did wonders for my fragile self-esteem. (He was also the first man I'd ever met who admitted to problems with a vasectomy which was a very useful reference point for the future.) However in due course he renounced the pleasures of London for a closer watch at his wife's side and the whole episode would have faded pleasantly from memory had I not re-encountered Brother One just after the Frost interview was confirmed.

After congratulating me on what seemed to be my progress in life, he remarked thoughtfully that he didn't wish to cast aspersions on my powers but he really thought some television training would be useful and would I permit him to arrange it? It had been made very clear to me how much IPC wanted the interview to go well, so I said yes please and thank you to his offer, secure in the knowledge that, Frost or no Frost, television was television and if the training got in my way, I'd dump it.

I was sent to a company called HyVision where I met a man called Peter Tidman who has since started his own company. The first thing I remember about Peter Tidman is that he had read everything he could find about me. This is always very consoling as well as ego-boosting because there's nothing more demoralising than having to go through the same patter about yourself again and again (which is why the really famous often become drunk, bored or ratty, as it is a frequent experience for them).

'Right,' he said, 'sit down and summarise your job and the way you're going to tackle it in three words. Then I'm going to sit you in front of a camera and we'll tape what you say. When it's taped, we'll criticise it.' I did as he asked – it's the sort of challenge, I like – and he was very pleased with the result. 'Now I'm going to interview you,' he said, 'but I'm not going to be on your side. I'm going to press you and harass you and throw you every curve I can think of and you must keep coming back. OK? For 15 minutes. Let's go.' And he contorted his face into a News of the Screws leer and went for the jugular. When we played it back, he nodded thoughtfully. Next he sat me in front of a camera and threw every kind of question he could think of at me for 15 or 20 minutes. Some of the questions were ordinary and friendly enough, but others were openly hostile. It was confusing, it was supposed to be, like a variant of the hard man/soft man technique used in interrogation.

'You can come out now,' he said and sat me down on a long sofa in front of the video with a quiet northerner called Stanley Hyland, the senior partner. Every time they saw something they liked particularly or didn't like at all, they pressed the stop button. And as they weren't there to sing hymns of praise but to eradicate bad television habits as quickly as possible, they were more critical than laudatory. Gradually my adrenalin turned to water and a large tear slipped down my nose. 'Listen,' said Stanley Hyland, northern man affronted by emotional display in southern woman, 'if you're going to carry on like that, we can't continue.'

I sniffed. 'Mr Hyland, you don't have to stop just because I cry. I won't cry on the night, that's all you care about. Now for goodness' sake, say what you have to say.'

I know that the techniques of television training gone into more thoroughly are a good deal more complicated than the hors d'oeuvres I experienced, but the advice and comments I received from those excellent men did one thing that could only be good for me: they made me feel there was nothing I couldn't manage. They showed me I had a nervous trick of throwing back my head like a rearing horse and that on television, this enlarges your neck so that you look as if you have goitre. They showed me that looking away from the camera doesn't make you look shy, it makes you look shifty. They taught me that women have a compulsion to smile at the camera which lessens the impact of what they have to say. They warned me against hair-twiddling, hand-wringing and lip-biting, irritating enough in real life, and a thousand times more disagreeable when magnified on television. And right there in your living room too. Finally Peter Tidman told me, 'You're a natural for television. The cameras like you, your energy comes over. Forget sitting like the queen and folding your hands like a schoolgirl. Keep your back straight, yes, but your hands help you to speak. For everyone who dislikes them, somebody else will be fascinated. Look the camera in the eye and get on with it. And you're fast. Use it. Good luck.'

On the day in question I planned to have my hair done. The National Union of Journalists called a mandatory meeting of members on the *Woman* staff but God smiled and I made it to the hairdressers. At Television Centre I was whisked into a nicely appointed dressing room where I began to make up. I don't like heavy makeup but television deals in images and if you don't wear enough, there's no image to see, still less an appealing one – you just look ill.

As the programme went out late in the evening and I was still rather over-weight, I chose to wear a lupin blue cotton caftan and a couple of decorative necklaces. If I had lost any weight, and I had been trying to, it showed in the face, which was all to the good – cameras add between 20 and 30 lbs. I had even painted my toenails, not that anybody would notice, but I'd know and it might make me feel good. And I prayed repeatedly, Please God don't let me fall flat on my face, not this time, if it be Thy will, Amen.

There was a knock at the door. Enter the producer, very white and tired. In the course of our chat, the tiredness was explained. The team had been in three different time zones that week and were all living on downers and uppers to get them to go to sleep and wake up again at something like the appropriate times. He reminded me that they were shooting the interviews back to back (i.e. in pairs) and that I would be on before Walter Probyn, bank robber and habitual escapee. And then somebody came to take me upstairs and introduce me to David.

Frost came out of his dressing room resplendent in a very expensive lemon yellow shirt and several layers of toast coloured makeup. We shook hands. He returned to his preparations and I paced a bit. A friendly assistant offered her hand. Clasping it tightly, I heard the countdown and then the introduction – nudge, nudge, wink, leer and a friendly crack about the young lady who was going from the whips and chains of *Forum* to respectability at *Woman*. I don't know what happened to my face (though I can imagine!) but the girl beside me squeezed my hand. 'Get him Anna,' she said. 'You can.'

Frost motioned me to join him and leading me to the chair in which I was to sit, asking in an aside, 'Introduction all right for you?'

I replied without thinking, still holding his hand, 'Listen you bastard, you talk to me like that on camera and I'll flatten you.'

I had forgotten the microphone was on. As we sat down, I heard the producer speaking from the gallery, 'Tape the introduction again, David, at the end.' I had no fear now, just energy and determination to give as good as I got. So we began.

I cannot pretend to remember everything that was said ten years ago, but I do remember that the reality of such an interview is easier to deal with than thinking about it. I remember that I told him off, even swore at him, made him laugh and was aware, even so, in the midst of it all, how very much he knew about the business of interviewing for television. When it was over, I walked the length of the studio towards the door at the back. The doorman, opening it, said, 'Good one miss.' I nodded thanks and gulped in air. I couldn't speak. I was numb. I stood in the corridor stunned. Suddenly I was warmly embraced by a woman I'd never seen before who turned out to be the assistant producer, while another equally enthusiastic stranger pounded me on the back. The producer appeared, smiling quietly, with Frost who took my hand and said, 'Anna, that was wonderful television.' I looked at him.

'And how much are you going to cut?'

He shook his head. 'Nothing.'

I was still angry. 'We'll see.' I regally inclined my head and went off to the dressing room.

As I sat in the armchair, staring at my hands, wondering if the day would ever come where I would know it was all right and not have to wait for somebody I could trust to put me out of my misery, there was a knock at the door. I went to open it only to be picked up and swung round the room by an old friend called Peter Foges, a longtime BBC employee and no fool. Such display was unwarranted from Peter. His antecedents may be Viennese Jews but his behaviour is almost over-English in its restraint. When he put me down (I think I was quite impressed that he'd lifted me up in the first place!), he was really excited. He told me that the producer was a friend of his, who'd invited him to watch the taping from the production box, and it was great, the interview was wonderful. After a few minutes, I asked him to stop, just tell me really what he thought and put me out of my misery. He pulled up a chair opposite and looked at me carefully. 'You lost weight for it – right?' I nodded. 'Did the television training that bloke suggested?' I agreed. 'You trained for it as though it were a fight?' I said yes. 'OK,' he said throwing his hands wide, 'you won!' Second knock at the door. Equally dramatic compliments from the director whom I didn't know and so I began to believe that it was all right.

At the dinner after the taping, I met Mrs Mona Frost, David's mother, who told me she was so excited that at one point she'd seized somebody's arm and exclaimed, 'Who *is* that girl? Nobody talks to David like that and it's so good for him!' I was to hear the same story all over again the next morning – the arm she'd clutched belonged to my secretary.

The Frost Interview paid £100 with which I bought the first two day length dresses I'd worn in years and what is called a prisoner's chain, that is without end, fashioned from ebonite, a rather sophisticated tortoiseshell patterned plastic. But what the show really did for me exceeded what money could buy. It is still often referred to when I meet new people and for six or seven years it was the way people generally identified me. It brought me 83 letters which I kept, good and bad, because whatever was there or missing, people were moved enough to watch and then write letters afterwards. The one I'm proudest of says in part, 'My wife and I watched you on David Frost's television show the other day and when it was over, we switched off and had the most rewarding conversation we've had in 17 years of marriage, so good that we thought we ought to tell you.' I garnered some very pleasing reviews and comments and the kids (my affectionate nickname for the younger staff members at *Woman*) were thrilled.

It brought me dinner with an Arab prince and all sorts of new acquaintance. Most importantly, it established me with sufficient authority to get me more television and radio work. So that was work and work was fine – but I wasn't.

When Michael and I split up, I didn't think that anybody would ever love me again. It never occurred to me to think of it the other way around. Loving people, though it obviously comes in various degrees, seems to be a case of trying to and wanting to, along with the innate personality. I was not unable to love, I therefore thought, as much as unlovable – because, of course, it's always easier to blame the other person. So the first person who showed the slightest interest in me was almost drowned in the flood of all the wounded feelings inevitably attendant upon a broken marriage or long term relationship.

When I moved out, Michael led me to believe that I was breaking his heart. All I know is that within a month, he had moved in Heartmender Number One and she remained with him for thirteen months, so he was a great deal more self-preserving about the disintegration of our marriage than I was. Of course if I'd had as much idea of self-preservation as an apple, I wouldn't have known as much about all this as I did. But when I left, I wanted us to be friends. We had spent five years together, we had loved each other, I thought, and we should be able to salvage a friendship from the ruins.

Unfortunately you can only have a friendship with your former marital partner if you are both at the same stage of emergence from the past, and we never were. So while I was trying to be a friend, he was still reaching out for me. And when he went off and reorganised his life the better to advance it, I felt unreasonably rejected and hurt. That the tenses had changed, that I was part of the past, was brought home in a very painful way when a friend of ours was caught by the Luxembourg police smuggling cannabis. He was extradited to London and held in the Scrubs. Michael rang me up, Phillipe was very down on his luck – wouldn't I go with Michael and his girlfriend to visit him? Not wanting to be a spoilsport, I agreed.

The afternoon began in a civilised way. We collected another friend and took it in turns to sit with and talk to the defeated Phillipe. When we left at the end of visiting time, it was suggested that we went somewhere to have a cup of tea. By now I knew that at every opportunity I was watching my replacement out of the corner of my eye, observing her carefully when she wasn't looking at me, considering her and Michael and there was a great lump of something burning just under my rib cage, as if I was pushing something hot and molten back so hard under pressure that eventually it must explode. I decided to go while the going was good. In keeping with my woman of the world image (I thought) I pecked all three cheeks goodbye and fled. Round the corner from the cafe, I began to cry like a child, in gulps and sobs, head held firmly up, daring anybody to acknowledge how distraught I was. When I came back into the flat where I was staying, I was confronted by my image in the very large glass just inside the door. And what I saw was horrible. My face was white with great purple smudges under the eyes, I could see the wrinkles beginning, my hair was standing on end like a cartoon cat after an electric shock and I could see the white in it. All I could think was, she's 23 and I'm 30. In that struggle to make films, he has stolen my youth. And I look so wretched when I cry.

Needless to say, I was torn between never wanting to love anybody again and thinking to hell with love, let's just prove I'm attractive to somebody. In the latter mood, I fell in with the first contender I recognised – there may have been others but I'm not always the most observant person about who's interested in me, especially not in that way! That Jonathan was younger than me flattered me to death and his approach was so direct that I was too outfaced not to comply. I was also grateful to him ('Gratitude is a very dangerous emotion,' said my mother more than once, and she was right) but as he was looking for an older kind of broken blossom than me, with a few more material enhancements than a good job, I didn't last long. He did take me to see the Allman Brothers in concert at Knebworth though.

And then there was Leon, a friend of an acquaintance whose own marriage had shattered ahead of mine leaving him looking for love or something similar. He was enormously likeable and with him I learned that no matter how scrambled my head was, everything else was in ace working order thank you. There was just one problem. He had recently concluded a formal psycho-analysis and believed that I wouldn't make much headway until I had committed myself in the same sort of way. He also believed in old-fashioned fidelity, which was fine in its place but its place was not yet because I couldn't help but feel that my fidelity was just to make him feel more secure about me. Sometimes he was very proud of me, sometimes he dismissed me and he did both all too publicly for my peace of mind. Arguments led nowhere, he turned and twisted my words until our conversation was like a sewing-box when the kittens have been at it. It was all very tiring and I was just trying to decide whether to dismiss or pursue him when I met John.

Because he worked for a very prestigious paper, I was impressed that John should even want to meet me though I admit that when he first took me to lunch, I thought it was for an item in his column, not in his bed. We met a few times before he departed for the country (to his wife's house) to finish a book and I decided that I must take evasive action. I've never been keen on married men. Although they are the same as any other kind of man in all the obvious ways, they are in fact spoken for and an alarming proportion of them intend to stay that way. Besides I tend to identify with the wife. If you wouldn't like it to happen to you, why make it happen to someone like you? So I moved in with Leon.

I realise this was hasty but I was unsettled, and unsure about buying a house on my own. When I was thinking about this period of my life prior to writing about it, I recalled that remark of Mrs Patrick Campbell's: 'Ah, the peace and tranquillity of the marriage bed after the hurly-burly of the chaise longue!' What a well-ordered existence that was. My problem was that in my mind marriage and affairs had all become one. I entered my affairs with intensity, moved in, lived with and tried, I suppose, to live through whoever I was with. There wasn't much time for over-commitment in this case however, because within a few weeks, my mother came to stay overnight as she and I were en route for Norway. Ma had always longed to go to Scandinavia and I could at least give her that.

This holiday was very important. First of all, it was the longest time we'd spent together without other people since I was a child. Secondly it confirmed that I really liked my mother, as you would a dear friend, apart from loving her as a parent, and thirdly it was a time of discovery, as time spent together without the duties of dealing with others always is. So we flew to Bergen, investigated everything, walked and talked and shopped, and in the privacy of our Spartan hotel room we had some very important conversation.

Ma asked me what really happened with Michael and me. I said that I doubted I'd ever know, that there was wrong on both sides but part of the story undoubtedly was that I should have been his mother. He'd have done well with a mother like me, I'd have been thrilled to have a son like him. Sadly however I married a tall child with a beard. 'And I wasn't much help to you, was I?' she asked quietly.

I shrugged. 'I don't see how you could have been. It was way out of your ken. Whatever went on between you and Pop, you loved each other. I know he wasn't good with money but he never deliberately did you down or reneged on anything important.' She shook her head fiercely. I wanted so much to tell her about the child that Michael and I never had, that my throat ached. She saw and misread my face.

154

'Poor old darling,' she said. 'Did I let you down badly?'

I looked at her. 'Only once,' I said and I remembered every detail of it including the smell of the dirty telephone box.

When I was about 30, my sister and I were as far apart as we could be. We were careful to observe the niceties and we still had considerable affection for each other but we were effectively estranged, so you can imagine how desperate I was to telephone my sister in the hope that it would deflect me from ringing my mother. Lesley was helpful and positive and consoling but when the receiver went down I still wanted my mum, so I rang her. I moaned and shouted while she tried to be reasonable and finally she said, almost breezily, 'Well, don't worry darling – you'll manage, you always have.' I recounted this to her, concluding, 'If you'd been there, I think it's the only time in my life I might have struck you. I knew I'd manage, I'd have to bloody manage. I just wanted you to tell me you loved me anyway, failed marriage and all, and then I *could* manage.' Her dear face fell, she knew she'd let me down. So I hugged her and she hugged me and after a while, as it has been in rows or disagreements or painful moments all through my life, she let it pass and so did I.

Somehow only a few minutes later the subject turned to jewellery and I persuaded her to try on a ring of mine. Rings are my favourite jewellery because I actually like my hands. To my surprise, once the thing was in place, she turned her head away as if in pain. When I asked her about it, she answered so quietly it was as if she were talking to herself. 'I never thought I could wear a ring as big as this, I always wanted to but I was afraid my hands were too ugly.' Which is how my mother came by what we laughingly refer to as her 'rich bitch' ring, the sizeable moss agate I bought her on our return.

My mother never pressured me about children but on that trip she didn't have to. I knew I wanted a child, I wasn't obsessive about it but I'd known that was a goal in my life since my middle twenties. But you need a man and a home for a child, I thought, and I'm nowhere near either of them at the moment. I could hear myself saying threateningly to Michael, 'And I'm not having a first baby after 30 –' and where was 30? It had come and was going and I was further away from the possibility than ever. Leon liked the idea of a child but when I mentioned it to my mother, she said drily, 'He won't last. You're not in love with him, you're in love with his house. And anyway, he's too young for you. They all are. Sometimes I don't think you'll get anywhere until you meet an older man.' And of course I'd already met one. He was married but if he was older, you'd expect him to be. So I made the sort of farewell speech to Leon that leaves you writhing in the dark when you think of it, and the scene was set for John.

Chapter 15

John was first, last and always a writer – sometimes a poet, sometimes a journalist but always with a shorthand notebook in his mind if not in his hand. He started writing me notes and postcards just after we met and continued to write letters of every colour of the verbal rainbow throughout our time together. And it did seem at the outset that he was very right for me having lived long enough to make plenty of mistakes of his own. If I'd paused and thought clearly, I might have seen the complexity and compromise of the life he was offering me – but pausing and thinking clearly were always things I was better at doing for others than myself. After all wasn't he an older man? Seventeen years older than me chronologically. It took me some time to learn he was emotionally deep frozen at nineteen. But at least I didn't live with him. Well, not really. I sublet a small flat in Islington which I visited at least once and maybe twice a day before climbing into the taxi or John's car to spend the rest of the time with him. It wasn't much of a stab at independence, but it was a beginning and if the odd dark cloud hovered over my personal life, at least as far as work went, there was more good news.

Some months before, while I was still employed at *Forum* and in the first year of the licensing of commercial radio, I had put together some ideas for a radio programme. Accordingly I went to see the then programme controller at Capital Radio, an ebullient and forthright man, now head of the National Broadcasting School with a second incarnation as Mike Barry the Crafty Cook. I had various ideas of which only one was using a telephone connection to discuss sexual problems. I don't remember talking about 'sexual, emotional and personal problems' but then I wouldn't. Life is life and pretty odd most of the time. And I already knew that if you mention anything

157

to do with sex in the majority of media ears, they don't hear anything that follows. However I did feel that people discussed things much more realistically than pundits and that was the basis on which I proposed to build. Michael Bukht (Mike Barry's real name) appeared to consider all this but asked me over and over again how I'd handle this or that, brought in colleagues, debated it with them, and the general conclusion seemed to be that the subject matter was too risky – or risqué – and so was any association with me, working as I did for a very questionable publication.

But now that time had passed and I was at *Woman*. What could be more respectable? So I was telephoned and offered an hour's 'phone-in on 'personal, sexual and emotional problems' and would I like to have a crack at it, and wasn't it a good idea? Yes, I said, I thought it was, but then I had initiated the idea, if not the format. Roars of good-natured laughter. At the subsequent meeting it transpired that Bukht and his colleagues were taking a risk on this. Because nobody quite knew what would happen if such a show were trailed (that is advertised on air), Capital had had to obtain special dispensation from the Independent Broadcasting Authority, which was initially granted for five shows only.

In due course I turned up at Capital Radio one Wednesday night at 8.30 to go on air at 9.00 with Brian Hayes. I couldn't prepare the show; it was going out 'on delay', which meant that the audience heard it seven seconds slower than it was happening, a device designed to protect the gentler ears from anybody using inappropriate language – but seven seconds isn't long, and effectively, it was going out live. Brian Hayes was a wonderful man to learn radio with because he'd presented every kind of show there was at one time or another, so he was immensely reassuring. I didn't think about doing anything but my best. Technically I had nothing to do but sit in front of a microphone and listen to what came through the earphones ('cans' to you). Mechanical control in the studio rested with Brian and beyond him with the engineer. And the calls came in. When it was over, I was surprised to find how drained I felt, it was even a bit embarrassing, but my colleagues thought that was to be expected. We went off to a large room to have a drink and get our breath back. The telephone rang. The producer answering it said, 'Well, tell her yourself,' beckoning me. I took the receiver and a man's voice said, 'I just asked if anybody had signed that girl because she's wonderful!' The girl he meant was me and the caller was Dave Cash.

After those five shows the IBA in a rare display of feeling wrote a letter to the then managing director of Capital Radio to the effect that not only would they permit the programme, they endorsed its usefulness. They did, however, recommend that I had a doctor to field the medical side of the questions. I had a man in mind from my *Forum* days, a psychiatrist who wouldn't falter at the sight of a microphone. Capital duly offered us contracts which were perfectly acceptable except for one clause which I refused to sign. It bound me to seek no publicity for the first six months. When I was asked why I'd refused to sign it, I said because I wanted such an agreement to be mutually binding. I wouldn't seek publicity but I didn't want Capital to either. That way, if the show established itself, it would be because people wanted it, not because they'd been hyped into thinking they wanted it. And anyway without direct publicity, we would escape the dragons of respectability breathing down our necks. Capital agreed and we signed.

Radio work provided me with a wonderful counterbalance to my week's stint in a magazine. At *Woman*, as with every other co-operative effort, there were always so many people involved, such delays and considerations to be dealt with. On Wednesday night on Capital Radio it was me, the doc and a microphone. It took me a long time to recognise the importance of the backup team from producer and presenter to telephone receptionists, but the immediate shock was the mail, which has arrived fairly steadily in sizeable chunks from the beginning.

Nor had I considered that anybody would take exception to or try to stop what I was doing. So Capital Radio was not on my mind when one day I was called to the office of my publishing executive. When I arrived, she stuck her head round the door to say hello and then left me to the tender mercies of another officer of IPC who told me that I could not continue with the Capital show. When I asked, somewhat taken aback, why not, he replied that 'it wasn't what IPC had in mind for me.' I cut across his next sentence. 'The agreement I have with my editor and Miss Lambourn, the contractual agreement I made with IPC, says that I may do anything provided it is not to the detriment of the magazine as a whole or to my role on that magazine. Now what have I done that contravenes the agreement?'

'Well,' he said, 'some of the calls you take are a little far-fetched.'

I asked for an example and he chose the one really oddball call we'd ever had at that stage (there haven't been many all in all). I explained that open-ended (i.e. not pre-recorded) phone-ins have their risks attached and this was one of them. In any case I couldn't see how a call about loneliness followed by a reference to keeping a snake supplied with white mice was offensive. Peculiar – yes. In questionable taste, no.

'And then,' he went on, pursing his mouth as if he'd got pure lemon juice up his backside, 'there are the calls about premature ejaculation. . . . ' I said yes and waited. 'Well, that's not the sort of thing –'

'Oh excuse me but it is,' I said, 'and let me tell you something. The day I get a good letter about premature ejaculation, it goes in the magazine. Because it is a problem and it bothers people and wrecks marriages.'

He looked at me quite coldly. 'It seems to me, Anna, that you have to choose. Do you want to stay at *Woman* or work for Capital Radio?'

I couldn't believe my ears. I told him I had no intention of choosing. As far as I could see, the column in the magazine and the radio show complemented each other very well. In any case, he was getting free advertising on the radio every time I was introduced and we made a point of referring to the magazine I was working for. I had honoured my agreement with IPC and now they were going to have to honour theirs. Had he finished? He had. I left. For the next three years we didn't meet except to say good morning and that was fine with me. I continued to work for Capital Radio – I still do ten years later.

In personal terms, I find radio very satisfying. Although we try to fit in as many calls as we can, it is widely accepted that we give people as much time as possible, if we feel it's useful. You don't have to look like anything to work on radio, you just have to sound good. Freed of the image, people find it easier to say what they mean and I often think the content of the calls is much more intelligent than in most of the other settings in which such subjects are aired. Radio provides a remarkable mixture of intimacy and anonymity. Bringing a telephone into the picture just rounds off the idea. Telephones are representative of the idea of one to one. As far as I'm concerned, I'm talking to whoever is on the telephone and the caller is not deceived, because he or she knows that there's the presenter, the Capital Doctor and me – the rest are eavesdroppers, they can listen if they want to.

When I'm asked how people can possibly talk about 'such things' on the radio, let alone talk in good faith, I say I'm sure that they, like me, often forget that anybody else is around except for those in on the conversation. The set-up of using a presenter to run the technical side of the show meant that if anybody had to toe the line, he or she could: the doctor and I were free to have our opinions. Though I must say that I had very few refusals on subject matter during my four years at *Woman* either. It was just a much more complex system through which you had to negotiate your material before you could start to respond to your questioner.

The radio show has been many things to me. It has been the fulfilment of a great wish to see an intelligent programme prosper. It has been by turns tiring and restorative, upsetting and uplifting, often deeply saddening, sometimes gloriously rewarding. My dream has long been to have a Christmas party for all those devoted listeners who've stayed with us, or gone away and come back, who've written to tell us what they think in praise or criticism. I didn't begin it thinking I'd be doing it for ten years. I just did it, exactly as I have just done all the other things in my life as they came along, fully aware that if I didn't seize the chance by the scruff of its neck and give it full blast on every available cylinder, I might never have another break.

And in the meantime John, the Older Man, was showing me his world and I was not reacting the way I thought I would be. He half-knew half of London, certainly literary and theatrical London. I thought I'd love it but I didn't. Certainly I felt like a fish out of water but not because I didn't know anyone – that I'd expected. More because it was all so incestuous. They all figured in each other's stories, slept with each other's spouses, and they were with rare exceptions very ordinary people making a living. I'd thought they'd be more than that and like a child was disappointed to find that most of those who populated circles I aspired (I thought) to join, had feet of clay – and then some.

I don't think John and I discussed this much. We discussed the passion we shared, though if either of us had a shred of honesty we must have wondered privately where it was leading. He had left his wife once and had a sort of collapse – couldn't write, couldn't think. When he went back, they mended the fences and he returned to working in London Monday to Friday and spending weekends at home with her. He wrote better there. He had been, by his own account, systematically unfaithful since the sixth year of their marriage. London was littered with all sorts of people that he had known, biblically of course. He didn't want me to ask awkward questions. Still less did he want me to have the same freedom to move around as he did. He couldn't see that I was only a few months out of the kind of marriage where I was absorbed to the point of unreality. He couldn't see that I was raw. Wasn't he with me now? Why wasn't that enough to comfort me? He couldn't see how much I feared just fitting into his life, his organised life – work, friends, wife, grown-up children, perks, professionalism and civilisation. I loved it and hated it and wanted it and was afraid of it. Never has civilisation seemed more like the mouth of a mocking croco-dile, where it's lovely to lie in the warm bit in the middle but hell if you come up against one of those very sharp surround-ing teeth. It seemed to me that he was asking me to fit in with an awful lot without ever having the opportunity to debate it. And what was I to be in all this? The town wife? No, not wife. 'A wonderful bonus' he called me in his letters, 'you've given me back my life'. Well fine, that told me about him. But what about me? And yet he was so generous and funny and tender and loving as well, that I'd feel like a heel for even thinking of questioning what he said he wanted for both of us.

So perhaps it was predictable that when I told him first a lie and then the truth about spending the weekend with some-body else while he was away in the country, he would throw a glass of whisky straight into my new extended wear contact lenses. As I peeled them out of my eyes, he flung me to the floor. In the course of the next few minutes, he did quite a lot of flinging and slapping and started calling me 'babe', an absolute incongruity in his very English voice and a sign that bad times were upon us. When I locked myself in the bathroom, he made so much noise that I was afraid the neighbours would hear. I emerged to more cuffs and cursing. I tried being reasonable, which was ineffectual in the face of his rage. Suddenly he stopped. 'Get dressed,' he said. 'We'll be late for George.' George was a very pleasant man who with his wife had invited us to dinner that evening. I asked him to telephone George and excuse us. He refused. Dreading more of a scene, I prepared myself and we turned in Academy Award winning performances of affectionate devotion for three hours.

When he parked outside my flat, I asked him to please leave me alone. He pushed past me into the house. He was quieter. I was tired. 'Come and sit here,' he said, patting the bed. 'Anna, why did you lie to me?' I didn't answer and he began methodically punching my head, just round the hairline. I couldn't believe this was happening. I remember in one of Erin Pizzey's books a battered woman talking about how she felt when she was being hit, about how cold she grew, cold and patient, until the beating was over. I kept thinking that if I let him, he'd stop eventually. So I didn't move, I just kept saying, 'Not my eyes, John – mind my eyes.' Wump. 'Why did you lie to me, Anna?' After a while he left.

The house was very quiet. I didn't know my neighbours. I needed the sound of a human voice. I rang Jeremy with whom I'd spent the weekend. He was shocked and offered to come over. I said no. If John came back, God knows what would happen. I just wanted to hear a voice. Jeremy urged me to call the police. When I put the telephone down I could just imagine some gently cynical, patient policeman telling me that it was a domestic matter, nothing they could do. And John had a public name. (The fact that I did too didn't occur to me until the following morning.) Besides, hadn't I brought this on myself? If I had done as John asked me to do, this would never have happened. I had brought it on myself. I should either have stayed at home that weekend and waited for his return or I should have lied in my teeth and stuck to it. So much for the liberation of women. What a choice. So I called the Samaritans. I know they do wonderful work but that night I got a sweetness-and-light merchant when what I wanted was somebody who would empathise. Ten minutes in, I said, 'Forget it, thanks anyway' and went off to make tea.

The next day in the office my departmental head, Dee Remmington, looked sharply at my arm and asked to have a word with me. 'What happened to your arm?' she asked. (I bruise if you look at me.) Before I could reply, she said, 'I know what happened. Dump him. Don't let him do that to you again.' I promised and went home to pack to go up to York for the second Annual General Meeting of the Campaign for Homosexual Equality, at which I was guest speaker. That night John, deeply apologetic and genuinely shocked at himself, reached me by telephone in my hotel bedroom. After asking if I was all right, he said, 'You don't seem to realise, I could have killed you.' I forbore to remark that it had not felt as if we were practising Morris dancing. 'And your poor eyes – have you got a shiner?' I replied that I had not. He sounded so comically dismayed and self-righteous, all at once, that I was very near giggling. 'Thank God. How would you have explained that?'

'I'd have worn my dark glasses on to the platform,' I said, 'and removed them when I had to speak, beginning "Brothers and sisters – this is what you get for a straight relationship!"' But I didn't break off with him there and then because it was easier to give in to the not-inconsiderable force of his personality and try again. Besides, if I broke it off, it was I who had failed again, failed at another kind of relationship and it seemed I was running out of options. I couldn't face failing again. But if we danced the masochism tango to get into the relationship, we damned nearly killed each other emerging from it.

We went through the same patterns again and again. Each of us attempted to avoid the other and then made pleas for clemency by letter and telephone. First one, then the other stood on dignity and let the other grovel. Then we tried talking about it and being grown-up which culminated in blinding, blistering rows. No wonder describing people as being in love always makes me think of two people drowning in a bath of blood and treacle. When I got sufficiently desperate I talked in confidence to two women, both of whom had known him for twenty years and more, one of whom was my agent. 'Every time I really try to bring it to an end,' I snivelled, 'he talks about the Chinese having a proverb which says that if you save a person's life, you are responsible for it. And then he talks about Lavinia, you know, the girl in the car crash.'

My agent smiled a wintry smile. 'Yes, I'm sure he does. You see, my dear, Lavinia had the good sense to get herself killed and so she achieved instant canonisation.'

And a little light was shed. Michael used to talk about our lives together being ruled by the principle of 'kill, or be killed.' Well, I didn't want to kill or be killed. I wanted to live, hard work and awkward though it often was. Dying wasn't high up on my list of things to do. So, somehow, we made an end of it.

Among the best things that John did for me were to buy me my first painting (incidentally introducing me to the cartoonist Mel Calman); to give me the *Oxford English Dictionary* for Christmas and to take me to stay for a few days at a 12th century manor house in the Welsh Marches where I learned that even I could like the country sometimes. He also introduced me to Deirdre McSharry.

Deirdre was then and still is the editor of *Cosmopolitan*, a success story unequalled in terms of British magazines. So I was rather looking forward to meeting her. And I was thrilled when she invited me to drinks and talked to me like a colleague. I remember she wore her hair cut very smooth and rather short in those days, in a shining red helmet, and I remember the ease with which she wore her clothes, an ease which came in part from having worn nothing but the best for 20 years. I liked Deirdre, I really admired her and she was kind to me, that careless kindness which was still the ultimate weapon as far as I was concerned, even at this stage. Throughout my life there had always been slightly older women whom I admired and respected (or wanted to admire and respect) and although I was now in my thirties, I still felt very much like an unfinished kid quite a lot of the time. So all that stuff I'd read about things getting easier when you get older still hadn't begun to happen to me.

* * *

As John removed his presence, so I got to know Jeremy rather better. Jeremy was a publisher, Jewish of course, very attractive if you like the idea of Paul Simon dipped in milk, with enormous, heavy lidded green eyes like Boris the Borzoi. Jeremy had had one long, long love affair with a girl he'd known in South Africa which comprised all sorts of ups and downs and after her, it was strictly heart in the safe deposit box and girls for amusement. He was a loner. He was used to being a loner. He was an affectionate man but so amenable that just as I thought I'd got hold of him, he slithered away again. He was so well socialised, so polite, so willing, determined to take care of me, to be there when I called, to give to me, that he was in many ways John's antithesis. One fought all the time, the other thought fighting was what people did when they ran out of words.

I don't think I cooked more than half a dozen times in the year and a bit I knew Jeremy. He was a wonderful cook. I did spend an inordinate amount of time doing his much neglected housework whenever I came to visit him, though. I was still firmly living in my own place, by now a rented flat on the other side of London. Actually it was rented from Michael with whom I was still trying to be friends. He got a film together which meant he'd be shooting in Africa and doing the post-production work in Sweden or Paris. He needed to let the flat for a year. I had to leave my flat in Islington and we agreed, in one of our more constructive periods of detente, that I would move in and be solely responsible for everything while he was away. If he returned, he'd want to borrow the place for a week or so at most and I could stay with a friend.

It was during this same period of detente that, at the urging of my mother, I announced to Michael that I wanted a divorce. I had never wanted a divorce, I had always thought that that was that, the marriage was ended but who needed a divorce? It wasn't something I was going to do again. But Ma insisted. 'Now,' she said, 'now, while you're on speaking terms, you never know. . . . ' Michael said he was unhappy about it but signed the papers. I put them in the brown box in which I keep all my most precious things. I did not yet file for divorce. And Jeremy drove loyally to collect me for the weekend, to hold my hand, most often to bring me back to share our work because, to counterbalance his amiability,

Jeremy was a workaholic. The only time I remember him free of unending money problems and piles of manuscripts in various stages of preparation was when we went on holiday to South Africa for three weeks.

But although he said and did a great many of the very rightest things, if you looked closely at Jeremy's life, it was nearly as disordered in its way as mine. He said that he wanted to marry me and that he would wait. But his business stumbled from one crisis to another, usually remedied by the supplement of a few thousands lent long term by another wealthy South African emigré. He said that he wanted a child with me but I couldn't see that I was a very good bet as a mother at that stage, and once I gave up my jobs, where was the financial security to build a home for us with or without baby? It wasn't that I expected to have a cut and dried future offered to me but rather that this was all so vague and hazy as to suggest no future at all. And I couldn't commit myself to him until he knew what he was about, or I knew what I was about – both of which events seemed to be pretty remote.

Meantime he retaught me to play tennis, very patiently and without mockery. We did a lot of shopping and talking and went out very little. I remember writing at five in the morning in his flat because one of the great advantages of living with a workaholic is that they don't mind if you're a workaholic too. It was all very nice – but nice was a word we were forbidden to use in composition at school because it was used to conceal all sorts of subtler and not necessarily acceptable feelings.

One night I stayed late at the office to meet a young man who had written me a letter about his girlfriend and asked for my opinion. I didn't see very many people, dealt mostly in letters and referrals but occasionally something moved me to see somebody. In this case the signature was so illegible I'd had to guess at his name when I telephoned him at work. I had spoken to him briefly, discerned an accent I couldn't place and moved by his sincerity and the pressure he obviously felt both about his difficulties and not being able to discuss them at work, had agreed to see him. I only ever saw anybody after 6.00 at night when I was on my own time, and only ever in the office.

When I went out to collect him from reception, I saw a mass of dark, thickly curling hair, a broad brow and a wide sweet

167

mouth, a bear of a man. Shaken, I immediately adjusted my perceptions. He was pale, tired and nervous. That made two of us. I took him to my tiny office. After a few sentences, I asked him the origin of his accent and learned that he was Israeli. I was further puzzled to learn that he was working for one of the German television stations with offices in this country. He shrugged. 'I am a good researcher and –' he spread his fingers meaningfully, arching his eyebrows, 'all the rest of it. Token Jew.' I asked him what he wanted to see me about. He told me about the woman he lived with, and the rest of the story. I commented, we debated. He began to relax. An hour passed.

'OK,' I said, standing up. He stood up too.

'Yes. Can I ask you something?' I looked at him. 'Will you be my friend? It's the one thing I miss very much here, I have no one I can really confide in.'

I said, 'I'd like that.'

'Here,' he said, 'I brought you a present.' He reached into his dark coat, handing me a copy of *The Little Prince* marked at the chapter about the Fox and Friendship, and a bunch of freesias. *The Little Prince* and freesias. Romance.

Chapter 16

How can you tell what draws you away from one person and towards another? Lust, say the cynics. I wish it were so simple.

Here was I jogging along in this nice amiable relationship when suddenly I was inexorably drawn towards somebody else. And when I asked myself, mentally begging both their pardons, what one had that the other hadn't – back came the answer: conversation, for one thing. Ideas about films and books and thoughts and theories. It was not for nothing that Dov (the bear) had read philosophy at the University of Jerusalem. The most damning thing about philosophers, I was to discover, is that they always sound as if they know, even when they don't. But Dov left academe, went into films, a short career culminating in heading the second unit on Norman Jewison's film *Jesus Christ Superstar*. Dov fought in the Six Day War, lost a good friend, remembered standing there, clutching his Uzzi machine gun to his chest and wondering, 'Why am I killing people when what I really want to be doing is eating ice-cream and watching the girls on the beach?' His parents were Hasidot, deeply religious, but he began to 'leave religion' (his phrase) then and it came to the crunch over the High Holidays when he refused to go to worship with his father. He went and ate a pork chop in the university cafeteria and waited for the sky to fall in. He loved his parents but he knew that, for all sorts of reasons, he wanted to leave. Where did he want to go? To London. 'Fine,' said his mother, the rabbi's daughter, her leg crippled from the DP camp in Ulm, the dream of Israel dying in her eyes. 'Go. I only hope you find some more like you out there.' He stayed first in Munich, then arrived in England for a three month visit. That was three years before I met him. When the Yom Kippur War broke out, he rang his mother to tell her he

169

wasn't coming home. At first she wouldn't believe that he was still in Europe but when he finally persuaded her that it was true, she said, 'Good. Stay there. Somebody has to survive.'

Choosing between Jeremy and Dov was very difficult. Perhaps, I thought, if I could just put the two together, all the good and none of the shortcomings, it might make one perfect person. But then of course even I knew that the problem wasn't either of them, it was me. So why bother debating this way and that? Almost every other convention had been dented somewhere along the way. Wasn't I liberated a long time ago? (Answer: if you have to ask, no.) I could have them both. So I told neither of them much about the other and I ran two lives, no past, no future, only now. Two different nows for two different men.

I didn't live with either of them. I lived in my own flat, which was an inconveniently long way away. I made it very clear that I hated surprise visits. They both knew I was jumpy and tense, so none of this surprised them. I had a drawer for the essentials at Jeremy's and a grass box from the Philippines for the same purpose at Dov's. Thus I never ran out of spare tights, clean underwear or basic toiletries. Everything else I brought with me when I came to visit, rolled up at the bottom of the large straw basket Jeremy had given me or, when that disintegrated, in a black canvas plumber's bag, which cost £5 in a sale at the General Trading Company. I chose these bags because they looked like the kind of bags people carried work around in, not as obvious as overnight bags or grips of one kind or another. And when I went to stay with one, I lied cheerfully to the other and the following night reversed the process. Occasionally I lied to both of them and had a night of delightful solitude, washing my hair and reading.

And what was my mirror telling me in all this? My mirror noted with some surprise that little green worms had not yet eaten the canvas of my face away. And when I asked her in the glass what was it she wanted, she would look back at me and then whisper, 'I don't know.'

'Perhaps what you need,' said Dov one day, 'is to have a relationship with more than one man at a time.' Oh dear, I thought, confession time again. At least this one won't want tears. As I opened my mouth, he said, 'You see, I know that's what you've been doing. With Jeremy. What I want to know is why you lied to me.' I gulped.

'Because I didn't think you'd put up with it,'

'What I will put up with is quite considerable, provided you tell me the truth. It's the lies, the uncertainties I can't stand. And what do you tell Jeremy – less than me?'

I nodded.

'And does it make you happy?'

I hadn't thought about happiness as a goal for some time. Things were agreeable, manageable. I worked very hard. I prided myself on the fact that I knew what I was talking about. Any good agony aunt would have told me that if you say you love two people at the same time, you don't love either of them. And I often said the words 'I love you' with my fingers crossed behind my back, to prove I didn't mean it, it didn't count. File love under the most misused and abused word of our time. But what else is there to say? Leave out love and provoke all sorts of questions? I didn't like questions.

Dov looked at me hard.

'Are you happy?'

'I don't know.'

The answer is a truism: if you don't know, you aren't.

All Dov asked of me was that I ceased to lie. Jeremy never got much of a chance to ask. Between his work load and mine, there wasn't much time for metaphysical conversation. So for a while I went on lying. There is a sort of sick excitement in waiting to be found out. And a crazy logic about 'if he loves me, he'll go on loving me anyway' – God knows where I got that from. From the depths of my confusion, I suppose. But then Dov came very quietly one morning to my flat, my holy of holies, rang the doorbell and marched past me looking very grim.

'If this was you, the real you, I would shut up. But it's not and you're hurting yourself and driving yourself mad. And you're hurting me too. So now, sit down and let's have this cleared out.' He didn't shrive me of my sins, he didn't attempt to influence me towards him but he did make me look at what I was doing to myself in the crisp light of morning. 'Running,' he said, drawing deeply on his cigarette, 'running. That's all you do.' Silence. 'Anna, do you want Jeremy?' I started to say I didn't know, I wasn't sure. The words died. 'Because the poor man wants you.' I shook my head. 'Then put him out of his pain and let him be.' He stood up. 'I'll see you another time.' I have blocked my mind totally against my final leave-taking of Jeremy. All I can remember is that we both wept.

In the middle of all this, Michael had managed to make friends with a very wealthy family who had a summer villa in Bordeaux. They also had a second villa next door which was used as a holiday house for their friends and their children's friends. Michael rang. Would I like to come for an inexpensive holiday? Somewhat shaken by my recent adventures in the unconventional, I answered that yes, I would provided there was no misunderstanding about my status – I would come as a friend, to my own separate bedroom, preferably with a lock on the door and if that wasn't possible, forget it. Michael laughed the lock away but said that he understood, so be it, and it would be nice to see me.

Did I dare to hope that it wasn't too late to repair our marriage? Well, at least I went with an open mind. When I arrived, his girlfriend was very much in evidence, although he'd told me she would be back in Paris by then. Much practising of sickly grins. I couldn't stand Annie. Never mind – grow up Anna – it's only for a couple of days. It's a cheap holiday remember. But it wasn't, it was cripplingly expensive because we were in a very chic resort and of course Michael had run out of money. And it rained. To begin with I thought I would pack up and go home, or kill myself, or Michael, or possibly both. A holiday house with inadequate heating and not enough to read is no place for a long-separated, not entirely cordial couple. Then the sun shone. I sat on the terrace and thought very hard.

Could I reconcile with Michael? Not a chance. I expected for the rest of my life in some painful knotted corner of my heart to cheer for his successes and wince at his troubles but I didn't want to live with him ever again. John was out, Jeremy could be attempted again – but to what end? And Dov? Suddenly I began to laugh. I remembered a girl on the radio I'd spoken to, divorced from her husband, torn between the two suitable men her family were pushing at her, with another choice of her own in the wings, and how I'd advised her with some force that she didn't have to take up any of those options

– that there were, or shortly would be, others. And here was I thinking about my immediate male acquaintances as if they were the last men on earth. Much cheered, I enjoyed the last few days of my holiday and returned to London to be met by a smiling Dov who above all else wanted to be my friend. When I arrived home, I took the divorce papers out of their safe place in my brown box and sent them to my solicitor.

Dov lived in a house in Kentish Town owned by a fierce German film editor called Hilde and apart from the rent, the terms under which she let him a room included that he cleaned the whole house every other week. Dov the demon cleaner. He was weighed down with so many different responsibilities – the burden of money, his parents, his past, knowledge, Hilde's housework and me. When he slept he ground his teeth constantly, often till he woke with sore jaws and an aching head. Tension was as much a feature of him as the nose on his face but he was generous, bright and thoughtful. Perhaps his very 'foreignness' made him easier for me.

In time we decided that we were subsidising the cab companies of London as neither of us owned a car and we lived so far apart. So Hilde rented me a room which I used to store my numerous possessions while I lived with Dov in one big room with a fireplace. One of the last things I remember about the faraway flat is that it was there I received my divorce papers and finally understood that my marriage was dead.

During the time I was with Dov I wrote several freelance articles including one or two for *Cosmopolitan*. I never had to ask Dov to take me seriously, he took everything seriously. And one of the things that I loved about him was that he could speak Yiddish, the almost forgotten tongue of the Eastern European Jews among their own and one of the most magnificently expressive languages on the face of the earth. So he would go into a routine, usually about food, in Yiddish, while I tried to follow and laughed and felt obscurely comforted. I also encouraged him to speak Hebrew when he was moved to do so. He protested that it wasn't fair, I wouldn't understand. I didn't care. I loved the sound of it and in time I did learn to understand some phrases just by intonation and context. What an effort to have to express yourself all the time in somebody else's language.

Apart from talking, of which we did a great deal, Dov

wanted to write and to write in English. I encouraged him to read much more widely, especially the American writers banded loosely under the title 'The New Journalists' – Herr, Capote, Wolfe, Didion and Dunn to name but a few. I also bullied him to learn to type. In turn he complained that I didn't read what he bought me – Fanon, Marcuse, Goethe and Camus – but he introduced me to Isaac Bashevis-Singer and I read everything he wrote that I could find. But if I was happy about Dov's Jewishness, he was not. He talked a great deal about Israeli politics, he talked again about leaving religion. I told him that he might have left religion, but religion had not left him.

My mother's first reaction when she met him was 'Well, I can see why you fell for him, he's beautiful.' Pause. 'But he's a boy.' I thought this was unfair given that he'd seen me through one of the most ungraceful periods of my life. Then she asked, 'What happens if you get married?' I didn't know, I wasn't sure. 'Because *you* may get out of the marriage but if you have a child, forget it. The Jews will not give up on a child.' Where did my mother get her ideas about the Jews? Anyway, there was no hurry. Marriage was something that happened to other people.

Our life was narrow. We didn't have many friends, either individually or as a couple. Dov was my retreat and I tried to be his. But the routine of our lives drove me mad. He withdrew into a great deal of dope smoking and loud anguished music which he played at volume through earphones into his head. To this day whenever I hear Pink Floyd I see Dov, stretched out in the darkness, joint glowing in his hand, gone walkabout in his soul. I bought a few more clothes, a few more books, haunted the antique markets and tried believe it would all get better when we got a house.

We'd talked about a house for a while and I had always insisted that, although I would buy it, it would be his home too. To that end, we saw houses, I was gazumped five times and lost a fortune in conveyancing. But somewhere in there, things began to change and we began to drift. Perhaps he felt I couldn't leave England though I'd always held that I could as long as there was emergency money to get home to Ma if anything was wrong. Perhaps it was because he wanted to go to America and I didn't want to live there again. Perhaps it was because he was always the stranger, quite comfortable but not really happy anywhere and least comfortable of all where he was happiest – in Israel. And he divined wisely that I wanted to settle but he wasn't ready to and he didn't want to play househusband.

Anyway he decided to go and see some old friends in Munich and to travel a bit and stretch his legs. He was away for several weeks, so was Hilde and the house was very quiet. Hilde's cat fell ill and I nursed it. I went to work and missed Dov and read a lot and slept. Our reunion was sealed by the gift of the Spinoza coat, as we called it, a velvet jacket bought from a barrow near the synagogue in the Hague where Spinoza used to preach. But the pleasure didn't last long. We were both restless. Whether I left him or stayed with him, I was no nearer having children. Because I wanted a man to have children with, a man who wanted them too. I'd had a lovely father, I believe in fathers and I wanted a father for my children. Dov was no more interested in marriage than I was but he wanted a child. It was like having all sorts of bits and pieces floating on their individual ribbons up in the air. How could we put them together? I was at a loss.

It seemed quite clear that life wasn't going to be anything like the shape I'd originally imagined it to be. Perhaps passionate love, in which I'd always believed, was really myth. Or just not for me. I cared for Dov. He cared for me. He was all the right and good things and we did quite well together. Maybe that was all there was. In the meantime I continued to work and he continued to write whenever he wasn't working, finding his feet in something he really wanted to do.

He decided to go to Israel and see his parents. It was always a source of pain to me that as far as his parents knew, I didn't exist. As far as they knew, he shared a house with a friend in London. He had lived with the lady from whom he was disentangling himself when I met him for three years, had his father visiting him in London and still maintained the same sort of fiction. If we were not Jewish, we couldn't exist. I had pet names for his parents. I knew things about them, we talked about their past and their health and their characters but I could never say 'Give them my love' at the end of a letter. As the time for his departure drew near, we entered one of those mellow phases almost as if we were reassuring each other that everything would be all right. Maybe neither of us felt we could face any more disappointment. Maybe drawing together is what lonely people do when they sense some more loneliness is on the way.

One day I reached for all those half-worked out ideas which had been floating around for so long and came up with the only way out I could see. I asked him, 'And are you going to tell your parents about us?'

He replied carefully, 'If there's a right time.'

I said, 'Dov, I will make an orthodox conversion.'

He was shocked. 'You know I'd never ask you to do that.'

I nodded patiently. 'I'm offering.'

He looked at me almost angrily. 'You don't know what you do.'

But I insisted. 'Yes I do. I've asked and I've read and I've thought. You know that I'm with my father in this, you don't make a Jew by conversion, you have to be born a Jew. But if the only thing which stands between your parents and their grandchild is my conversion, then I will convert. And you know nothing will do for them but an orthodox conversion.'

Dov smiled his dazzling smile. 'Ah,' he said, 'so now you want to marry me.'

'I don't know,' I said, 'but I'm tired of being hidden. It hurts me. If this is the only way in, I'll take it. You want a child, so do I.'

So he hugged me and called me all the wonderful nicknames he had for me, laughed as he packed his shirts – 'My mother will know I didn't choose these!' – and went to Israel.

* * *

In the background of all this, there were some changes at *Woman* which began when I came into my little office at High Holborn rather early one morning. I was just sitting there, sorting through letters when my editor Peter Lawrence put his head round the door. He asked if I was busy, I said no and he said he'd like to talk to me for a minute. He sat down and I waited. 'Anna,' he said, 'I've had some bad news. I have cancer.' The cheerful beam of sunlight in which he was sitting suddenly looked very cold.

'What are the chances?' I asked quietly.

'Not good. I'm having treatment of course, but it's pretty final.'

I was watching him. He raised his eyes and smiled at me. 'I just wanted to tell somebody . . .'

'Thank you for telling me,' I said. 'You know I will do anything I can.'

He nodded. 'Just don't tell anybody,' he said and I didn't.

Peter wasted to transparency while his stomach swelled. There was remarkably little talk among the staff. What was happening was painfully obvious although the official line was still that 'investigations were proceeding'. He suffered terribly with chemotherapy, the drugs made him sick. The magazine staggered on. His young wife was pregnant with their second child when he died. Jo Sandilands succeeded him as editor.

To begin with, the difference wasn't very great. She was courteous to me, I returned the compliment but as time wore on, it became clearer and clearer that we might get on well seated together at the occasional lunch but as employer and employee, we were in trouble. But I'd made my deal with IPC long ago and I'd stuck to it. So inevitably we crossed swords. She liked what I'd written in a longer format, especially one or two items she'd read in *Cosmopolitan*. Would I write longer features for *Woman*? I submitted a list of over a dozen ideas. She took six months to set up a meeting to discuss them. Although I was approached for promotional or advertising work, it didn't often work out but now various things came up I was interested in. Jo vetoed them. Then she wanted me to write a piece about rape. I did. She employed the time honoured technique of magazine editors everywhere and argued over one line or one paragraph taken out of context. I rewrote and rewrote. She haggled some more and I dug my toes in.

In the meantime I was telephoned by a personable voice asking me if I'd consider membership of the board of Apex, a charitable organisation for the rehabilitation of white collar offenders. I said yes and the voice made an appointment for himself and his placement officer to visit me. The voice was owned by a tall dark man with the curiously opaque eyes of a snake and a great deal of natural charm which is, if you don't know it, as rare as hen's teeth. His name was Nigel Lilley. He talked about recidivism, prison life, reintegrating prisoners

177

into the work place. He presented well. I said I would read the papers and let him know. But I felt that it was a field where there were too many amateurs already and it required more time than I could give it. When I rang him to refuse, he took it gracefully and invited me out for a drink. I couldn't think of a way to say no so I said yes and cancelled, something I did a great deal in those days. It saved explanations.

Then an acquaintance rang me from a freelance film production company to ask me to come and meet a director who was interested in putting together a documentary on rape. His name was David Munro and he is now better known for his work with John Pilger on thought-provoking documentaries about Cambodia, Vietnam and the arms race. David spoke about the reaction he'd already had among the powers that be in television to the subject matter, while I told him how frustrated I was by the general unwillingness to write an other than carefully slanted feature on the subject in women's magazines. Would I like to present the film if he could get it off the ground? Yes, I would.

All the way back to the office I debated how to tell Jo Sandilands what I was doing without living in fear of losing my job. (One of the things which drew Dov and I together was paranoia – dictionary definition: 'systematic hallucinations of a persecutory nature' – with a rider: just because you think there's somebody after you, it doesn't mean there isn't.) Jo played into my hands. The deal was still as it had been in Peter Lawrence's day, that I submitted a list of my extramural activities every month. As I carefully buried the *Man Alive* documentary on rape (courtesy of Aubrey Singer, who had always admired David's work) two-thirds of the way down the page, in amongst Radio Four and speaking engagements, my editor departed for a two-week holiday, returned for a few days and flew off again to New York. We began shooting the documentary in the middle of that.

Filming the rape documentary was harrowing. Rape is not a subject that anybody with any feeling can be in much confusion about and even when you're prepared as we were to consider rape fantasies, the manipulation of men, the enshrinement of man active/woman passive in every kind of literature from Mills and Boon to *Men Only*, there is still no case *for* rape.

178

Back at the office, I was now on my second secretary. Christie was a mate, a true friend and never did she show it more than while I was off on the first of my endeavours to fit 48 hours worth of emotional work into 18 hours, five times a week for the foreseeable future. Christie was my age, had been a secretary at IPC far too long and my first meeting with her occurred in the corridor outside my office in the old building at High Holborn. By the time we reached the unlovely tower block on the South Bank where most of the IPC publications are now housed, she was fed up to the teeth with working for the home department and had been typing my Capital letters at home for several months for extra dough (£2 per hour). I had a disastrous few weeks with a little girl who thought I'd end up in Madame Tussaud's and then I asked Christie very hesitantly if she'd work for me. She was so bored and desperate, she was thinking of leaving but for some reason or other, working with me seemed an appealing prospect. And for a long time she spoiled me for anybody else. She was bright, intelligent, nearly as drama prone as I am, and we were great friends. She gave me to understand that she would do anything in her power for me, and she did. And now Dov went away so there weren't the ups-and-downs of home to deflect me from working very hard.

While we were making the film, the schedule was that I arrived at the office at 6.00 am and hit either the typewriter or the tape recorder until 9.00 am when I donned the lilac dress I never wanted to see again by the end of the shooting, checked my make-up and left. As long as we were filming in London, I checked in wherever I was told to go and worked until lunch. At lunch I rang Christie, made calls if I had to, corroborated her statements and tried to give some idea of when I'd be back in the office plus preparing a covering story in case I wasn't back early enough. I may add that a lot of this was only possible because once again my office was a tiny inner sanctum while Christie fielded all comers in a much larger outer office. How I got all this space when offices for the editorial staff were at such a premium, I don't know. Maybe the rulers of our little kingdom fancied I could give the staff moral malaria. All I know is that for the four years I was there the staff regularly beat a path to my door in confidence, sending Christie out ahead of them to check that the coast was clear and they could return to their desks unobtrusively. The fact that I was geographically cut off like this plus the fact that I wrote without the hair-raising supervision and interference of earlier days made my absenteeism possible. Whenever I finished what David had for me to do, I made my way back to the office, somewhere between 4.00 in the afternoon and 9.00 at night. There would be all sorts of notes and messages, the tape of the morning clean and ready to go again and I would begin another four or five hours' work. Never let it be thought that Mrs Thatcher is the only person who can work like a fiend. We all can if the incentives are right.

When my editor returned from holiday, she summoned me to check up on one or two details and then asked about the rape documentary. I answered as if it was still not confirmed. 'And what will happen,' she said, 'if I tell you I'd rather you didn't do it?'

'That might be a bit difficult,' I replied, 'because I've got several days' material in the can.' After some vituperation on her part and some explanation on mine, we called it a day. But I had learned something. Displeasure doesn't mean discharge. I was always too anxious, too agreeable to fight until I felt I was justified. How could it be wrong for me, the problem page editor of a women's magazine, to be involved in a documentary about rape?

Within three days all was forgiven because *Woman* had spent a great deal of money on computer time to set up a big survey on sexual behaviour in the eighties – or something like that – and needed a comment from their own agony aunt and all the help with the publicity they could get, both of which I was delighted to give them.

I now received a telephone call from Nigel Lilley who had left Apex for a senior recruitment consultancy, to invite me to lunch. If talking to one man about another is unflattering, then it was the most unflattering lunch Mr Lilley had ever bought anyone. Not for nothing had he been in the police for years and lectured on interrogation. I didn't even know how well I was being questioned. And in the course of telling him all about my hope and fears, my life and times, I gathered quite a bit about his too. The whole episode seemed very important, though for the life of me I couldn't tell you why. Two weeks later I returned the compliment of Mr Lilley's lunch. Christie regarded me thoughtfully when I returned to the office. I asked why she was looking so wise. 'Apart from natural vivacity and vinous good spirits,' she said, 'you do look exceptionally happy.' I insisted that it was all very nice – just – very nice.

Remember what I said about that word 'nice'?

Two hours later a telegram arrived which read:

Have now recovered from your overwhelming deposit to Lilley Corporate stop Advise you now have majority share-holding and unlimited funds to draw on at any time stop love Nigel

We began to speak to one another rather frequently.

* * *

The biggest difficulty with the organisation of the rape film was that the BBC had just screened Newman's *Law And Order* for the first time and relations between police and television were strained. Try as we might, we couldn't find a policeman to interview in London or environs. Eventually we went down to Bristol and Avon where the interview had been OK'd, only to discover that the superintendent in charge of public relations sat with the officer we were interviewing and told her exactly what to say. What the superintendent really thought about rape came out later over a cup of tea and I just wish we'd taped that. And then I thought of Nigel Lilley. Hadn't he been a policemen for 13 years, cadet at 17, CID at 21? Hesitantly I told David that I knew an ex-policeman who might be worth looking at, now involved at the other end with rehabilitation of offenders, having himself been accused of perjury in a Drugs Squad trial and having served one year of an 18 months' sentence. I was hesitant about making an inappropriate suggestion, hesitant about how N. Lilley him-self might respond to being seconded into a film about rape, but the one thing I was sure of was he would be good on camera. David felt I should approach him and when I did, he agreed to have dinner with us to talk it over.

Over that dinner I learned that Nigel was frequently called Nick, that he spoke eloquently about the police, that he loved animals – tigers and dolphins best – and that when David questioned him about trying to change attitudes towards prison and authority, his eyes filled and his voice, which was curiously light and anonymous for such a strong presence, shook. He offered to drive me home in the very small car he had at the time and I offered him coffee. I showed him books I liked, played him some music, I talked, I waited. He spoke very little and then he did something that threw me. He began to weep and I sat beside his very large person and tried to wrap my inadequate arms around him. 'Damn you, Anna Raeburn,' he said through his tears, 'I love you.' And damn it was right.

Chapter 17

To write about someone you love is to risk derogation of the person in particular or the subject in general. It came as quite a shock to realise that I had given up the idea of loving anybody more than I loved Dov, not that I had much option where Nick was concerned because I might just as well have argued with a tidal wave. He didn't overwhelm me. It did. For several months, my instinct and respected 'gut' told me that everything was fine while my poor head was still trying to work out what, quite, had hit me. However, nothing very much could happen immediately. Although Dov was away for several weeks, I remained in the flat I shared with him in north London. Nick, although already divorced from his wife, was living with her again, a situation which developed partly out of disorientation when he first emerged from prison and partly because of her ill health. They were at the end of a long marriage begun when he was 21 and maintained for so many years in part because the police force is not keen on divorce. That they were not going to continue to live together was decided before I came on the scene – perhaps you might say I crystallised it. So, in between commuting from his office to Windsor, Nick began to look for somewhere to live, while I made it clear that I would join him as soon as I could.

We went to bed together twice and then we embarked on several months which we referred to as the Victorian courtship. Whereas both of us had played very indulgently heretofore with anybody we fancied, whatever it was we had was different. It could not be treated the same way. Our motto became 'Accept No Substitute' until we could be together properly. We both had some sorting out to do and my timing was regrettable as Dov had just decided to see if he could hold a British as well as an Israeli passport, a process which made him feel more vulnerable that ever.

The rape film involved interviewing among others one rapist, three rapees, two police surgeons, a representative from the Rape Crisis Centre, a psychiatrist treating rapists in prison and a former police officer (because serving ones weren't allowed much in the way of freedom of speech). There was a great deal of other material too, much of which necessitated my speaking to camera. Both David Munro and I felt that if we had a chance to examine the subject, we should try and do so as comprehensively as possible. We filmed outside much of the time and it was so cold that I could only move my mouth with difficulty. During the last day's shooting, on that part of Putney towpath directly on the flight path to Heathrow and in competition with a municipal buzzsaw, I shook visibly until the soundman fused two batteries together to make me a handwarmer.

Once it was 'in the can', we began eleven months of arguing and recutting. The process is regarded as standard by freelance film-makers. The television company agrees that you should have a go at the film because its representatives think you will do a good job and or it saves producing it in-house, that is with a company producer as well as crew. But then your efforts are clawed in and shaped to fit the slot for which the film is earmarked, regardless of previous agreements, intentions and aims. There is a story Dov told me about the BBC being so obsessed with balance that their edition of the Second World War consists of thirty minutes Hitler, thirty minutes Jews. My most vivid memory during this long haul is of Desmond Wilcox as the head of department, wanting yet another recut and musing aloud . . . 'lack of balance and you see, it's so one-sided and angry!'

My eyes met with David's and I exploded. 'Oh do tell me,' I blazed, 'do let me know – what is the case *for* rape?'

He yelled back, 'I do wish you'd stop treating me like the enemy, my dear – I'm on your side.'

'Convince me,' I said. A year or two later, he told me that Esther thought the show worked.

When it was released, the rape film was a shadow of what we'd intended. We'd gone from the possibility of devoting two fifty-minute slots to it, to one and a half with a studio discussion for the balance of the time, to one – just. We'd cut out a lot we deeply believed to be important. The idea of rape as a serious subject for debate was not appreciated by the press, who gave us nil coverage. *Time Out* commented that I sounded like every other BBC mouthpiece. But the public response was gratifying.

Dov came back to London during the filming and I told him that I'd met Nick. The second time I mentioned him, he said, 'You sound as if you'd like to go to bed with him.'

I replied that I had.

Dov swept me his most cynical grin. 'And how was it?'

'Very nice thank you,' I said but I quailed at the prospect of telling the whole truth. Nick and I continued to speak on the telephone, meet for lunch or drinks and talk about everything under the sun. There was no impatience, just determination to be together soon.

Then one day I was doing a discussion programme with young people for BBC Regional Television in the south, near where my mother now lives. Nick offered to take the afternoon off, come and collect me, take me to my mother's for tea and drive me back. Ordinary enough, wouldn't you say? I regarded the whole idea with appalled fascination. This was all too fast for me. But since I couldn't think of how to say no, I said yes. The discussion programme was great fun and I complimented the producers and the participants. Nick arrived and hit the right note with everybody as only those with enormous self-assurance and a graceful spirit can. And then we drove off to see my Ma. My sister was there which was a bonus, and we had a cup of tea. And in that couple of hours I learned that Nick had decided the afternoon was going to be all right and so it was. He met with my family on equal footing without apology or explanation and they responded to that approach most comfortably. He had remarked very early on in our relationship that I didn't laugh enough, that he wanted to make me laugh and I remember laughing a lot that afternoon. He is a remarkable and outrageous storyteller. So there was no reason why, on the way home in the car, I should begin to cry. But I did and I couldn't stop. After two or three wet miles, Nick pulled over and tried to comfort me, asking what was the matter. I couldn't work it out for several hours. It had all been blessedly easy. I wasn't used to anything being so easy. That night I telephoned my mother in fear and trembling. What was I going to do if she didn't like him? Rhetorical question, I knew what I would do. I just hoped I wouldn't be called upon to do it. When I asked her what she thought of him back came the reply with all the warmth that well-loved voice could muster, 'Oh darling, I'm so glad you brought home an adult at last!' In my mother's moments of deepest love and pride, a spade is never less than a bloody shovel.

In the months between our meeting and moving in together, Nick and I talked about our pasts a good deal. We both felt the failure of our previous relationships (God knows there were enough of them!) and the necessity to learn from them and not make the same mistakes again. We talked a great deal about marriage. It was not uppermost in either of our minds. When I told him about offering to make a conversion to Judaism in order to have a child with Dov, he was horrified. 'If he wouldn't have you as you are, how could you have a child with him?' he asked. I hadn't until then thought of that offer as a compromise but then I saw that, however sincere, that's exactly what it was and a very risky compromise at that. Which led us (Nick and I) into discussions about children, futures, families. We talked and talked, held hands and talked some more. How grateful I am for that talking, which made for the beginning of a real intimacy; how grateful – when I know how much easier it is to go to bed and articulate your present wishes rather than discuss in real terms what's gone wrong before and what you really want. At this stage, we added a second rule to the existing canon which was that Things Must Be Said. Of course some tact in the question of timing would be nice but Things Must Be Said. What one friend of ours called 'the secret agenda' – the things you want to believe you desire mutually, only slowly to discover you don't share at all – had nearly destroyed our respective marriages, aided and abetted by our inability to commit.

We sat and talked most evenings on the way home in the quiet bar of a West End hotel, now sadly all glass and jazz and noise. Our preferred evenings were Wednesdays when I only had to leave in time to get to the radio station and Fridays when anything can happen to anybody and almost everybody comes home a bit late. But sometimes the balancing acts – of our jobs, our pasts and presents, plus the pull of whatever future we might have together – combined with two large drinks into a fairly lethal cocktail, the kind that lifts you up to the heights and drops you back down again to the depths very hard and very fast. One evening, thus afflicted, I began to say something as Nick was driving me to Capital Radio. When I heard in my own head what I was going to say, my mind cautioned me to shut my mouth – fast. But not enough to escape the attention of the eagle eye sitting beside me.

'What were you going to say?' inquired Nick.

I said, 'Please don't ask me. I will tell you, really I will, but not now.'

'Not on,' averred the Big Fella, parking the car.

I tried to evade him again but he insisted so I said in as deliberately level a voice as I could manage, 'I was going to ask you to marry me and take me away from all this.'

'Don't worry,' he said calmly, opening the door for me. 'I intend to.'

I looked at him. 'Then please,' I said, 'don't give me more than a week's notice. Just time to organise Ma and a dress. I'll only panic if I have more time to think about it.'

I find it hard to tell you how different all this was for me. I have played most scenes somewhere along the line – declaration, persuasion, passionate lover, world-weary mistress (a pity I wasn't as good on the stage as I was in life!) – but I had never experienced anything as beautifully matter of fact. And for the first time since I could remember, I had no residual misgivings. It would work because we would work to make sure it did. I trusted Nick.

Sometimes our partings left us armed for the ensuing separation but still we had very little time together without the risk of somebody seeing us. I don't know how much Nick's wife knew about his move to London at this point. I think she knew he was looking for a flat but perhaps not why he was looking with such enthusiasm. And I was still trying to find a kind way of letting Dov down gently. So we learned to cherish the odd day that Nick brought the car up to town or the few minutes of glassed in privacy we shared in the back of the taxi taking him to Paddington. And in case all this is beginning to sound like so much whimsy and love's young dream, Nick commented drily that many's the time he got into his train with a lump in his throat and another in his trousers. I would frequently have been grateful to have him behave according to pattern because then I could have rationalised my way out of whatever we were in. But it didn't happen.

We had one weekend together when Dov was working in Germany and Nick moved up to London. There was nobody else at home in the house where I lived and he shouted up to me, grinning like a schoolboy. I came flying down the stairs with no feeling but utter joy that he would be there when I opened the door. However, when I first saw the flat he had found, I gulped hard. Somebody had taken yesterday's rhubarb and custard and made it cloth – it was hanging at the windows masquerading as curtains. It was in fact this flat that taught me why such a unit is referred to as a 'pied-à-terre' – because you can only put one foot on the earth. It was pokey and drab with a cupboard for a kitchen and a large bath in a tiny bathroom but it had a telephone and it was PRIVATE. Nick gave me a key and I hugged him.

Weekends generally were the worst and we developed all kinds of dodges just to spend an hour together including the time-honoured 'I need to be alone' on my part. On one of these sojourns we went to Camden Passage where we found a magnificent ring which I had to buy as Nick hadn't brought his chequebook. I couldn't wear it yet, but I could keep it against the day that I would be able to. He knew me as an inveterate shopper and it wasn't a lie to say that I had bought it. But I was too superstitious to wear it and carried it in my purse.

At last it became clear to me that, far from sparing Dov anything, I was just insulting him by backpedalling into past unfortunate habits. We were not good at going our separate ways on the same turf. He knew I was lying, I knew he knew and when I finally got round to telling him the truth, his first question was 'Will he make you happy?' I said yes. 'Then I'm happy.' A pause. 'And did he really buy you that ring you carry but won't wear?' I said yes. 'Will you show it to me properly, please?' I did so. He asked me what the stone was. 'Black opal,' I said very quickly, 'set in white gold with diamonds.' His response was an impressed exclamation which I won't insult my Jewish friends by trying to translate into print. It made us both laugh and cry. 'Now,' said my friend Dov, 'let there be peace.' Shortly afterwards, he got his British papers and I moved out into the most cramped flat I'd ever seen.

188

Living with Nick Lilley was so natural it's hard to look back and discuss it. In a way, writing about everything else is easy by comparison. I can never take my good fortune for granted and I worry that to write about it is to risk it. We just did it. We lived very near to the West End so we made full use of all the cinemas and cheap eating places. Nick could walk to work, I was just a short distance from my office. We talked and ate and worked and celebrated finding one another.

* * *

Now that I was more settled in myself, I began once again to enjoy my work at *Woman* more though I still felt very strongly that the only way to stay fresh as an agony aunt was to do something else as well, other different things, and this was still not easy to negotiate. However the principle seemed again, 'Don't talk about it, just do it,' and in order to set the scene, it is again necessary to go back before we go forward.

In amongst the interviews I had done in the first two years at *Woman* was one with Len Richmond, for *Time Out*. The subject was rather less *Woman* magazine and rather more about the Capital Radio show. The tone of the interview was very candid, inevitably involving a question or two about homosexuality, for Len is the only gay chauvinist pig I've ever known. He really thinks that straights are missing out on the deal. I have always believed in framing your interview to its medium and in those days I had some regard for *Time Out* as a publication. But I had reckoned without the hoohah this would cause at *Woman*. Just to make matters worse, I had never heard of the ruling whereby one publication is allowed to extract a certain number of words from another (under 400 I think) without interfering with copyright. So the *News of the World* extracted just under 400 words' worth from *Time Out* and ran it under a heading 'The Agony of Anna'. It was a perfect example of how words could mean one thing in one context and sound completely different in another. Blood pressure at IPC was considerably raised. They were not used to their problem page editors acknowledging the existence of lesbianism, still less speaking about it in the first person. (When Len asked me about love between women, I had inevitably mentioned Nat.) But the storm blew over (and I still have a letter sent to Michael Raeburn, care of his union, the ACTT, asking if my sexual proclivities were the cause of the breakup of our marriage). And from then on, Len and I became friendly. We saw each other intermittently until I was settled in my new found cocoon of happiness with Nick, when he rang me to ask if I'd discuss an idea he had for a TV situation comedy.

It was about the women who settled the Wild West, drawn from a book of carefully researched anecdotes about the mail order brides, shady ladies, school mistresses and all those other frontier heroines who were a good deal grittier and more interesting than the one or two stereotypes we're repeatedly offered in western films. So we met a couple times a week for six weeks or so, trying to come up with a working method and a story line. Len liked writing plays. He had been an actor and had masses of nervous energy. He decided he wanted to work with me because he liked me and I had a name. But the name was no use in America and it rapidly became clear that this project had nowhere to go in England. We fought over my lack of commitment to the idea and his inability to see that working very hard into a void was a shocking waste of energy. In the meantime he was putting himself about with a view to writing for television and one day he rang me very excitedly.

He had written some sketches and sent them to Humphrey Barclay, who was then head of comedy at London Weekend Television. Humphrey offered him an appointment and allowed, in the course of their meeting, that he could set Len to work writing additional material and sketches for various shows, if that was what Len Richmond really wanted. 'What I really want,' said Len, 'is to write a situation comedy about an agony aunt and Anna Raeburn will help me.' HB was interested. Len rang me, an exercise in tact I much appreciated because he was only just up the street – the LWT and IPC buildings virtually adjoin – but he knew that I was not good at being dropped in upon. 'They've offered us a meeting next Monday,' said Len, 'so will you come with me?' Of course I would. 'God, Anna,' he said, 'I don't know what to do next.'

'But I do,' I said. 'We tell 'em why it's funny and why it's sad and why the two have to combine. And she has to work in a radio station as well because that's a whole different thing–'

'Oh great,' said Len, 'so now we can have a DJ! Great, so I'll come and collect you.'

At the first meeting with HB and a producer called John Reardon, the main thing seemed to be to convince them of the tone we both believed would be right. Len taped this conversation and most of the meetings we subsequently had. I told stories about what really happened, the awful, amusing things that are all part of being around other people's problems. They suggested it might be very difficult to write but we wanted to try and they wanted us to. The unexpected pluses were that Len and I were in agreement about the kind of humour we wanted to put across and the kind of heroine we wanted to have. We defined the humour as 'funnybone humour', when things are so painful you have to laugh, like the Howard Hawks comedies of the 1930s – *His Girl Friday*, *Bringing Up Baby* – and more recently, Woody Allen's films, especially *Annie Hall*. Len, as an American, had a strong leaning towards *Soap* and *Mary Hartman, Mary Hartman* but although I admired the speed of American sitcom, I felt that both of these series were farce and I wanted our characters to be real because I believed that would make them acceptable, so freeing us to have some very strange people in the show whom we could laugh *with*, not at.

So we began.

* * *

We worked in Len's flat, my office and once even in a hotel room he was temporarily staying in. When we began we improvised situations between us for the characters and acted them out on tape. When we thought we'd hit something, we typed it. Correction. I typed it. I type faster than Len. We worked into the afternoons because then I could keep my paperwork under control and be seen about in the mornings, obviously doing my job. It was always easier to absent yourself from work after lunch at a magazine because lunch can last a very long time and if the executives don't come back, it's rare for anybody to go looking for them.

We soon discovered that Len was a worrier. He wrote pages and pages of notes and suggestions and dreadful jokes at various stages between our meetings. While I cogitated about

191

one development or theme, Len would attempt to write a book overnight, staying awake, getting high, whatever. Our meetings often began acrimoniously with him asking me whether I'd really given the matter we discussed the previous day any thought and with me systematically destroying an insomniac's ration of paper. There was rarely anything we wanted to keep in the cool light of day from those mammoth worry sessions, but the characters grew like Topsy.

I wanted the heroine to have a very classless name, one syllable, like – Jane. We agreed she should be Jewish. The four best known agony aunts in Britain at the time were all Jewish or had Jewish antecedents – Marje Proops, Claire Rayner, Irma Kurtz and me. Len's eyes lit up. If she were Jewish, she could have an impossible Jewish mother like his. And her husband isn't Jewish, I added. So her mother doesn't really get on with her husband, said Len. Point of conflict, points of conflict are good, Anna. But he's dishy. They met at University, I volunteered. Where he was very talented and popular. But when Jane got bored and went and got herself a job, concluded Len, their positions changed. She is now the name in the family and – what are we going to call him? Laurence, I suggested. Great – Laurence can't stand it. What does Laurence do? We debated various occupations and concluded he was a psychiatrist because they're often in a lot of personal trouble and agony aunts frequently do their job so much better (!) We decided that Jane had a fantastic secretary who was crisp, well put together and organised, everything Jane wasn't – and that their relationship was built on a sparring partnership. Jane had to cope with an editor – and what an editor! – based on what Len and I knew of them as a breed which meant she despaired of Jane's lack of glamour but was unable to outmanoeuvre her in her own field.

When we got to the possibilities of the radio station and a phone-in programme on people's problems, Len was salivating. He announced that the DJ was called Andy and he became Andy Evol – Evol is love backwards and Capital DJ Adrian Love did everything he could to help us and Peter Blake, the actor who played the character. Jane has to have neighbours, neighbours who are both a boon and a curse. Len wanted a gay couple. When, he demanded, did you last see gays portrayed as humans, the nicest and most reasonable humans in Jane's life, irritations excepted (or do I mean accepted)?

We made each other several solemn promises. We would not withhold criticism from each other. We would level with each other. We would stay solid in the face of all outsiders, even if we fought like mad in private and we would split everything fifty fifty. To this end we endured some acrimonious afternoons in each other's company and frequently one or the other felt that he or she was actually not able to make the necessary contribution. We both hit the biscuits like a junkie coming out of a cure. We had some loaded confrontations but we did manage to stay friends. And in view of the route we took with the series, that was a miracle.

When the pilot for *Agony* was accepted, Maureen Lipman's name was far from the top of the list. But when we'd seen her as Jane, we couldn't imagine anybody else in the part. The actor who played Laurence in the pilot was replaced and I remember that Maureen and I were equally surprised when Simon Williams read for the part. I went to a meeting with him, HB and Reardon and he read for us again. We talked about the character and I was sure he could do it but . . .

'Come on, intelligent lady,' he said. 'What are you thinking?'

I'd never thought of Simon Williams outside or beyond James Bellamy in *Upstairs, Downstairs* and I wanted him as far from that as possible. Given that he will always be tall and lean and rather aristocratic in appearance, I felt we must play against that to establish Laurence as himself. 'Will you wear your glasses?' I asked. He agreed. 'And not have a moustache.' He agreed again. We had our Laurence.

Len went to many of the casting sessions. I stayed away. Once the pilot was accepted, we launched into writing and rewriting six scripts over and over again. When people say, 'How did you know what to do?' we didn't. We just tried hard and kept on writing. One of the greatest difficulties in writing for film or televison and in particular for TV sitcom, is that you have so little time in which to accomplish so much. Well, we did. Judging by a great deal of British sitcom, nothing happens from start to finish. As an experience in receiving confusing and contradictory messages, ours is unlikely to be surpassed. The producer John Reardon, the executive producer Humphrey Barclay and Michael Grade, then Head of Programmes at LWT, wanted the series to be new, fresh, provocative, outspoken. But they didn't want to upset anybody or break any new ground. They wanted each segment jam-packed with action and happenings and so did we, but life doesn't always work out as neatly as art. We wanted a few untidy endings. They refused. Once on the umpteenth rewrite of an episode, I remarked bitterly that what they really wanted was *War and Peace* on ice with jokes in 22 minutes. Everybody laughed and agreed. It wasn't reassuring.

In the middle of this we dispersed for our holidays. I knew that I didn't want to continue at *Woman* and Deirdre McSharry of *Cosmopolitan* took me to lunch and made me an offer. So did Christopher Ward, then with the *Sunday Mirror*. I decided I wasn't ready for the *Mirror* and accepted Deirdre's offer which gave me a small increase in salary and total control over what I wrote. Then I wrote my letter of resignation to Jo Sandilands. We had a remarkably candid conversation about my leaving but apparently it fluttered the dovecotes because the publisher of *Woman* then took me to a totally gratuitous lunch at the Savoy. He made it clear that I would never be allowed to become an editor at IPC although they were sad to lose me, and then asked me what sort of magazine I was really interested in. To answer that, I explained a bit with particular reference to the appearance of *Elle* and – 'What's that?' he asked. Not jolly-old-buffer-missed-it but sorry dear, never heard of it. I spelled it. He had never heard of it, he said. Power resides in strange hands.

Nick announced that I had a week to find a dress. Dee Remmington took me to lunch to wish me luck for the wedding and to tell me I was mad to go to *Cosmo* for so little money. I was so excited that I bought two possible wedding dresses but of course I should have known that the closet Italian I was marrying loved the idea of his bride in a classic black and white small print silk dress, the dress I call my Ferrari, the most expensive garment I've ever owned. Nick booked my mother and his sister Vivien into a nearby hotel and we invited those we knew best to lunch after the event.

I wrote a paragraph for *Woman* handing over to Virginia Ironside, in which I said that I had come to *Woman* at the end of a marriage, desperately hoping that I was good for something and that *Woman* had made many things possible for me, professionally and personally, which had healed me, I was now leaving, with much gratitude to the readers, to marry again. I left *Woman* on a Friday afternoon with my arms full of files and the Le Creuset ironware Christie had insisted I was given in farewell, guiding the powers-that-were away from something, she hinted darkly, totally unsuitable. That night my mother, Vivien, Nick and I dined in a candlelit restaurant in Covent Garden and I spent the night in the hotel with Ma. Nick came to collect us at 8.45 the next morning and we had a cup of tea in an adjacent Wimpy while waiting our turn in the registry office. At 9.15 we were married by a delightful northern gentleman who gave me the wedding lines with a friendly admonition to hang on to them. I had the square gold ring I'd bought so long ago on my wedding finger, my beautiful opal on the third finger of my right hand and we both had heavy Russian wedding rings on the little finger of the right hand.

We had hardly arrived home when the *News of the World* appeared on the doorstep to be dismissed with white-faced self-control by Nick. We left for Bianci's. Bianci's in Frith Street is owned by Lino Ricci and his family and Nick has known them for many years. We had sat and eaten and drunk and talked and argued many times at the corner table. Lino had offered to close the restaurant for me, a special menu – I'd refused. All I wanted was to go there and feel comfortable and private. When we arrived he had decorated the tables with the darkest red roses I'd ever seen and the whole occasion was quite beautiful. We sat down and tried to eat and talk. We did quite well until they brought in the cake.

I had not asked for a cake. It was Lino's gift to us. I had not wanted a cake. In some way I felt that every time I eschewed these ordinary things, it was tempting fate. It was asking for more than I had a right to. And there was a cake which couldn't have pleased me more if I had planned its details myself, dripping in Strega, bearing the legend 'Happy Days', cream and green and decked with every symbolic decoration ever put on a wedding cake. Trust the Italians to make a wedding.

Chapter 18

We spent our wedding night at my sister-in-law's house in Irby in the Wirral because, on the Sunday after my wedding, I had to take part in the last of a series of 'God slots' (TV jargon for religious programmes) I'd been involved with at a rather fine noncomformist church in Blackpool, in company with Canon Bryan Green. On Sunday morning Nick was in the garden playing with his niece and her brothers when, in lifting her up and twisting away to avoid the boys, he slipped a disc. The first I knew of it was when he walked into the kitchen with the tread of Frankenstein's monster to tell me. One of the drawbacks about big men is that there is an awful lot of body to be out of action if anything goes wrong and me attending upon a lumbering Lilley resembled nothing so much as a rather anxious tug bobbing alongside a stunned liner.

The programme we taped that day was the most satisfactory of the series (excepting the one with Dr Una Kroll), and Bryan Green was and is a joy. We then drove back to London with Nick in considerable pain, not knowing whether our longed for 'holimoon' – I was too superstitious to call it a honeymoon and too honest just to call it a holiday – would indeed come to pass. Fortunately Nick's doctor (who also took care of Arsenal football team) was able to manoeuvre the disc back into line and dole out some much needed painkillers. Nick had to go into his office that day for some reason and as you might expect, the story of how he hurt his back was greeted with much disbelieving hilarity. The consensus of opinion seemed to be that I must have learned a trick or two during my years at *Forum* which had proved too much, even for Nick. The next morning we departed for Crete.

We spent two weeks in the sunshine and beauty of a place I'd always wanted to go to, where I feel indefinably at home.

Its scenery is so various, its people fine companions, the food good, the water clear and the sun shone. We hired a car and travelled and as the wind and the sun beat on our happy heads, he told me about himself and I told him about myself and we talked and talked. We also swam and slept a lot and there were even English bookshops to browse in. As Nick's eyesight is better than mine and his ears considerably longer he was privy to the two or three times we thought we were sighted, of which my favourite runs:

'Hey, Anna Raeburn's here on honeymoon.'

'Yeah, I know. She's over there.'

'Oooh – where? Oh yes, so she is. Who's that fella with her?'

'Dunno. Must be her husband.'

'Mmm. Don't think much of him – do you?'

Greek met Greek as far as the shopping went and we investigated every store frequently and thoroughly, returning with all sorts of things for the new home we knew we were going to have to have. Summer in our hole in the wall was one thing but spending another winter there, trying to cook on a Belling circa 1932, never mind wash and dry clothes in no space at all, wasn't on. Upon our return, after a saga of conveyancing with which I will not bore you, we finally became owners of a maisonette in Hampstead. It took me a year to admit that I lived in Hampstead. When asked, I ducked and said North London but after a while I stopped feeling apologetic. Now I just think we're very lucky to live in such a pleasant place.

* * *

Len and I continued working with each other and arguing, arguing rather more strenuously with Barclay and Reardon. Slowly the scripts shaped up. In retrospect I think that we were both very naive but I don't know how you're supposed to learn anything except by getting on and doing it. There is no question that we were both so happy about what we were doing, about what we were aiming for, that it never occurred to us that other people would not see that willingness for just what it was. Everybody in the cast invented business, contributed lines, suggested how a situation could be improved. We thought that was part of the wonderful teamwork we'd both loved briefly in the theatre and longed to be part of again.

Then suddenly I received a very excited telephone call from my agent who told me LWT wanted me to front a show for them about the differences between men and women. It meant co-presenting with Clive James. I was delighted. I was floored. I shook myself firmly and reminded myself that a job is a job is a job. *A Question of Sex*, as it was called, was a salutary experience for Clive James and for me. He was then writing regularly for the *Observer*, appearing on *Saturday Night People* and undoubtedly had other irons in the fire. I had a new job at *Cosmopolitan*, Capital Radio every week and *Agony* to complete, plus other little things from time to time on the appearance/public speaking front. Into the hands of our producer, we kidded ourselves, believing that the series would only take two and a half days per week, maybe less, and that all we had to do was to be ourselves. It was a mistake we paid for.

A Question of Sex was a wonderful idea but television resounds with lorryloads of wonderful ideas that die between conception and birth. Sadly *AQoS* was no exception. Building a series around debating the differences between men and women via interviews with related specialists and research projects, with the use of two presenters and a lot of props, was risky. The first episode was filed in the dustbin, all £40,000 worth of it. We were choreographed around like drunken skaters, how we were supposed to move only explained to us on shooting day because the rehearsal space was restricted. Clive discovered that he couldn't move and speak at the same time with a camera trained on him. The live animals we had waiting for their appearance took it in their heads to whoop at the wrong time and the props weren't finished for the final rehearsal. So there we were, going for a live recording, only to discover at the eleventh hour some very real problems in the matter of the aforementioned properties. For example we had two walls of brick, one pink, the other blue, to demonstrate why women live longer than men and what kills men off on their way through life. We were to dismantle some of our respectively 'sexed' bricks at every indication of loss, which naturally speeded up as the incidence of male death increased until Clive was supposed to knock down whole chunks of the wall. But the bricks were made of steel girders. They weighed a ton, couldn't be moved swiftly and trying to knock them down in quantity threatened a fracture of the hand and made a noise like the Blitz.

Apart from this, what Clive James and I learned was that never again would anybody else write lines for us. But right there and then we didn't have time to start into a battle to take over the scripts, so we wound up reciting pages of material to camera and trying to bounce off each other to enliven the proceedings whenever we could. Among the small successes of the series, I learned to use an autocue and I wore my glasses on television. A tiny step for womankind. I have kept the letter from the executive producer half-ordering, half-begging me not to wear them. Another kind of success was that anything you do that you haven't done before teaches you something – handling props, 'busking' some of the audience through an experiment – but the biggest success was the chemistry between Clive and me. This was aided by the fact that I was just married and couldn't have been happier, which tends to protect you against a lot, but it was down mainly to the luck of the draw and the fact that I was, as far as I could see, one of only two women in his immediate vicinity not pursuing him for reasons of venery.

So *AQoS* and *Agony* were prepared side by side. Suddenly it seemed we had agreement on everything with *Agony* and Len announced that he hated the British winter and wanted to go home to California for a break. I was bemused. I thought he was mad. It was obvious that such an absence would be regarded as a breach in the wall we'd been fighting to build around our baby series to protect it from some of the surrounding heavy hands. But he went. From the day he left, some of those previously agreed scripts were suddenly open to question again. I found my position invidious. I could not stall further consultation on the scripts. I felt that if I was obstructive, that would make matters worse, not better. So I co-operated. I stayed pragmatic and I stayed on the scripts. Compromise is a very ambivalent business.

One day in the middle of shooting a sequence for *AQoS*, Len Richmond walked back into London Weekend Television and gave me to understand that my co-operation in his absence was equivalent to Elia Kazan's co-operation with the House Unamerican Activities Commission under McCarthy i.e., unforgivable. I made some pithy response about his winter vacation and went back to work.

So we rejoined forces with the clash of verbal steel in several different directions at once, pressure being now well and truly upon us because the studio dates were approaching. There were some royal fights and a great deal of trying to find ways of relating to each other in various permutations of pairs without losing face. But Len and I were still basically in the same corner when it came to *Agony*. We just wanted it to be as good as it could be. Len wanted to attend every rehearsal which was firmly vetoed, so I now tended to come when I was called and not otherwise. When it came to the first recording, done live in front of a studio audience, I didn't know whether I was supposed to be there or not and I didn't ask. I went to the theatre with Nick to see Barry Humphries being Dame Edna Everage and it was wonderful to see somebody else being funny. When I appeared in the rehearsal room the next day, my absence that first night was described to me by Maureen as 'the most unprofessional thing I've ever witnessed in my life.' I apologised and was there for the rest of the tapings. Just as well. Aided and abetted by a suspiciously innocent sounding Nick beside me in the producer's box, Humphrey Barclay in his executive producer's hat and Len in the audience, I fought to reconstitute lines and jokes, even at that late stage. Somewhere around this time, HB asked me how I would feel about giving Maureen Lipman a writing credit. Her contribution was considerable but then so was everybody else's and the only way she'd get my OK for a writing credit was if we gave one to every other member of the cast too – something I would happily have done.

The reception of *Agony* was enthusiastic, even if Len did feel that I got more publicity than he did and even if most of it was tosh. From the night of the second taping to the end, I was asked to introduce the cast of *Agony* and outline the story to the audience after the warm-up man (the comedian hired by the company to take the chill off the studio audience) had finished. That done, it was back to battle stations, me behind the scenes and Len in the audience. Nick and I worked out a gracious appearance in the bar afterwards to thank everybody for ten minutes after the taping, then we beat it to a quiet place where I drank and nibbled and 'came down' after what was always the most intense adrenalin rush.

I'm often asked if I really wrote *Agony*. I did. Len and I had a good writing relationship. We often made quite different contributions. We drove each other mad, argued and shouted, disagreed over jokes and points of character, but remained a good team. There was a time when I could go through an *Agony* script line by line and tell you where each idea emanated from with appropriate credit to all the contributors. Whatever its faults and flaws, *Agony* worked, so I wasn't really surprised to be told that a second series was planned. But Len wanted to go home. He's a California boy and they always go home, and in addition the gay scene was a good deal more congenial out there, he said. In personal terms, I was glad for him. He asked me how I felt about it. I said I felt fine. He had been living out of a suitcase mid-Atlantic for some time. He asked me what I'd do. I said I'd have a crack at the next series by myself and then we'd see.

The to-ing and fro-ing began almost immediately and lasted the better part of a year. I tried to write a script on my own. Len and I had had some idea about where a second series might go and anyway ideas weren't my problem, but I couldn't manage it. I was asked if there was anybody else I'd like to work with but the only person I knew who was funny and wrote scripts was Bob Monkhouse, then under exclusive contract to ATV. LWT then selected a variety of writers and let them loose on half a script, saying I could choose somebody I'd like to work with from that selection, provided they were happy with my choice. I chose Andrew Marshall, who was highly attuned to everything we'd tried to do in the original series and very funny too. Humphrey Barclay chose Andrew Nickolds and Stan Hey whose principal claim to fame at this stage was writing some episodes for a detective series called *Hazell*. When I tried to reason with HB, he gave me to understand that Andrew Marshall was an unacceptable choice (why then was he proposed to me?) and that I was going to be working with Nickolds and Hey. How in the name of reason I was supposed to muscle in on an established writing partnership has yet to be explained to me. Once the deal was set, however, Nickolds and Hey simply retreated behind the impossibility of working as a threesome. They couldn't pick up where we'd left off because their humour was essentially north country muck-and-brass while ours was more metropolitan and Jewish. I attended meetings after they'd done a first draft since they wouldn't actually consider writing with me (I must say in their defence that the logistics were a bit beyond us all) and they made it clear that, as far as they were concerned, they were writing *Agony*.

Their material was flatter, broader and less trouble. The producer and Maureen Lipman approved of it. Here at last was her chance to play Mary Tyler Moore, Hull-style. The producer was still John Reardon. For many months my name was tied up with *Agony*. There were many people (there still are some) who thought Jane Lucas was just a thinly veiled portrait of me and LWT banked on the fact that I'd take the money and shut up.

By now there was something else to be taken into consideration. In between the first and second series of *Agony*, Nick and I had begun to consider whether or not we would have a child.

We talked about it exhaustively – did we want one, would we regret it if we didn't have one, could we have one (me with a gynaecological history like the Hundred Years' War and Nick having been told that he was unlikely to father a child)? How much would it change our lives? Were we prepared for that? We'd found each other comparatively late and having a baby was a real choice in the sense that we both felt very strongly about people who have them for the lack of anything better to do. We decided we wanted to have a baby. Right. How were we going to feel if we couldn't conceive? If I lost it, miscarriage was unhappily all too familiar to me, but how would he react? We decided to try on the basis that if it happened, it was meant, and if it didn't, that would be meant too and we would still have a rich and satisfying life with one another. I couldn't invest in all the tubes and charts and investigation in search of a baby. If I wasn't to have my own, then doubtless the Almighty knew what he was up to and the world was full of all sort of other babies, womb-size to rugby forward, who could do with the love and care we had to offer. Nick agreed.

In the middle of all this song and dance about *Agony*, I duly had my IUD removed and we made our second trip to Crete. Several associates from LWT also holidayed in Crete but we only met the producer Reardon once, when he made mention of a particular episode needing my attention as soon as I got back. Mercifully the spell of the Aegean still worked its rehabilitative wonders, more or less, but something was amiss.

I felt very odd, quivery, like the string of an instrument, and while sometimes we seemed to be very close, other times we were far far apart. I remember Nick read the short stories of John Cheever, which Christie had introduced us to, and that Ma insisted I read Mary Stewart's trilogy about Merlin and King Arthur. Thank heaven she did because I felt rather lost and very much in need of the comfort of something simply written and appealingly imaginative, rather more than my usual introspective 'I really should read this' holiday reading. At the airport on our way back we had one of our rare disagreements and I buried my nose desperately in *The Greek Tycoon* until it was time to fly. I sat on the aeroplane saying goodbye to Crete where I'd been so happy – it now seemed a very long time ago, waves of regret and remorse washing over me, thinking something had gone wrong, really wrong and it was my fault. I shouldn't have got married again, I wasn't the type, how could I have been so silly and kidded myself, even composing in my head the letter I'd leave for Nick and working out how to get away clean, as it were.

The next morning, still hugging the dreadful secret of my failure to my chest, I burst into hysterical tears at some quite reasonable suggestion of Nick's. When I'm in that mood, which is mercifully rare, everything is my fault and I become so defensive it's nearly impossible to have a sensible conversation with me. Nick sat beside me and asked what was the matter. And from the pit of my stomach I reeled off my fears and my confusion which was (do laugh!) mostly to do with the fact that the hotel did not have a double bed available for us and we'd spent two weeks sleeping in single beds pushed together. Greek beds have flat wooden frames so there was about eight inches of no man's land between us when we slept. I suppose on the purely practical level of hot nights, curling up in separate sleeping territories was acceptable and even desirable but we had no choice, we were separated and I felt lost without the affectionate continuity of touch. To my relief Nick not only listened, he understood and even agreed, so that

I was soothed into relative calm. And a couple of nights in our own enormous bed helped still more.

In the weeks that followed, I developed a heavy chesty sinusy cold and began feeling very sick. It was true that I hadn't had a period for about six weeks but in all that emotion, I wasn't surprised that the hormones were a bit awry. But the sickness got worse and eventually Nick and I went off to see our doctor. While Nick waited for me, Peter Vernon looked down my throat and discussed how I'd been feeling. Knowing my history, he thought he would then examine my chest and as I took off my bra, he pointed to my already burgeoning bosom and inquired, 'What's all that?' I admitted they'd enlarged a little of late. He asked about periods. When I told him, he laughed and said, 'Well dear, I'll check your chest for infections but judging by that little lot, what you've got is a bad cold masking morning sickness. I'll do a test by all means, but believe me, it's unnecessary.' When I went to tell Nick, he told me he'd already thought I was pregnant in Crete but was determined not to mention it until I did. My test confirmed what we all knew. Baby on the way.

I didn't tell my LWT colleagues. Why should I? They all thought I was pretty odd already. Pregnancy would presumably make me odder. I don't know how soon anybody guessed but I didn't discuss it until towards the end of our association.

Meantime, back on Series Two, the shit really hit the fan over Episode Five in which one of the gay boys has to come out and tell his parents the truth about himself. This idea was as dear to my heart as it was to Len's and although there undoubtedly were ways of writing it which would have highlighted the humour along with the pain the version which saw light dissatisfied me in every way.

We finally met – Nickolds and Hey, Maureen Lipman, Humphrey Barclay, John Reardon and I – for a meeting which lasted some seven hours and I fought until I couldn't fight any more. When I left the LWT building that night, I got into the car knowing that I had just bowed out. It was and is the most profound defeat of my professional life.

The way I saw it, I had what gamblers call a stacked deck. I couldn't win. I could carry on fighting and win some small concessions but they would be so small that they would be lost in the overall changes which in my view took all the life and freshness out of *Agony* – however flawed it was. LWT had signed me up to do something which I now was unable to do – writing – and I wasn't having my name on what remained. I got in touch with my agent and asked to have my name removed from the series. It was only to remain with Len's on the 'created by' credit. I returned money so that there was no further misunderstanding. I understand it cost LWT £1,800 to reshoot the titles for the series without my name. I said nothing to anyone except my own circle of friends to whom I said so much, so often, and so bitterly, that I'm sure they thought I'd finally flipped.

My Ma, ever my captain and my guide, was enormously relieved. Her greatest fear was that I would carry on bashing and lose the baby. I hadn't even thought of that but once it had been mentioned to me, by heaven, I did think about it. But the bad times weren't over yet.

Chapter 19

Thank heaven I was still gainfully employed at *Cosmopolitan* which was, for the most of my time there, a satisfactory writing experience. For a start one of the things I'd always had to do at *Woman*, though I did it much less than originally envisaged, was to contract everything down – write briefly. Suddenly I had the time to develop themes and look at ideas from more sides than one or two. It was lovely. When I began working for *Cosmo*, the offices were in Victoria but by the time I'd joined the magazine, they were just off Carnaby Street. Contrary to what you might perhaps expect, my colleagues at the magazine were not aggressively modern neurotic women. They were intelligent, kind and pleasant to be with and although I found the enormous open plan office presided over by Deirdre McSharry (or D McS as she calls herself in the editor's letter) intimidating to begin with, this was a monthly magazine, not a weekly and I did most of my work at home.

That caused its own problems. I had been going to work in offices for most of the preceding 17 years. I didn't actually grumble very much about it either. In my younger days, office hours were something you kept if you wanted to keep your job, and by the time I'd got to *Woman*, I'd discovered that you used your discretion, they used theirs and we were all principally concerned with getting the work done. Suddenly I didn't have a mental time clock to punch and it took me a year to pace myself so that I gave myself time to write the piece for *Cosmo*. Very often the only way I could manoeuvre myself into sitting down to confront that blank sheet of paper which leered ominously at me from the typewriter was when the deadline was upon me. I know it was silly but that's what I did. And I returned with joy to my teenage reading habits – a book a day.

The magazine promoted me heavily when I joined them with advertising copy to the effect that 'Anna Raeburn can say anything she damn well pleases in *Cosmopolitan*'. My mother rang me smartly. 'Make sure they stick to that,' she warned. (My mother is always telling me how little she knows about the business world and I remain, on the evidence received down the years, totally unconvinced.) Almost immediately the letters began flooding in. I had warned Deirdre that whether or not we asked for them, I would get letters. She promised me a secretary. Meanwhile I faced a decision.

Did I prove what a willing ninny I was by settling in to working eight hours a day answering these letters or did I stand my ground? It took eleven months to get a secretary. I acknowledged the most urgent letters and kept the rest in files. When Nicky arrived and applied for the job, I warned her that the backlog was now several hundred letters and I wanted to answer every one. She gulped hard and said she thought she could face that. I also warned her that at *Cosmo*, as in many places, secretaries are regarded as a lesser form of life. And 'proving themselves', which is supposedly the golden carrot, frequently requires the guts to rebut exploitation rather than seizing the opportunity to express any particular talent. She said she thought she could handle that too. And she did.

Everybody has teething troubles when they begin a new job. I was fortunate in having far fewer than many, for the same or similar reasons that I'd had some kind of autonomy at *Woman* – I wrote opinion pieces, on very personal subjects in a very personal way. But I learned in the early days that the delightful flannel I'd been dished as a cherished freelance contributor was a thing of the past. Now I was staff, and staff existed to prove their worth by survival. I wrote my first and second pieces for *Cosmo* before I went away on honeymoon. When I returned, I found my second piece refused at the 11th hour. Deirdre had asked me to write about my marriage, which I preferred not to. Although I wrote on another subject she declined this at the last minute and re-iterated her original request. Now, if you're in the business of regular jobs, you're in the business of keeping them. There wasn't much point in throwing a resounding tantrum. I wrote the piece.

I joined *Cosmo* during what I consider was its best period when, in spite of the *de rigueur* sex piece lifted from the

American parent magazine, the same old psychologist examining the same old themes with an air of concentrated trendiness, it was making a real effort to be relevant for those readers (and there are many) who live outside London. It carried some very good, seriously written, informative pieces about a wide range of subjects and it looked lovely. The offers have always been just about the best of any British magazine although the front covers have always been too close to the American progenitor for comfort. But by and large it was doing something I could relate to and respect. It was saying, 'We're here, we're established and therefore it follows that our readers will trust us to be adventurous.' In other words, it was growing up. During this period, while I could always point to its faults, I was proud of *Cosmo*.

Successfully briefed to write the equivalent of personal 'think' pieces every month, I did some good work. I liked the photographs they used which were done by Laszlo Zatecky, the first photographer I'd met for years who didn't spend his time repining about my nose, or the circles under my eyes, and trying to make me look 'pretty'. He just got on and shot what was there.

I liked the staff meetings we all attended and to which we were obliged to contribute not only debate but ideas. And I respected my deputy editor Brenda Jones, an intelligent, enormously capable woman. It was Brenda who rescued me from a morass of frustration over an article I had written on abortion. Little I write satisfies me and I usually feel it could have been better but this time I knew it was good. However, I also knew it was very heavy duty and I wasn't quite sure how Deirdre would react. I was probably more nervous than I usually am when the person I have to get past is reading what I have written but at long last, she called me over.

'Anna,' she said, 'it is very strong and rather grim and it brings me to something I have been meaning to say to you for some time. You see, you are very good at this powerful, passionate stuff but sometimes I really do think you go over the top. Something like this would be much better handled more calmly and coolly like, say, Jill Tweedie, so would you go away and have another think about it.'

I said tremblingly, 'My name is Anna Raeburn. If you want Jill Tweedie to write on this subject, you are at perfect liberty to ask her to do so but I don't write like anybody else.' I removed myself to what was laughingly called my office – a typewriter on a table between two bookcases and admittedly more private than any other available location – and shook. I then put the paper in the machine and tried to think about rewriting it. As I sat there, choking with misery, Brenda Jones came over and spoke to me. She asked me if I was all right. I said I was not. She asked what was wrong. I explained. 'Just wait fifteen minutes,' she said. Brenda Jones read the piece and made minor suggestions for changes in what I'd written, which I was happy to agree to. And she ran it.

The sequel to this is interesting. A couple of years later I became friendly with Sue Slipman, former secretary of the National Union of Students, now with the SDP and working in NUPE. She shared a house with another woman who was also a trades' union representative. Before the TUC decided to back abortion formally, they debated long and hard in closed session and apparently this friend rose to her feet and read them what I'd written. I'd be very proud to think this was so and even more grateful to Brenda Jones.

But by and large things weren't that dramatic, though I could never get through to Deirdre how much I wanted to like and admire her. She had been very good to me. She had approached me within the first year of my employ at *Woman* to see if I wanted to join *Cosmo* instead and when I declined, handled it with good humour and tact, promptly commissioning me to interview the black American writer James Baldwin for her. Baldwin was somebody who had always fascinated me so I leapt at the chance. I saw him in the Savoy, surrounded by his publisher, publicist and travelling companions. They all talked and the telephone rang frequently and I was overawed by the complexity of the little dark man with a face like a Yoruba god who sat on the sofa beside me. The main problem for me about interviewing Jimmy Baldwin was that no interview in the world could reproduce the magic of his voice but at length we were done, he signed his latest novel for me and I went away to write up the piece. So unsure was I of myself, the glamorous editor of *Cosmopolitan* and the final result that I didn't send it to her, she didn't ask for it and we started all over again a year later. But she gave me another chance, so I was even more willing to like and admire her. She made a real effort, or so it seemed to me, to keep in touch with me and encourage me along.

Even if you're used to being lonely, you can get sick of it and I was always ripe for what seemed to be a rewarding friendship, particularly with somebody of the same sex – which would be less complicated than with somebody of the opposite sex – who'd been in the industry to which I was new for longer than me and could perhaps take me under her wing. She evinced great admiration of me. It was flattering and comforting. She liked my work, she said she liked me and I referred to her as my Professional Fairy Godmother.

As I say, the first real change was when I stopped being freelance and became a regular employee. The second was when I married, but that was containable. In any case she seemed to think that Nick was devastatingly black Irish handsome. And he was charming and courteous to her to the extent of taking her to lunch when I was worried about her to see if we could help. But it is significant that in all the years I knew her, I never entered her private social world, though I was often invited.

What happened from the date my pregnancy was confirmed until I left the magazine is an unpleasant story, best left untold, not because I lack the skill to tell it. Throughout this last period of my time at *Cosmo*, my self-preserving paranoia was on the upswing and though I tried to control it, I had little enough to counter it with. And by the time the end of that road was in sight, I felt I had tried in every way to save the situation, short of a knockdown, dragout fight which might have spared me a lot of discomfort. I still wanted my job but eventually, it wasn't worth it. So I left.

Until recently I was the only person on the staff of *Cosmopolitan* to have gone through a pregnancy while working there in the ten years of its existence and even now there are two of us, you couldn't call the occurrence common. So much for prestige, position and all the rest of the illusions, and God knows what happens to women who are less fortunate and working in less enlightened surroundings. For it seems that in spite of all that has been written about women combining their professional and personal lives – and the most challenging way in which we do this is by combining paid work and motherhood – all that has really happened is that the number of stereotypes has increased.

Once there was the Career Woman – well-cut suits, manicured nails, facials and financial success. Her opposite number was the Mother – Laura Ashley dresses, climbing cigarette consumption, nips from the cooking sherry, homemade bread and lack of acknowledgement. To them add a third – what I call the Professional Mother – breastfeeding at Fortnums, staff of three to run the house you haven't got the time for (and eventually kids ditto), jogging suits, personal manager and Valium. These images are over-simplified but recognisable as the kind of fodder we're all fed. And if you decline any or all of these three, you are imponderable and should be dismissed from further consideration. As a friend remarked bitterly, 'Down here (she lives in a rather smart suburb) they understand fulltime mothers and they understand professional women. The inference is that the rest of us who work and have families aren't doing either kind of work really well.' You don't fit. If you don't fit you aren't acceptable. And so I found myself at yet another crossroads. But you don't arrive at such a pass unless it's time to start anew. So, when I'd finished feeling miserable and rejected, I began to see the bonus, and the bonus above all others was the baby.

Chapter 20

When I told my mother we thought we were pregnant, she laughed, cried and jumped up and down at the same time. She was then 80, I was 36 and Nick was a year older. Once I'd decided to deal myself out of *Agony* and setting aside the ups and downs of *Cosmopolitan* life, it was a lovely pregnancy. I became very large very quickly and was very happy, proud and well. It came as a bit of a shock when the newspapers broke the Debendox story. Debendox is an antinauseant and as I had morning sickness 20 hours out of every 24, the doctor recommended it. Like a fool I took it for two months out of the first three. However, when it came time for my second scan, the baby was all in one piece, so we were lucky.

The only other furrow on my relatively serene brow was who was going to deliver the baby, as my gynaecologist doesn't deal with confinements. His choice was Mr Pinker and I acceded because the latter had already been briefly involved in a much less happy period in my life and sentimentally, I suppose, I wanted to show him that things had worked out in the long run. But Mr Pinker was not sure that he would be available on the indicated dates as he was due to go abroad. Eventually I rang my own gynaecologist once more and asked to be referred promptly to Professor Norman Morris at the West London Hospital, my original choice.

The West London maternity outfit is famed for their thoughtful and helpful approach and Norman Morris and his registrar Jeremy Wright (grandson of the famous birth control pioneer Helena Wright) were wonderful. My last public engagement was to address a meeting protesting at the threatened closure of the West London and a week later my son was born there.

Throughout my pregnancy, I referred to the bump as

Ithimshe, a name which mightily tickled Nick's Nigerian clients because it sounded like one of their own. I wasn't getting into the debate about its sex. All I wanted was a healthy child and I would be very grateful for whatever we got. All this was the conscious level but a few layers deeper down, I was terrified about having a son. When the third person in as many weeks said that it must be a boy because of the way I was carrying, I wound up clutching Nick and saying rather desperately that I didn't think I could face having a boy.

'Why?' he asked.

'Because I'm so acid and emotional and intense about everything – I can't Nick, I just can't – I'd really make a mess of it.'

If the truth is told I had no intuition about which sex the child was, no wish about it either – at least consciously. I just assumed that I would be having a daughter and interestingly, as you can see from the above, that she would be able to handle whatever I was.

Of course half the publishers in London sent me maternity books, most of which contradict each other, and after I'd read about ten, I ditched the lot and commenced living through *my* pregnancy. I ate very sensibly, took regular exercise, went off my beloved red wine and cheese for the only time (till then) in my adult life and was grateful that I didn't have to worry about smoking. Ma was tremendously impressed that I rested every afternoon and indeed I only did two risky things with Ithimshe on board.

We went to see *Apocalypse Now* which was thunderously noisy and titanically emotional. I explained beforehand to Ithimshe that I wouldn't normally take such a person to such a place but that this was very important to me. I cared deeply about the whole issue of Vietnam, had found Michael Herr's book *Dispatches* remarkable in many ways and the film was very much influenced by the book.

And the second walk on eggs came when the pro-abortion movement mounted a demonstration in opposition to John Corrie's proposed Abortion (Amendment) Bill. I was then seven months pregnant. Somebody rang me and asked me to go and I knew that I must. In the most personal way, it remains one of the bravest things I've ever done. I really kept waiting for the Finger of Fate to push through the clouds and a voice to say, 'Raeburn, you're pushing your luck!'

It was bitterly cold on the march which met at the House of Commons and I shall never forget the nurses who joined us. Forbidden to wear their uniforms, they arrived in mufti and changed in the ladies' loo opposite. They were young and strong and lovely because they cared so much and I was quite taken aback when several of them recognised me and thanked me for being there. 'Boot's on the other foot,' I said, 'thank *you* for coming.' So often the speeches at the most heartfelt demos are disappointing or go on too long. These were impressive. Central Hall was so packed that I couldn't get from the main room to the canteen for tea or to the lavatory, a rather pressing need for an expectant mother. Somehow I made it through nearly four hours with various journalists asking how I could be pregnant and still be on an abortion march. When I came home, I knelt down and prayed with every ounce of my intelligence and conviction that God, the God I have always believed in, the God of my fathers, the God my father taught me was far above the hearts and minds of men and women, would understand and would still grant me our child in one piece.

At Nick's very carefully timed and lovingly considered suggestion, I did not have natural childbirth. I wasn't as young or fit or strong as I might have been and I have an unusually low pain threshold. And I had an induction because at what we estimated was the due date, the scales registered over 12½ stone. When the medical staff protested, I said rather firmly that by my calculations, this was D-Day and if we left the Bump in there any longer, we'd need a can opener to get him/her out. I was given an epidural anaesthetic, monitored very carefully and 12 hours later, a very long boy made his debut into the world, hands folded and smiling as serenely as any Leboyer baby. I felt so many things simultaneously that it would take another book to document them all. I remember very clearly Jeremy Wright explaining that he was going to use forceps, saying in his most reasonable sherry-offering voice, 'Now Anna, push down when I tell you. It will hurt like hell but not for long.' I perceived the pain quite clearly as a thing apart from me. And I cherish the memory of Nick patting my green draped knee and reassuring me that Jeremy Wright was making 'a beautiful job' of stitching my epesiotomy (cut to you!). For the splendour of the baby, I have no words.

There was no question about his name. We had been down to see Ma just before he was born and she was a bit blue. She felt old, she missed my father. When we left, Nick said to me in the car, 'I think if we have a boy, we should call him Taylor. Your mother would like it.' She did and he was. He is called Taylor after my father, Edward for my mother's father, Sturges which is Nick's favourite family name and for the first year of his life we called him so many nicknames and pet names that one little boy asked me curiously, 'Is honey his name?'

Taylor thoroughly approved of the superstructure I sported (bust 44D) and having started life at 10lbs all but an ounce or two, continued on his jumbo-sized way. But the first year of his life was awful as well as wonderful. I loved him to pieces but I felt absolutely inept. Everybody seemed to know more about babies than I did. Everybody could tie better nappies, soothe him quicker, settle him more easily and I was just about to give up breastfeeding, in spite of the two pyramidal peaks, when a kind Capital listener sent me an excellent book on the subject and I discovered that was one thing I *could* do for him. But I began to realise how much of my self-esteem was tied up in a kind of adult work pattern rendered nearly impossible with a young child. I always hated being over-weight but I was. I couldn't get to my hairdresser, had my hair cut locally so I looked like a fat refugee. I loved him helplessly and adoringly and practically and in every other way but I couldn't escape the feeling that this mothering game was not something I was very good at. Surrogate mothering was much easier. I didn't really know any other young mothers in the area – you don't if you work full time – and I hired temporary nannies when I had to go into the office. Like an idiot and totally ignorant of what was involved, I had commissioned myself to do a programme for the BBC about *Antony and Cleopatra*, one of a series (*Shakespeare in Perspective*) in which well-known people precis'd and commented on various plays, as part of the BBC's mammoth endeavour to mount productions of all Shakespeare's plays.

After a couple of not entirely comfortable episodes with

babysitters (one leading to a complaint on my part, countered by a death threat letter from the girl of whom I complained!), I found the British Nursing Association and they in turn found me Deirdre Begley. She was a small, stocky, overqualified New Zealander with beautiful hands and she gave me the confidence to do anything. I left for the first day of filming so nervous that I couldn't express milk, which is how my indignant son came by his first and only formula feed. 'He looked at me as if I'd crawled out from under a rock,' recounted Deirdre gleefully in her Antipodean twang. But from there on in for the two weeks of filming, we never looked back and I remain undyingly grateful to Sister Begley and the BNA for helping me to enjoy what I feared might be traumatic.

My contribution to *Shakespeare in Perspective* was a delight all round. I worked with people I liked who liked me and when we couldn't film because the weather was uncertain, to put it mildly, the crew sat round and told stories about the other series they'd worked on, the famous they'd worked with including Peter Ustinov and Richard Burton and we had a highly entertaining time. And at 4.30 or so when the light died, I fled home, milk seeping to the knees, thinking that this dual role was really rather nice and wasn't I lucky it was working out so well. When *Cosmopolitan* and I parted company, I was not unnaturally shaken and found that the lure of international stardom (media now as opposed to movie) paled in comparison to the delights of my son's company. But it seemed silly to give up everything I'd worked so hard to achieve and besides, we soon learned I couldn't afford to.

The accountants I'd taken on to help me make proper arrangements during the period of my highest earnings were very expensive. Very expensive, very good at spending my money on legal fees and consultants' advice but totally inefficient in advising me about how to order my savings or arrangements with the Revenue or the Customs and Excise. The only consolation about the awful mess they made of my affairs is how often you hear the same story. It seems you only find reliable accountants by trial and error. Well, I had tried, they had erred and now I was almost back where I started from – skint. So at the end of my son's first year on earth, I had no permanent job and no prospect of one, tax debts beyond my wildest nightmares, a great feeling of shame that I'd ever let myself get into this mess, 21 extra pounds I didn't need and a son who was really much more interested in his father. Thank God for the Capital show.

I couldn't go out and earn with my small son on my arm and I wasn't about to leave him with just anyone. I appealed to my health visitor for help. She introduced me to a tiny Welsh woman who'd been a nurse for 30 years, a health visitor for 12, who was a widow with a grown up son, herself the daughter of a Keir Hardie socialist. Her name was Dot Pracy and she came to look after my son three days a week so that I could go about getting some work. Taylor loved her and she loved Taylor.

If the world were to be divided into givers and takers, Dorothy Pracy is a giver. Sometimes she is so spendthrift with her gifts, that those of us who love and cherish her have tried to curb her but all of us who have benefitted from her can only be everlastingly grateful she's around. She has the rare gift of tactfully doing whatever there is to be done, so you're freed to get on and do whatever it is that's bothering you. As Taylor became more mobile, it was clear that writing in what is essentially an open plan flat wasn't very practicable. 'Use my flat,' said Dot, who lives ten minutes down the road and without that flat this book would never have been written.

In the year that followed Nick spent a great deal of time trying to find out what I wanted to do. We chewed over *Agony* and *Cosmo* till they tasted like poached doormat. I didn't want to write for TV, I wasn't ready to try on my own. I didn't want to go back into magazines. What did I want to do? I couldn't answer. Slowly it began to emerge that I was still in love with the idea of books although the contract for £50 with two options drawn to Reg Davis-Poynter for the book he had wanted about group sex was still round my neck. Nick's former solicitor introduced us to one of his partners at Kingsley Napley, Laurence Shurman. At Mr Shurman's suggestion I approached Davis-Poynter (for the third time of asking) about releasing me from the contract if I returned his payment of £100 which was given in equal payments to my then partner and me. He kept the cheque for so long that we thought we were in with a chance and then he refused it. At this point I was becoming quite desperate. The only thing I wanted to do was write and here was this publisher sitting between me and it, refusing to release me. I was invited to take part in a function at the Liberal Jewish Synagogue to raise funds for Leo Beck Rabbinical College and among the others contributing to this effort was the man who had drawn the contract, making it, Davis-Poynter held, unbreakable – Lord Goodman. When I mentioned this to Mr Shurman he advised me not to mention the contract unless Lord G. brought the subject up. And of course he didn't. But Mr Shurman now brought the matter to the attention of Sir David Napley, who in turn raised the matter with Lord Goodman. It took months and a considerable amount of prodding – Shurman to Napley, Napley to Goodman, Goodman to Davis-Poynter – but eventually Mr Shurman advised me that Reg Davis-Poynter had agreed to release me from the contract for £1,500. So eleven years after I signed the contract, at a cost of eleven months' negotiation, £575 legal fees and with the payment of a borrowed £1,500 – I was free to think about books, the writing of. And the moral of that story is not to sign contracts out of obligation. When Reg Poynter-Davis offered me the contract, I felt I ought to sign it and I can't think of a worse beginning for what is essentially a business agreement.

In that lean year I was approached by a marketing and sales company I'd done some work for before to make a promotional film for a new sanitary towel. My mother laughed out loud. 'Other people's daughters,' she said, 'are asked to advertise Blackglama mink. Mine is offered STs!' So I flew to New York for three hectic days where I stood, clad in white and pastels to soften my 'hard' face, in the middle of Madison Avenue, in a very plush office and at the airport, declaiming about modern woman and press-on sanitary towels. A very acceptable product, they seemed to be, and the money paid off one section of that dreadful tax bill.

A little later I was invited to speak at the London College of Printing, where it emerged in discussion with the course tutor afterwards that they were very enthusiastic about but desperately short of part-time contributors to the two year combined journalism and business studies course, particularly on the journalistic side. So I became a part-time tutor for a year. I loved it and I think my father would have approved.

In the meantime I received a letter from an independent film producer asking my advice about a film script concerning an agony aunt – not, he wrote, farcical as *Agony* had been but a serious treatment. I went to lunch to advise him and came home writing a script on spec (with nodding gratitude to John Gregory Dunn who'd just written an article on how to write a script in *The New York Review of Books*). While all this was going on, I had withdrawn from my previous agent and was looking for a new one. I saw 12 that year, one a month and I wasn't entirely happy with any of them. Nick asked me the same question every time I came home from yet another agent. 'Don't tell me what you're going to do for them,' he kept saying. 'We both know you're a workhorse. Tell me what they are going to do for you.' As I could never answer this question to his satisfaction or my own, though there were one or two near misses, I didn't have an agent. Then at last I thought I'd found someone, and he persuaded me that the script outline I'd already written for the independent producer wouldn't make a film but it might make a novel. I'm not good with the word 'novel'. It's a specialised form of writing and I'm chary of it. I preferred to call my fictional endeavours stories or just books and anyway, I'd already thought of the sort of book I'd like to write, a personal book, a sort of tale of my pale purple past and eventual growing up. But no, contended the agent, no. I must do a novel first because otherwise no-one would take me seriously. (If this comment were made to me now, I think I'd rejoin rather smartly that if people didn't by now, they never would. But then I was still busy being led.)

So we approached a publishing house and a contract was drawn up. When I said rather humbly that the sum involved did seem a bit on the lean side, I was told (since verified six times over) that first novels don't bring much money. (It therefore follows that Clare Francis and Shirley Conran, for example, don't write first novels. They market product.) But I wasn't happy about the whole set up and I kept the contract unsigned while I thought and worried and thought some more.

Then one day I was having lunch with Nick (we manage this half a dozen times a year – his schedule makes mine look staid). My eyes filled. He asked me what was the matter and I told him. Once again I was about to do something because somebody else, somebody who was older than me, somebody I was a bit in awe of, said I should – although what was suggested was directly in opposition to my own feelings. 'What are you going to do?' he asked and I said I knew one person in publishing I could rely upon. His name was Roger Houghton and at the time I approached him he was in charge of Elm Tree Books at Hamish Hamilton.

Accordingly I rang Roger and threw myself on his mercy. I told him what I'd got arranged and my misgivings about it. I told him that the book about me was the one I wanted to do at the moment. He asked me if I had anything written down. I said yes, an introduction (well, a cod one really – you can't write an introduction for an unwritten book but I've always found it helps to have something written down – you can always dump it later), a chapter breakdown and a first chapter. He asked if I could drop them in to him and made an appointment for 11.00 the next morning.

The next morning he informed me that the introduction was dismissable, he wasn't enchanted with the chapter breakdown but he liked the first chapter and could I give him more of that. I left the meeting knowing that a contract would be prepared for a sum of money which meant survival if nothing excessive and that I could now write a first book. I rang my then agent, who was disinclined to have anything further to do with me, and that's how the long haul between talking about a book and writing it began.

I had various battles with different bits of this book. But I wanted very much to include what I suppose were the events by which I grew. Not all of them were comfortable in the telling and many sent me home shaken and drained with a nasty dose of introspection. If, during the course of writing this book, I relived the death of my father, then life went on and it wasn't always kind. My mother fell, breaking her right wrist and her left shoulder, just as I'd commenced writing. Within six months she was registered blind with only residual sight so she, who has read so much and with such pleasure, will not be able to read this book. She will be able to hear it, but that's not the same. I know that well because one of the aspects of writing that has haunted me for years is that people expect me to write as well as I speak. But nobody writes exactly as they speak. They may seem to but what really

220

happens is that you learn to write so that it sounds the same. Materially it is always different.

At one point I was halted dead in my tracks when I read of a well-known American actress asked what she would be doing when she was over 40. 'Well, I'll tell you one thing I won't be doing,' she laughed, 'and that's writing my autobiography.' Perhaps the whole idea was a terrible mistake and I should have suffered and strained to produce a novel after all. I got into such a state about it that I stopped writing. I could feel the block building up. Suppose the whole tone rang false, suppose the press and the public who have for the most part been kind to me for many years, took it into their heads to have a go at me over this? I could hardly be more vulnerable than when I'd offered a warts-and-all edition of the first half of my life. This particular horror was resolved for me in a most unexpected way.

Laurence Olivier had just published his memoirs. In a subsequent interview a journalist pointed out that his friend Sir John Gielgud apparently deeply disapproved of the frankness with which Olivier chronicled the descent into awfulness of his marriage to Vivien Leigh. What did Lord Olivier say to that? 'I don't give a bugger,' Lord O. was quoted as replying. 'I was there and if I'm not going to write about it the way I saw it, I might just as well not write the book.' The message cleared my fuzzy head for the rest of the assault. It is after all my life. Many other people contributed to it, without two of whom it would never have been begun. But I have lived it.

If what my parents told me about their lives and if what I knew of them was interesting, then it wasn't nearly so easy to write about my sister. I shrank from even trying to write about that until she gave me the key. When I was nearing the end of the first draft, we all went down to spend the weekend with my mother and my sister came over, accompanied by her black labrador, Ben, whom Taylor adores. So we three plus the dog went off for a walk. It was a beautiful day, the sky was very blue and my small son romped with the dog and fell about on the fallow ground.

I was talking to Lesley about the visit I'd made to Dublin a few weeks earlier to promote the Erno Laszlo cosmetics I use and how I was barely allowed to get my plug in for them on the *Late Late Show* (Ireland's top television show) before Gay

Byrne the presenter asked me about abortion. I can only be as I am but answering such a question live on Irish television, studio audience and all, was hair-raising. Lesley said reflectively, 'You feel very strongly about that don't you?' I agreed. 'You must never hesitate to tell them about the other side,' she said. 'Tell them my story, you have my permission. Because honestly, there isn't a day goes by that I don't regret . . .' We were then 39 and 52. I had never heard her say such a thing before. She had never said very much on the subject anyway and still less that I could understand. I squeezed her arm. We looked with mutual approbation at the spectacle of child and dog and field and sky. I said almost apologetically, 'I – I sometimes call him Buster, you know.'

Her face swung towards me. 'Do you? Do you really? How lovely.' And we flung our arms around each other and wept and I felt the long shadowy fingers of her unhappiness ease their grip on my past. She was never my enemy but I lost her for many years and through my son, I got her back.

So, what would you? It's not a very traditional fairy story. It begins with a family instead of a stepchild or a romantic orphan, and it ends with two families – the one I regained and the one I made with Nick. In fairy stories you don't marry the prince at 34 but I did. And he was worth waiting for. And as for the ending, I intend to live as happily ever after as I can.